"The rise of the biblical counseling movemer [...] important developments within evangelical C [...] most promising. In this timely book, Heath Lar [...] tory and theology, offering the most helpful book yet to appear on this movement. I am deeply thankful for the return to the sufficiency of Scripture as the foundation for all true biblical counsel. This book will serve generations to come as a guide to the biblical counseling movement and its significance."
R. Albert Mohler Jr., President, The Southern Baptist Theological Seminary

"Like any significant church movement throughout ecclesiastical history, the biblical counseling movement has been subject to many changes and considerable growth. It has become a worldwide, multicultural agent of change for the church of Jesus Christ. Heath Lambert has written an amazing account of key influences that God, in his perfect sovereignty, has brought about in this movement. This factual account is an important contribution to understanding how and why the biblical counseling movement has had such a profound and lasting impact. It is a must-read for anyone who desires to understand the movement."
John D. Street, Chair, MABC Graduate Program, The Master's College and Seminary

"Having been a part of biblical counseling for some twenty-five years, I greatly appreciate and wholeheartedly endorse Dr. Lambert's incredible work. He informs the novice, the veteran, and the critic on how the great heroes of the biblical counseling movement have built upon one another. He shows how an understanding of the movement must proceed from both historical and biblical contexts. And, as he reflects on the past one hundred years of church history, Lambert contributes a clear perspective on present day biblical counseling by demonstrating its strengths and weaknesses. He does this work in a way that leaves readers challenged, more unified, and strengthened in their faith and resolve concerning the sufficiency of the Scriptures."
Stuart W. Scott, Associate Professor of Biblical Counseling, Southern Seminary; author, *The Exemplary Husband* and *Biblical Manhood*

"A thoughtful analysis of the development of a growing discipline, Lambert offers a careful assessment of the intriguing history of the biblical counseling movement. He goes to great lengths to help the reader understand the rich heritage of biblical counseling, transitions in its development, and wise recommendations for its future. Definitely an insightful read!"

Jeremy Lelak, President, Association of Biblical Counselors

"I deeply appreciate the impact Jay Adams's teaching has had on my life, writing, family, and ministry. His emphasis on progressive sanctification, of continually growing and changing as followers of Christ, has been especially meaningful. This volume is a fascinating story of how Jay's students, building on his remarkable foundational work, have caused the biblical counseling movement to grow and change for God's glory. Thanks, Heath!"

Randy Patten, Executive Director, National Association of Nouthetic Counselors

"This book is an excellent resource for explaining the history of the biblical counseling movement, including the successes and failures along the way. Lambert presents a great framework for all who want to grow in and advance biblical counseling."

Dennis Lee, Program Manager, Hebron Center Addictions Recovery Program

The
Biblical
Counseling
Movement
after Adams

The Biblical Counseling Movement after Adams

Foreword *by* David Powlison

HEATH LAMBERT

WHEATON, ILLINOIS

Cover design: Studio Gearbox

First printing 2012

Printed in the United States of America

Trade paperback ISBN: 978-1-4335-2813-2
PDF ISBN: 978-1-4335-2814-9
Mobipocket ISBN: 978-1-4335-2815-6
ePub ISBN: 978-1-4335-2816-3

Library of Congress Cataloging-in-Publication Data
Lambert, Heath, 1979–
   The biblical counseling movement after Adams / Heath Lambert ; foreword by David Powlison.
      p. cm.
   Originally presented as the author's thesis (Ph.D.).
   Includes bibliographical references and index.
   ISBN 978-1-4335-2813-2 (tp)
   1. Pastoral counseling—History. 2. Adams, Jay Edward. I. Title.
BV4012.2.L245   2012
259—dc23   2011020714

Crossway is a publishing ministry of Good News Publishers.

CH   25   24   23   22   21   20   19   18   17   16

To Jay Adams,
who reawakened generations
to the sufficiency of Scripture, and
to Norman and Belita,
whose kind and gracious care
made this work possible.

Contents

Foreword by David Powlison   11

Acknowledgments   19

1 The Birth of a Biblical Counseling Movement   21
   and the Need for Growth

2 Advances in How Biblical Counselors   49
   Think about Counseling

3 Advances in How Biblical Counselors   81
   Do Counseling

4 Advances in How Biblical Counselors   101
   Talk about Counseling

5 Advances in How Biblical Counselors   121
   Think about the Bible?

6 An Area Still in Need of Advancement   139

Conclusion   157

Appendix   165

Bibliography   171

Notes   197

Index   217

Foreword

The people of God have a huge stake in the issues captured by our word *counseling*.

What problems impel or compel a person to seek counseling help? The answer is simple, though the problems are complex. Emotions play in darkly minor keys: anxious, embittered, guilty, despairing, ashamed. Actions run in self-destructive ruts of compulsion and addiction. Thoughts proliferate internal chaos, obsessing fruitlessly. Sufferings hammer a person down until the experience seems unspeakable.

But something important often goes unmentioned in mentioning the obvious. Such life-disabling problems are complex intensifications of the utterly ordinary. The human condition intrudes brokenness into everyone and everything. Things go askew inside all of us. We live for good gifts, not the good Giver. Our instincts run to self-serving, even with the best of conscious intentions. We invest life energies in vanities and reap confusion. We addict ourselves to follies and reap pain. Relationships disappoint, and fragment, and alienate, and isolate. Others hurt you—and you hurt them. We find ourselves without resources to face suffering and feel crushed and overwhelmed. Young or old, you suffer a cascade of losses, and then, one way or another, you die. We are more like each other than different, when you look below the obvious differences.

It is a wonder that more people aren't in continuous emotional lockdown, in the fatal grip of panic, despair, and bitterness. The apparent stability of "ordinary life" bears an eloquent triple witness. God's providential goodness shines in all that's fair—*Thank you for all the blessings of this life.* Humankind is fascinated lifelong by schemes for earthly joy, sowing seeds of self-destruction—*Have mercy on us, Father of mercies.* What appears stable and ordinary is extraordinarily fragile—*You alone are the way, the truth, and the life.*

Failure and fragility, whether ordinary or intensified, can open a person to seek help or force a person to need help.

So why should the people of God care about these things that impel and compel people to seek counseling help? Because as ordinary people, these troubles and struggles are ours. And as God's people, in particular, such waywardness and woe is exactly what our Bible is about. This is what Jesus comes to do something about. This is what church and ministry are intended to tackle.

Or is it? Are the Bible, Jesus, church, and ministry about *counseling* problems? Or is our faith preoccupied with a religiously toned set of beliefs, activities, places, and experiences? Do counseling problems belong mainly to secular mental-health professionals? Make no mistake: according to Scripture, Christian faith and life are occupied with all the gritty, grimy, sad, or slimy things that make for human misery. Jesus came to start making right all that has gone wrong. And we are his living body put to work here on earth to keep making right whatever is wrong. And never forget: we are part of what is wrong. One and all, we need the give-and-take of wise counsel: Hebrews 3:12–14; Ephesians 4:15, 29; 2 Corinthians 1:4. In fact, we need Genesis 1 through Revelation 22 and the well-honed practical wisdom of brothers and sisters, both past and present, who have taken this God to heart.

We ought to be good at counseling, the very best at both receiving and giving. No one else's explanation of human misery goes as wide and long or as high and deep as the Christian explanation. No one else can account for the complexity of factors while keeping the actual *person* clearly in mind and heart. Think about this. Other counseling models never notice that actual persons are made and sustained by God and are accountable to God, searched out and weighed moment by moment. They never mention that actual persons are sinful by instinct and by choice; that we suffer within a context of meaningfulness; that Jesus Christ entered our plight; that we are redeemable and transformable by intimate mercy and power. Every other supposed explanation and answer looks shriveled when juxtaposed with the breadth, length, height, and depth of the love of Christ.

We should be very good at counseling. After all, Christian faith invented the hands-on care and cure of souls (the root meaning of *psychotherapy*). Intentional, life-transforming discipleship is a Christian distinctive. That's not to deny that many other intentional discipleships have arisen in the last one hundred years. But given their intrinsic and relentless secularity, other proposed psychotherapies cannot avoid "heal[ing] the wound of my people lightly, saying, 'Peace, peace,' when there is no peace" (Jer. 8:11). They offer Band-Aids and analgesics by essentially seeking ways to augment self-reliance. But we can heal deeply, forming essential reliance on the God of life. They hope to shape happier, more constructive human beings, a bit less self-destructive and others-destructive. But we aim for the faith that works out into self-giving love, that drinks from the springs of joy, that finds peace and knows how to make peace.

We should be good at counseling—caring, skillful, thoughtful. We should become the very best—careful, helpful, practical. But more often than not, we have been poor and foolish, rigid or inept. The pat answer, snap judgment, brisk manner, and quick fix are too often characteristic. Where is the patient kindness? Where is the probing concern and hard thought? Where is the luminous, pertinent truthfulness? Where is the flexibility of well-tailored wisdom? Where is the unfolding process? Where is the humanity of Jesus enfleshed in humane, humble, sensible people? Have mercy upon us, Father of mercies.

You are reading a book about the people of God attempting to become good at counseling. Notice four things about this book.

Notice the significance of the fact that Heath Lambert traces a story. A good story develops, unfolds, and goes places. It is like life itself, never static, frozen in one time, place, and person. This book traces a good story: we, God's people, can cooperate, building together to become good at counseling. We are becoming better at counseling. We will get better by far. Jesus is the best and wisest counselor. It does not yet appear what we shall be, but we know that when we see him, we will be like him. Such a hope gives us reasons to set out in his direction. The vision of Ephesians 3:14–5:2 will be realized in times, places, and persons. Wiser counseling will be realized in your life, in our lives, in the real-time-and-place story of the church of Jesus.

Notice the significance of the fact that Heath Lambert is in this story.

He does not stand outside, pretending to dispassionate objectivity. He cares about what happens. How will this story go? Where will we end up? This is his story—and yours. You and your church have a part to play in what happens next.

Notice the significance of the fact that Heath Lambert treats other people well. Yes, he's candid about the shortcomings he perceives; he is willing to disagree. But he notices strengths, too, and he is constructive in his candor. He wants us to rightly understand the points of essential continuity so that we all appreciate the organic nature of godly wisdom. He also wants us to rightly understand the significant points of difference so that we all appreciate the organic nature of growing in godly wisdom.

Notice the significance of the fact that Heath Lambert proposes some desirable next steps in the unfolding of our corporate wisdom. There are more chapters to be written in this story. Where are we heading? How can we go forward in a good direction?

Our trajectory into the future is the most important part of all this. As I look over the landscape that this book describes, I see a progression of six stages in the development of our collective wisdom. This is the process any one of us goes through in awakening and maturing into the wise love of good counseling. These six stages also describe the process all of us will go through as we grow up together.

First Stage. We each need to hear—some of us for the first time—that the church has a unique and significant counseling calling. The Lord interprets personal struggles and situational troubles through a *very* different set of eyes from how other counseling models see things. He engages us with a *very* different set of intentions from how other counseling models proceed. We, as his children, are meant to counsel according to how he sees and proceeds. The fruition of that vision may seem far off. Your church currently may be doing a poor job of counseling, or counseling through deviant eyes, or abdicating the task entirely. But as you come to realize that the Wonderful Counselor intends to form his people into, well, into pretty good counselors—and getting better all the time—it makes you stop and think. Until we know that something *might* exist, we can't envision participating. Participation becomes a possibility when something rises above the horizon. I hope that you hear the call.

Second Stage. We need to agree that the vision is a desirable one. Not only could the church become good in counseling, but we *should* become wise and fruitful in counseling ministries. Our God calls us to grow up in this area of ministry. You might want to read Ephesians 3:14–5:2 through the eyes of the question, "What does this imply about mutual counseling ministry?" Every sentence has implications. Hearing that it is possible to counsel in biblical wisdom—that God wills us to do so—leads to assent and commitment. I hope that you say, "Yes, this should be so. I may not yet understand exactly what it will look like, but I agree it ought to happen."

Third Stage. We need to personally embrace and embody the vision. This is the decisive step, the *sine qua non.* Scripture teaches you how to understand both your deepest struggles and your best gifts. God shows you how to face your heaviest troubles and how to respond to your greatest blessings. I believe that the Lord's vision of my sins and sorrows, of my graces and felicities, is the true understanding. I believe that the Lord's way of engaging broken people in a broken world is the only truly loving engagement. I take all this to heart. As we take it to heart, we enter into the lively dynamics of transformation portrayed in Psalms, Proverbs, Prophets, Histories, Gospels, and Epistles. You enter into God's counseling process for yourself. You become his disciple, learning his ways. You join the wise saints of all ages.

God's take on things becomes yours. You increasingly come to live in reality, leaving the shadowlands behind, forsaking the imaginary virtual realities. Whatever the configuration and severity of your personal problems, you come to understand yourself in a new light. That we must personally embrace biblical reality registers something very significant. I am not committed to biblical counseling because it's a theory that I happened to find persuasive, or because one killer Bible verse turned the lights on. I am committed because God tells the truth about me, about my world, about the Father, Savior, and Friend who has taken me to heart and takes me in hand. And I come to know any other human being—you, my fellow struggler, my brother or sister—by the same light in which I am coming to know myself.

The fact of personal embrace and embodiment is no oddity unique to biblical counseling. There is something essentially autobiographical about *every* counseling model ever proposed—Freud, Adler, Jung, Wolpe,

Rogers, Frankl, Gestalt, Glasser, biomedical psychiatry, MFT, CBT, ACT, DBT, EFT—or any eclectic combination. Each theory and practice reveals its author's core personal faith. Any ABC theory and XYZ therapy invented a hundred years from now will proclaim something essentially autobiographical. It will offer some way of interpreting and then reconfiguring humanness, according to where the author stands personally. If that understanding is not true to Scripture and to Christ—the Word written and the Word incarnate—then it will be false to humanness. If that interpretation and reconfiguration is not true to Scripture and to Christ, then it will be false to humanness. In a commitment to biblical counseling, I bear witness to how I understand life and to how I live. I hope that you enter into the call to wise counseling as simply one outworking of your call to live in Christ.

Fourth Stage. We need training, teaching, mentoring, practice, and supervision. Maturity always involves an educational process, a discipleship. You read books, talk with others, take classes, give it a try in practice, get feedback. If you are humble, you grow wiser. Your comprehension grows in scope and depth. Your skills in loving develop more relevance and flexibility. We rarely grow to understand anything without conscious application. Some of you will start to read good articles or books. Some of you will form discussion groups. Some of you will enter a graduate program for systematic study in biblical counseling. Some of you will take part in training in your church. I hope that you seek out the sort of learning appropriate to who God has made you and how he is working in you.

Fifth Stage. We need to become good at counseling. Excellent, in fact. You can enthusiastically embrace biblical counseling as an idea, even go to school to learn more, while still remaining inept. Perhaps the most accurate synonym for *counseling* is *wise love.* Wise love makes a huge difference in other people's lives. Both the receiving and the giving of wise love make a huge difference in your life. Genuine care, a searching question, sympathy and understanding, a timely and true word of God, practical aid, patience in the process—these are life giving. Here's the bottom line: you must become better able to help people. This contains a divine paradox. All genuine life transformation is the direct work of the life giver, the Shepherd of his sheep, the Father of his children. At the same time, this living God willingly uses us to give life to each other, to shepherd each other, to nourish, protect, and encourage each other. Skill takes time and experience. Skill calls you to the humility of a man or woman who is always learning. Skill bears fruit. It sweetens and brightens the lives of other people. I hope that you pursue the goal of becoming good at counseling.

Sixth Stage. We need to develop leaders. Counseling wisdom is a communicable skill. It must be communicated to others, spread around, passed down the generations, developed further. Three kinds of leaders will be raised up.

Some people will become leaders by their skillfulness in teaching others. They are able to break a complex process down into its component parts. They have a sense for the scales and arpeggios necessary to learn to play beautiful music. They possess some of the many sub-skills: assessing others accurately, selecting good candidates, hands-on training, face-to-face mentoring, insightful supervision, careful coaching. Leadership means not only the ability to counsel strugglers but also the ability to help someone else learn to counsel strugglers. It replicates skill. It's not a given that skill in practice (fifth stage) leads to skillful teaching (sixth stage). Think of a basketball player who can routinely nail the 24-foot jump shot. What if you ask him to teach you to nail your jump shots from downtown, and he tells you, "I just shoot the ball, and it goes in." He may make the Hall of Fame as a player, but he'll never be a coach. Will God call you to train others?

Other people will become leaders by their ability to contribute to intellectual progress. Biblical wisdom must always be sharpened and developed. It is fashioned by engaging new problems, meeting new threats, interacting with new contenders, and identifying new needs in order for us to grow up into greater wisdom. It helps all of us when someone can put familiar truths into unfamiliar words and can point out unexpected implications. It helps all of us when one stands back and reflects on what we are all doing and then points out both our strengths and our weaknesses. It's so easy for any of us to stagnate or get into ruts. We need to be refreshed, to extend the range and depth of what we understand to be true. Will God call you to contribute to the R&D work that refreshes ministry? Will he call you to push the envelope so that we all become more faithful to the God who speaks and acts?

Still others will become leaders by their talent as entrepreneurs and managers. Counseling needs a home. The care and cure of souls calls for organizational structure, institutional development, delivery systems, support staff, financial underpinning. All ministry costs time and money and occurs in a context. Leaders with gifts in startup and in administration are able to create, maintain, and re-create appropriate structures and support systems so that counseling skills are best used. Will God call you to help build healthy churches or healthy parachurch ministries so that the body of Christ can deliver the goods of good counseling to people in need?

I hope that someday some readers become such leaders.

Whether you are just considering the possibility of biblical counseling, or flourishing already as a leader, or somewhere in the middle, I trust that the pages that follow will nourish your wisdom. *The Biblical Counseling Movement after Adams* is a story about our growing up. Make its story your story. As you work your way through the book, let me encourage you to take the next steps. Commit yourself to choose one of the books or articles mentioned and put that next on your reading list. Commit yourself to talk with someone else about how your church might become better at counseling.

Most of all, may each of us live our lives within God's reality, becoming good at receiving wise love (stage three). And may each of us thus grow up toward wise love in helping others (stage five). Here's one way I weigh whether a counselor is good: would I entrust my mother, my daughter, or my wife into your care? Would you handle their honest struggles well and wisely? Would I entrust the fine china of my own life into your care? Would you prove truly helpful? And do I give you reason to trust me with the hardest things in your life? May we give each other good reasons to trust, as Ephesians 4:15–16 becomes the living reality of our life together, bringing the peace of Christ into this broken world.

David Powlison

Acknowledgments

A project like this always represents the labor of many people. This reality is certainly the case in my situation. I am deeply indebted to many who have contributed in countless ways to the completion of this project. I am thankful to the members of Crossing Church in Louisville, Kentucky, whom I serve as the pastor of biblical living. It is a joy to live the Christian life with them. As they speak to me and let me speak to them, I am learning to be more like Jesus.

I am also thankful to the many students I have had in class at Southern Seminary and Boyce College. Their questions, criticisms, and comments have helped me think through much of what is written here. Their reflections spurred me to make many improvements to the ideas in this book.

I must thank Stuart Scott. It is a joy to stand beside him preparing future ministers for service in the kingdom of Christ. For years he has been a treasured mentor, guide, and friend. In our numerous conversations, he has been a source of wisdom and encouragement as well as an example of how true and loving conversation should happen in the Christian community. This book would look very different were it not for his influence on me.

Before this was a book, it was a PhD dissertation, and so I need to thank the members of my doctoral committee. Chad Brand and Randy Stinson have given of their time and wisdom, and I am profoundly thankful for each of them. These men—apart from helping me to improve what is written here—have encouraged me greatly. In my life up to this point, I have never worked under men who were so interested in helping me arrive at excellence and success. Working with each of them has been an honor.

The supervisor of that committee was David Powlison. He has walked with me every step of the way through this project. Without his wisdom and care, this project would never have been written. Without his living example of Christlikeness, I would be much less than what I am. One of the greatest honors of my life was doing my doctoral work under his leadership. I am repeatedly thankful for his friendship, wisdom, and input.

I also need to thank the entire team at Crossway for their confidence that this dissertation could become a book. Working with everyone on their team was truly a blessing. I have deep appreciation for the work of Lydia Brownback, in particular. Her meticulous work of editing caught errors that many other people missed. She took the book to the next level, and I am very grateful.

My dear and precious wife, Lauren, is more responsible for the completion of this project than any person under heaven. During my work on this dissertation-turned-book, she has cooked one thousand meals, changed a million diapers, given birth twice, and cared for me day in and day out. She is God's most precious gift to me, and I love her more than I could communicate in a work one hundred times as long. "Her children rise up and call her blessed; her husband also, and he praises her" (Prov. 31:28).

Finally, I am supremely thankful for the sustaining grace given to me by God. The completion of this project is one more demonstration that his strength is truly perfected in weakness.

Heath B. Lambert
Louisville, Kentucky
January 2011

1

The Birth of a Biblical Counseling Movement and the Need for Growth

This is not a book about counseling. Even though you might be tempted to think it is a book about counseling, it is really a book about ministry. The fact is that counseling is ministry, and ministry is counseling. The two are equivalent terms. *Counseling* is the word our culture uses to describe what happens when people with questions, problems, and trouble have a conversation with someone they think has answers, solutions, and help. Those kinds of conversations are what ministers do every day, all day long, and the ministers who don't do this know that they could spend their time this way if they wanted to. So don't think that just because this book is about counselors, it doesn't have anything to do with your ministry. That it is about counselors means it has *everything* to do with your ministry.

If counseling is equivalent to ministry, it means that it must be informed by the Bible and that those who do it are theologians. Ministry always grows out of worldview commitments. As Christians we believe that our worldview is authoritatively informed by God's Word, the Bible; that is to say, it is *theologically* informed. Counseling is, therefore by definition, a theological task. Counselors may understand that counseling is a theological task or they may not. They may be good theologians or bad ones, but make no mistake: they are theologians who are neck deep in a theological enterprise.

I hate to say it, but most people don't understand this. In fact two very different groups have been guilty of cutting the theological foundations away from the counseling task. The first group is secular psychotherapists who are very well intentioned but ultimately seek to help people solve their problems while ignoring Christ and his Word. They have rejected the Godward dimension of counseling, moving in the opposing direction to claim that God and his people should have little or no role to play in the counseling task.[1] Their diagnoses of and their attempts at "curing" people and their problems are man-centered and so will always fall short of offering people true and lasting change for their deepest problems. Integrationists, taking their cues from this group, attempt to be theologically faithful but formulate the theology in an unfaithful way.[2]

A second group misunderstanding this issue is—ironically—conservative, Bible-believing, Christ-exalting ministers of the gospel. These conservative ministers fail to grasp that counseling is an essential part of ministry and so disconnect theology from counseling. They demonstrate the misunderstanding every time they say things like, "Oh, I don't counsel people; I'm a preacher," or, "Counseling takes too much time away from my other ministries," or, "I don't think the Bible has anything to say about this problem; you need to see a professional." Such people mean well, but they are wrong about the theological, ministry-driven nature of counseling. Each of these groups fails to understand the intrinsic connection that counseling has with ministry and theology. The truth of the matter is that I used to be in the second group. Let me tell you my story.

My mother was addicted to vodka during the first eleven years of my life. By the grace of God she quit drinking, repented of her sins, and became a believer in Jesus a few years before her death, but that was after I had grown up. A large portion of my childhood was filled with the roller coaster of my mother's months and years of drunken stupors followed by her many failed attempts to stop drinking. I would sit with my mother during her many visits to Alcoholics Anonymous meetings, and at these meetings I overheard a great deal of talk about "the disease of alcoholism" and statements like, "It wasn't me who did those things; it was my disease." At a very young age I remember thinking, "It doesn't *seem* like a disease." When my grandfather died of cancer I thought, "Now *that* seems like a disease." The point here is that even before I became a believer, I was not convinced about the application of a disease model to problems such as drunkenness that were clearly moral in nature, because such problems involved issues like self-control and avoidance rather than being merely physical.

Then, years later, after I became a Christian in my freshman year of high school, one of the first books I read was the first book Jay Adams wrote about counseling, *Competent to Counsel*. I read through the book in one sitting, and my mouth was hanging open the entire time I read it. I was captivated by Adams's vision to reclaim counseling as a theological and ministerial task and of his mission to make counseling an enterprise that was centered on Christ, based on his Word, and located in the local church. From that point on, I was a wholehearted believer in biblical counseling and wished the best to those who were a part of the movement. I only wished them well, however; I certainly did not want to *be* a counselor.

I wanted to be a pastor, and by that I meant that I wanted to be a preacher. By my second year of college, the Lord had created in me a strong desire for the work of ministry. I wanted to preach. I wanted to spend my weeks surrounded by commentaries unearthing the glories of God's Word. I wanted to spend my Sundays dispensing those glories to God's people. I admired preachers such as R. C. Sproul, John Piper, John MacArthur, and Tim Keller. A few years later I reported for duty to my first paid pastoral position and couldn't wait to hit the books. Little did I know that in that first week God was going to completely redefine how I conceived of pastoral ministry.

That very first week, three separate groups requested meetings with me. I wasn't sure what they wanted to talk about but was thrilled at the thought of conducting such meetings. I couldn't wait to answer the theological questions these people had. I was ready to deal with issues about the Trinity, inerrancy, Calvinism, whatever. Let me at it!

I was in for a surprise.

The first meeting was with an elderly couple who were having marriage problems and wanted advice. Their words to me were, "We've been married for more than fifty years and all of it has been bad. We don't know how much time the Lord has for us, but we want what is left to be good. Can you help us have a better marriage?" The second meeting was with a mother and her daughter, who had been molested, and they wanted help they had not received from secular therapists. The third meeting was with a mother who wanted help knowing how to control a difficult child.

To say that I had absolutely no idea what had hit me would be putting it mildly. I had no kids, had never been molested, and had been married for only a few weeks! What did I know? I realized in the span of one week that I should not only wish biblical counselors well but figure out how to do what they were doing. I realized that there was no arbitrary distinction between the public ministry of the Word in preaching and the personal ministry of the Word in counseling. I realized that being a faithful pastor and preacher meant also being a faithful counselor.

So I began to work hard to understand biblical counseling. I made friends with people who were committed to counseling and spent a lot of time with them. I also started reading everything I could get my hands on and even began formal study in the area. In fact, I got a little carried away and ultimately earned a PhD on the topic.

I tell you that story because I want you to know how I came to see that learning about counseling is really about learning how to do ministry well. Here is a fact that you'd better write down, underline, circle, highlight, and memorize: if you want to be faithful in ministry (I didn't say *successful*) you're going to have to learn something about counseling. There's just no way around it.

The other reason I tell you that story is to help you understand something I began to figure out about biblical counselors. As I read all the different books and all the different authors on biblical counseling I started to notice that not everybody sounded the same. Oh, there were plenty of strong similarities: everyone was committed to Scripture as the source of wisdom for change, to Jesus as the source of power for change, and to the church as the central location for change, but there were also a lot of differences. Specifically, people who wrote during the first twenty years of the movement often sounded different from those who have been writing in the last twenty years of the movement. I also noticed that these differences were really improvements. The movement was not merely changing but was changing for the better. I further noticed that there was actually a fascinating story that surrounded these changes and improvements.

The purpose of this book is to tell you that story and to describe the improvements that have happened in the biblical counseling movement. I think it is important to tell you this because I believe that if you know how the biblical counseling movement has advanced, you will be a better church member, friend, brother, parent, or minister who is more equipped to have the kinds of conversations Jesus wants his church to have.

The story of this group of men and women is actually the fourth part of an even larger theological drama. You see, the Christian effort to help people with their problems did not begin forty years ago but rather is as old as the Scriptures themselves. God inspired the Scriptures for the very purpose of helping people with their problems (2 Pet. 1:3–4). Throughout the centuries of church history God's people have been at times more faithful and at times less faithful to use the Scriptures in ministering to struggling persons. The last forty years have been a time when the American church has been growing in its facility to use the Scriptures this way, but it is not really possible to understand what has happened in the last few decades without a brief peak into the last few centuries for some historical perspective. The church's attempt to do ministry in the last several hundred years has unfolded in a drama of deep theological reflection, theological neglect, theological recovery, and theological advancement.

A Period of Deep Theological Reflection

The Puritans took counseling seriously. They didn't call it counseling, but they believed that ministry was important, and they began a particularly rich period in theological thought regarding personal ministry of the Word. Those men wrote hundreds of works to help people deal with their problems in living. It is impossible to survey all the literature there, but it will be helpful to mention a few works. Richard Baxter wrote *The Christian Directory*, outlining in exhaustive detail the spiritual problems Christians face.[3] John Owen wrote, among other things, *The Mortification of Sin* as a practical guide for dealing with the flesh.[4] *A Lifting Up for the Downcast* was intended by William Bridge to be an encouragement to Christians struggling with all manner of life's difficulties.[5]

Writing in the Puritan tradition in America, Jonathan Edwards wrote *A Treatise Concerning the Religious Affections* to deal with the pastoral issue of judging true works of the Spirit from false ones.[6] One of the last careful works was Ichabod Spencer's *A Pastor's Sketches* in the 1850s.[7] In this work, Spencer recounted his conversations with many troubled persons and showed—in the context of nineteenth-century case studies—how ministers might talk with troubled people about their problems. Spencer's work was not perfect. He could be a bit heady and ignored internal realities that helped some secular thinkers believe that Protestant reflection on counseling was a wasteland. Still, in many ways, it represented the end of careful and uniquely Christian reflection about the task of interpersonal ministry.

Theological Neglect

The next book after *A Pastor's Sketches* that would offer uniquely biblical insight into helping people with their problems was Jay Adams's book *Competent to Counsel*, more than one hundred years later![8] Why is it that Christians neglected a robustly biblical approach to counseling for more than a century? The truth of the matter is that there were many reasons why this happened, and here I want to address nine of the most important.

1) People Want to Understand and Help Other People

Just look at the best-seller list. Books written by psychologists thought to explain people and their problems typically dominate. Seen any TV lately? Talk-show hosts often serve the role of pop-psychologist to their viewers (when they are not professionally trained as such). With increasing frequency, news programs invite psychologists to explain the inner workings of newsmakers or the public that observes and responds to them. Psychology is the most popular undergraduate degree program in colleges across the United States. All of this is true, because people love to know how they and others function. But there is a rub. When people begin to discover how others function, they become aware of problems and want to help. This is where counseling and therapy come in: when you observe, you see trouble and try to give help.

This reality ensures that what David Powlison calls "the Faith's psychology"[9] will always have competitors. That competition will come from both inside and outside Christianity, but this drive to know about people will mean that many different philosophies of helping people with their problems will always be present and in need of critique and correction. Therefore, Christians must always be vigilant to strengthen their understanding of the problems people have and be aware of alternative positions so that such positions may be critiqued. When this fails to happen, the faith's psychology will recede and a faithless psychology will ascend.

2) Counseling Is Hard to See

Another consistent problem that makes it hard for Christians to engage in theological reflection on counseling is that it is hard to see. Think about it. Preaching is not hard to see at all. It's a public ministry visible to the masses. The opposite is true with the interpersonal ministry of counseling. Very often, those who are in the room at the time are the only ones aware that counseling is happening. Out of sight, out of mind—that is the problem here. People do not generally give much thought to things they never see.

As I mentioned earlier, the Lord used the preaching ministry of several men to ignite a passion for ministry in my heart, and this centered initially on preaching rather than counseling, because I could see the former and not the latter. There are thousands just like me in this regard. They think about and love the public ministry of the Word because they see it. Conversely the personal ministry of the Word doesn't occur to them, because they never see it. Because this is true, it is critical that Christians be vigilant to use the public ministry of the Word to exhort other believers toward the importance of the personal ministry of the Word.

3) Counseling Is Hard to Do

Another timeless difficulty of personal ministry is that it is hard. That is not to say that the public ministry of the Word is easy. I have spent years as a pastor preaching three to five different sermons a week, so I know it can be tough. I'm also saying, however, that the challenges of personal ministry in counseling are on display in a way that the challenges of public ministry—in preaching, for example—are not. Both the audience and the content of public ministry are general. However, preachers preach to crowds, addressing no particular person or problem. Because this is true, the sermons of a preacher could potentially fail to produce change in the lives of his hearers for quite some time before anyone caught on.

But personal ministry is the exact opposite. Both the audience and the content of personal ministry are, by definition, specific. The counselor counsels specific people with names, faces, and stories. Because this is true, counselors cannot fail to address problems and pursue change with their counselees. Failure is immediately apparent to real people with real problems who need real grace from a real God. Counselors cannot hide behind crowds but are always under scrutiny from the others in the room.

The difficulties of counseling are, therefore, more difficult to obscure than the difficulties of public ministry of the Word. Because this is true, some may be less inclined to engage in counseling ministry. Quite frankly, the level of scrutiny present in counseling is likely to make it an undesirable locale of ministry for many people. This reality makes it incumbent on those who would be faithful ministers of the Word in all its forms to be diligent to practice the personal ministry of the Word as well as to proclaim its necessity to anyone who would be an authentic servant of Christ.

These three issues make counseling difficult to reflect on theologically in all times and places, but Christians will always need to think through counseling in the face of these difficulties. These three factors are partially to blame for the failure of Christians between the middle of the 1800s and the middle of the 1900s to think theologically about counseling, but they are not the only reasons. There were also some important historical factors that caused the church to take its eye off the counseling ball and move away from the rich resources of the Puritan area. These historical forces came both from within the church and from the surrounding culture.

4) Revivalism

In the 1700s a religious phenomenon began to grip Christianity—revivalism. In discussing the history of revival, Iain Murray quotes eighteenth-century theologians Jonathan Edwards and Solomon Stoddard, saying, respectively, that revival is "a surprising work of God," and is "some special season wherein God doth in a remarkable manner revive religion among his people."[10] A century or so later, things were much different. Murray says:

> [By the close of] the nineteenth century . . . a new view of revival came generally to displace the old, and a distinctly different phase in the understanding of the subject began. A shift in vocabulary was a pointer to the nature of the change. Seasons of revival became "revival meetings." Instead of being "surprising" they might now be even announced

in advance, and whereas no one in the previous century had known of ways to secure revival, a system was then popularized by "revivalists" that came near to guaranteeing results.[11]

Revival, historically seen to be the unilateral work of God, had given way to revival*ism*, which was seen to be based on the engineering of people. There is a lot that could be said about revivalism, but for the purposes of this project, only two elements demand attention. The first is the focus among revivalists on drawing a crowd. The camp meeting was so called because spectators would travel long distances to the meeting and then camp there for several days. This ability to camp out in one location made it possible to have bigger crowds, since attendees could travel from long distances and stay for long periods of time. The crowds were often quite large. One revival, the largest ever, in Cane Ridge, Kentucky, had anywhere from thirty thousand to one hundred thousand persons in attendance.[12] Though this meeting was larger than most, crowds were typically in the hundreds and thousands—much larger than any single-day event could ever be.

The second element of revivalism that is important to address regards the purpose of drawing a crowd—conversion. The revivalist's motivation in drawing a crowd was to preach the gospel so that sinners would trust in Jesus and be saved. Other components, such as religious education, also occurred during revivals, but they were secondary to the primary goal, which was to preach sinners out of hell and into heaven.

Revivalism has been rightly criticized for much of its excesses,[13] and yet it must also be said that with regard to the elements addressed here, there is nothing wrong in principle with drawing a crowd and seeking the conversion of those in that crowd. In fact, it is a good idea. Having said that, revivalism's emphasis on these two aspects did over time have a devastating impact on the interpersonal ministry of counseling.

In many ways, counseling and revivalism have opposite emphases. First, revivalists concern themselves with drawing huge crowds and preaching to the masses, but counselors are concerned with individualized ministry and conversation. Second, where revivalists have conversion as the goal, a minister seeking to counsel biblically will have that same goal but is just as likely to focus on discipleship. Third, revivalists tend to focus on instantaneous change that is measured in a moment of decision; counselors tend to work in the details of change that happen in a process and over time. Given these emphases it is not difficult to see how a Christian culture that was consumed with revivalism for many decades had trouble reflecting upon and emphasizing the activity of interpersonal ministry.

5) The Fundamentalist-Modernist Controversy

The church was confronted by another significant challenge by the end of the nineteenth century. The problem was what came to be called "modernism." In this controversy higher criticism and Darwinism worked to undercut the confidence that many ministers and ordinary Christians had in the authority of the biblical text. The Bible's teaching on the origins of the world, its understanding of the problems of people, and even the words of Scripture itself all came under fire. George Marsden addresses this issue:

> The publication of Charles Darwin's *Origin of Species* in 1859 had sparked an intellectual crisis for Christians that no educated person could ignore. Darwinism focused the issue on the reliability of the first chapters of Genesis. But the wider issue was whether the Bible could be trusted at all. German higher criticism, questioning the historicity of many biblical accounts, had been developing for more than a generation, so that it was highly sophisticated by the time after the Civil War when it became widely known in America. It would be difficult to overstate the crucial importance of the absolute integrity of the Bible to the nineteenth-century American evangelical's whole way of thinking. When this cornerstone began to be shaken, major adjustments in the evangelical edifice had to be made from top to bottom.[14]

The church was in crisis, and its leaders sprang into action. Leaders of the so-called Princeton School were the first ones to deal with the crisis. The Princeton theologians famously addressed the issue of biblical authority in works such as *The Inspiration and Authority of the Bible* by B. B. Warfield.[15] Years later, *The Fundamentals* was published, which was meant, as the title indicates, to defend the fundamentals of the faith against liberal attacks.[16]

Such defenses of the faith were necessary. Defending the faith against liberalism was critical work. Such critical fights, however, have a way of marginalizing other important activities. *The Fundamentals* was a defense of important issues including the authority of Scripture and the origins of the universe; however, a biblical defense of theology that was pastoral, personal, and practical was not included in its pages. Counseling was ignored. As mentioned above, it was ignored for all the right reasons, but it was ignored all the same. This left an opening for the modernists to come in and take over counseling within the church. With conservative minds focused on defending the Bible, modernists began to be consumed with secular approaches to counseling in their excitement over the social gospel.[17] This modernist connection with counseling made it only more difficult for conservatives to reflect on the topic.

6) The Psychological Revolution

While the church was grappling with revivalism and modernism on the inside, there were also big changes happening in the culture. One big change was a revolution that occurred in the field of psychology toward the end of the nineteenth century. To understand the psychological revolution, it is necessary to understand two of its most important leaders, Wilhelm Wundt and Sigmund Freud.

Wilhelm Wundt founded the world's first psychological laboratory and is regarded as the father of experimental psychology.[18] Wundt is responsible for what he called physiological psychology. According to Wundt, all of a person's psychological processes are rooted in some element of their biology.[19] What this means is that basically everything you think and feel begins in your physical parts. This made Wundt years ahead of his time, as this is what most psychologists believe today, even though Jesus and the apostles said that everything we think and feel grows out of our heart or soul (Matt. 12:33–37; Mark 7:14–23; James 1:14–15).

For Wundt, then, psychology and physiology were intrinsically interrelated. Wundt is an important figure in the history of science because he is credited with rounding out the scientific revolution, bringing it into the field of psychology. He was among the first to bring the scientific method to psychology using experimentation and was the first to urge his students to find relationships between the physical and spiritual realities of people. If you are going to understand why the church stopped thinking about counseling in a theological way, you need to understand Wundt, because he took the first steps in making psychology a respectable scientific discipline based, at least in part, in a study of the human body.

Sigmund Freud is perhaps the most famous (and infamous) figure in the history of psychology. Here it is only necessary to draw out one main element regarding Freud's stated goal. He initiated a practice called "psychotherapy" or the "talking cure." As I argued above, historically pastors provided the guidance and wisdom for helping people with life's problems, but Freud thought the church had failed in this task. In his work *The Question of Lay Analysis*, Freud argued for a class of "secular pastoral workers" with the goal of secularizing the counseling task.[20] The term *counseling* was not in vogue in Freud's day, so, amazingly, he described the task of helping people as the "pastoral" task. In this book, Freud makes clear that his task was to remove counseling from the ministerial context and place it in a secular one.

It is essential to understand the work of Wundt and Freud to appreciate the decline in theological reflection on counseling. Once psychology began to be defined in secular scientific terms (Wundt), it became possible to argue that psychotherapy should be the prerogative of secular professionals (Freud). The emphasis on each of these elements resulted in a massive decline in ministers reflecting on this same subject. During another time such a decline might not have happened, but at this peculiar period of history, as has already been mentioned, the church was focused on other things.

7) A Changing American Economy

The transition from the 1800s to the 1900s was a critical period not only for the church and the scientific community but also for the American economy. The change happened in two respects. On the one hand, Americans began to move from the country to the city. On the other hand, and linked to the first change, Americans began to move from farm work to factory work.

The Industrial Revolution, as it was called, created a new category of person—the titan of industry. The titan of industry served to stoke a kind of tough masculinity that the culture found desirable at that point in history.[21] It highlighted the kind of strong-willed man that could hold the masses in his sway. As the culture became enamored with this type of individual, the effects carried over into church life as well and stoked the flames of desire for the larger-than-life preacher that was accentuated in revivals.[22]

The move from small towns to big cities and from farm work to factory work had another impact on the church's theological reflection regarding counseling. In the old agrarian economy, workers had to be experts with *things*—soil, farm equipment, seasons, and crop rotations. In the new industrial economy, the barons of industry had to be experts in, among other things, *people*. The larger a company became, the more employees it hired. The more employees a company hired, the larger was the necessity to keep those employees happy, cooperative, and productive. A historian by the name of E. Brooks Holifield describes what I'm talking about:

> [The new American] working as members of staffs, faculties, committees, and management teams . . . needed to be adept at handling people and manipulating abstract symbols. Their task was to maintain the morale and high motivation of people who worked under them, adapting themselves to the expectations of superiors who valued "well-rounded personality." . . . [This kind of economy] could not have been better designed to stimulate interest in the nuances of "personal relations." . . . Large corporations began to value good scores on "personality tests" as much as experience or intellectual ability. . . . [On the other hand], churches presented themselves as preservers of the family or as havens of friendliness.[23]

As the church was focusing on a revivalistic effort at soul winning and a defense of the fundamentals of the faith, secular psychologists were gaining ascendancy employing the scientific method with cutting-edge work in understanding people in their relationships with others. As it turns out, this was information that a changing American culture found useful, while the church sat on the sidelines. Christians were simply not involved in these activities. Psychology came into vogue, and the church was behind the times.

8) The Civil War

Christian reflection on counseling declined because of changes in the church and in the culture but was also brought about by three major wars. The first was the American Civil War. Between 1861 and 1865 America was involved in the deadliest war it had ever fought or would ever fight up to the present day. The American Civil War called upon countrymen to fight against one another, brother against brother. The war consumed the country, leaving no segment of the population untouched. The war also toughened the country. A brutal and bloody war served to emphasize certain masculine virtues such as strength and toughness. In the aftermath of the war, there seemed to be no time for casual conversation and discussion. Such activities were seen to be effeminate at a time when more masculine activities were prized. Holifield also refers to this phenomenon when he says:

> By promoting a cult of masculinity in intellectual circles, the war raised a question about the cure of souls: Was the whole enterprise perhaps unmanly? The question implicitly equated pastoral care with genteel and refined conversations that proceeded delicately in parlors and sitting rooms. Such an image of pastoral labor embarrassed ministers who had come to admire the "bold virtues."[24]

Ministerial embarrassment regarding the "gentility" of pastoral counseling is one element behind a decline in pastoral counsel. They were afraid to act like girls. The American Civil War coarsened the country, emphasizing a certain kind of toughness over against biblical reflection on the practice of interpersonal conversation.[25] Theological impoverishment was a direct result of this unhappy reality.

9) World Wars I and II

Wars bring trouble and massive social change. Psychology was introduced to the military during World War I in the form of placement tests to properly locate the vast numbers of manpower in the workforce. By the end of the war, the problem of "shell shock" presented an urgent need for the military to help those who crumbled under the intense pressure of battle.[26] During World War II, the United States government enlisted thousands of men as chaplains to assist those psychologists in counseling soldiers with their problems that stemmed from prolonged exposure to the violent and volatile battlefields of war. The involvement of chaplains in the war effort helped address the problem of effeminacy that came about in the wake of the American Civil War but, interestingly, created another problem.

Upon returning from the war, many chaplains involved in the effort expressed chagrin at their lack of preparation for the work. Many simply felt unqualified to help battle-torn soldiers deal with the complex problems they were facing. Holifield observes:

> When the service people began to talk to the chaplains, something often seemed awry. A study of veterans after the war revealed that their complaints about the wartime clergy returned almost invariably to one issue: The chaplains too frequently lacked the skills appropriate to the cure of souls.[27]

Christians serving as chaplains had the resources in Scripture to help these men but lacked competency in how to use them. For years secular psychology had been on the rise, while biblical reflection had been on the decline. Now, when placed on center stage in the war effort, the bareness was beginning to show. When this failure was placed alongside the relative success that psychologists had coming out of the war effort,[28] it resulted in more lost ground for those committed to a biblical philosophy of helping people.

Pressures from within the church and from without all played an important role in the decline of biblical reflection on how to care for people experiencing problems in living. Just as Christian reflection on these matters was decreasing, secular reflection and practice was on the rise. The work of Sigmund Freud led to the work of dozens of others until, by the middle of the twentieth century, most Christians who were taking seriously the responsibility to care for people's problems in living had adopted the person-centered approach to counseling of Carl Rogers. Christian thinking had given way to secular thinking in the ministry to persons. Original and distinct Christian reflection was not happening. Regarding counseling, the church had experienced a devastating theological loss.

Theological Recovery

The absence of theology in counseling was the order of the day when, in 1970, Jay Adams published *Competent to Counsel*.[29] In that book and many others in the 1970s Adams sought to alert Christians to their failures in the area of counseling and began pointing the way to the resources laid out in Scripture for helping people. It was the role of Adams to begin to restore to the church an understanding that it had held before the American Civil War, namely, that counseling was within the realm of the church, every bit as much as its counterpart in public ministry, preaching.

Adams believed that counseling was intrinsically theological. He claimed:

> All counseling, by its very nature (as it tries to explain and direct human beings in their living before God and in a fallen world) implies theological commitments by the counselor. He simply cannot become involved in the attempt to change beliefs, values, attitudes, relationships and behavior without wading neck deep in theological waters. . . . These theological commitments may be conscious or unconscious, biblical or heretical, good theology or bad, but—either way—they surely are theological . . . . Thus . . . the relationship between counseling and theology is organic; counseling cannot be done apart from theological commitments. Every act, word (or lack of these) implies theological commitments.[30]

Adams's conception of the counseling task was deeply rooted in Scripture and was, therefore, intensely theological. This conviction was the basis of Adams's work. A focus on counseling that was theologically informed, however, brought a problem into focus for Adams. As he looked over the counseling landscape, he saw a field full of compromise in the counseling arena. Theological reflection on counseling that had been in place at earlier points of history had given way to a thoroughly secular approach in modern psychology. When people conceived of counseling, their categories of thinking were not shaped by biblical presuppositions but by secular ones.

While this was perhaps to be expected, another reality that Adams needed to confront was that these secular categories of thought had infiltrated the church. Because that is true, Adams's theological recovery of counseling logically operated in two modes: a destructive mode and a constructive mode. On one hand, Adams needed a destructive element in his model aimed at discrediting secular approaches to counseling. On the other hand, Adams needed to build a positive biblical model.

Critiquing Secular Approaches to Counseling

Adams believed that secularists had commandeered the domain of counseling, which rightfully belonged to Christians. Because he believed this to be true and because the secular model for counseling was the dominant one, it was critical for Adams to make the case against it. Adams said:

> Biblically, there is no warrant for acknowledging the existence of a separate and distinct discipline called psychiatry. There are, in the Scriptures, only three specified sources of personal problems in living: demonic activity (principally possession), personal sin, and organic illness. These three are interrelated. All options are covered under these heads, leaving no room for a fourth: non-organic mental illness. There is, therefore, no place in a biblical scheme for the psychiatrist as a separate practitioner. This self-appointed caste came into existence with the broadening of the medical umbrella to include inorganic illness (whatever that means). A new practitioner, part physician (a very small part) and part secular priest (a very large part), came into being to serve the host of persons who previously were counseled by ministers but now had been snatched away from them and placed beneath the broad umbrella of "mental illness."[31]

There are several elements of Adams's view to note here. First, Adams denied the existence of inorganic mental illness. The operative term here is *inorganic*. Adams never denied the existence of physical (i.e., organic) problems and diseases in the brain. What he explicitly denied is the notion of mental illness that is disconnected from pathology. Adams argued:

> Growing numbers of authorities have begun to object to the concept of "mental illness," and the vigorous propaganda campaign, which has been conducted under that misleading misnomer. The fact is that the words "mental illness" are used quite ambiguously. . . . Organic malfunctions affecting the brain that are caused by brain damage, tumors, gene inheritance, glandular or chemical disorders, validly may be termed mental illnesses. But at the same time a vast number of other human problems have been classified as mental illnesses for which there is no evidence that they have been engendered by disease or illness at all. As a description of many of these problems, the term mental illness is nothing more than a figure of speech, and in most cases a poor one at that.[32]

Second, Adams argued that psychiatrists as counseling practitioners are illegitimate. Because inorganic mental illness is a nonentity, when psychiatrists attempt to help people with their problems, they are actually engaging in the work of the ministry. (As Adams said, they are functioning as "secular priests.") Adams said further, "Psychiatry's legitimate function is to serve those who suffer from organic difficulties. The psychiatrist has reason for existence only when he specializes as a physician to treat medically those persons whose problems have an organic etiology."[33]

Third, as Adams argued against the existence of inorganic mental illness and against psychiatrists as "separate practitioners," he did so standing on the authority of God's Word. It is Adams's reading of Scripture that helped him to see three legitimate problem sources: demonic activity, personal sin, and organic illness; and one illegitimate source: inorganic mental illness. It was Adams's further reading of Scripture that led him to rule out-of-bounds the psychiatrist's efforts at secular ministry. Adams's worldview was thoroughly biblical. God's Word stood as his standard, and he viewed it as a fundamentally faithless act to evaluate counseling—or anything else—by another standard. He said:

> The Bible itself provides the principles for understanding and for engaging in nouthetic counseling and directs Christian ministers to do such counseling as a part of their life calling in the ministry of the Word. . . . Therefore, those who develop other systems, based on other sources of information, by which they attempt to achieve these same ends, by the very nature of the case *become competitive*. It is dangerous to compete with the Bible, since all such competition in the end turns out to be competition with God.[34]

Adams, therefore, believed that secularists in the field of counseling were illegitimate. Their theories compete with God's Word. They engage in work reserved for Christian ministers. They misunderstand the problems that people have. Their solutions are false gospels.

While it was true that Adams had strong disagreements with those practicing psychotherapy, it would be going too far to say that Adams believed psychological science had no role to play. Adams believed that psychological science did have value when used rightly. In fact, at the very beginning of Adams's very first book on counseling he said:

I do not wish to disregard science, but rather I welcome it as a useful adjunct for the purposes of illustrating, filling in generalizations with specifics, and challenging wrong human interpretations of Scripture, thereby forcing the student to restudy the Scriptures. However, in the area of psychiatry, science largely has given way to humanistic philosophy and gross speculation.[35]

In other words, Adams believed psychology[36] could be useful when appropriately understood and rightly applied. When psychology stayed on its own turf and dealt with organic issues, Adams believed it could be helpful and beneficial. What Adams ferociously objected to, however, was the atheistic worldview of psychology as well as his perception that psychologists were meddling in the domain of the Christian ministry. It was crossing this line—not their existence in general—that earned them the ire of Adams.

Constructing a Biblical Approach to Counseling

Adams's fundamental task was positive. His critique of secular psychology and its encroachment into the church served to clear the ground so that he and others could construct a biblical approach to counseling and helping people with their problems.[37]

Adams's construction of a biblically based theology of counseling began with theology proper. An understanding of God's existence, power, and authority was central both to Adams's critique of psychology and to his own positive understanding of counseling. Adams said:

God is around us, in us and with us. He knows (and cares) about every word on our lips and every thought in our minds. He knows us—indeed has known all about us from all eternity past! The omniscient, omnipresent God is our environment, inescapably so! And though most people rarely recognize it, they are deeply influenced—in all their thoughts and actions—by their environment (I am not speaking about that truncated, superficial and distorted view of the environment that is so much a part of various counseling systems like Skinner's or Glasser's. Rather, I refer to nothing less than God Himself, and a creation that serves and honors Him). In this sense, every unregenerate man, and every system he designs, is influenced by his sinful failure to describe the environment properly and, as the necessary consequence, his inability to develop a counseling system (or counseling method) that corresponds to the reality of the environment as it truly exists. A false view of the environment, therefore, can lead to nothing else but a counseling system that is askew, and that rebelliously misrepresents man and the rest of creation because it misrepresents God. Indeed, because it is in such basic error—a system designed to promote life apart from God—it is in competition with God, and at odds with His creation.[38]

Several things are clear here. Adams wanted to restore a thoroughly theistic framework to counseling because he believed that God is the inescapable reality with whom all persons have to do. Secular psychology's failure to grapple with this fundamental reality led Adams to argue that such approaches to counseling were fundamentally wrong and, therefore, unhelpful. But Adams argued much more strongly than this; the atheistic worldview of those in secular psychology not only rendered their counseling systems "askew," but they themselves were "rebellious," "competitors" with God. For Adams, the only counseling model that could be helpful in any meaningful sense was the one that had a firm grasp on the God of the Christian Bible.

Since, for Adams, God is the "air" people breathe, all the problems people have are directly related to him and to their failure to reach his perfect standard. Adams argued therefore, for an understanding of problems in human living that was grounded in the doctrine of sin. Adams addressed his understanding of the problem of sin in his typically clear manner:

> Corruption of the whole person, but especially of his inner life, is a dominant and essential theme for every counselor to know, to teach and upon which to base all his work. Clearly, he cannot bring about biblical change by means of the old heart, since from it flows only sin. He will counsel, then, only believers . . . he will evangelize unbelievers. But, conversely, he also will recognize the tremendous potential of the new heart. He will not give up on truly regenerate persons (or those who through profession of faith he must presume to be so); in them is the capacity to understand and obey God's counsel (Ezek. 36:27). The indwelling Spirit makes this a genuine reality.[39]

Adams believed that the most basic problem people face is their separation from God because of sin, and this understanding held numerous implications for Adams's counseling model. To begin, Adams did not believe counseling was possible for an unbeliever, because counseling aims for the fruit of the Holy Spirit.[40] This belief underlined an important reality for Adams: the counseling task is an activity that has specifically to do with issues of sin and righteousness in a person's life. Because an unbeliever does not have the resources to obey God's counsel and to put off sin, the only option for such a one is problem-centered evangelism with the hope that true counseling then becomes possible.[41]

This understanding brought great optimism regarding the counseling task. Since believers do possess God's resources to stop sinning and learn love, the counselor and counselee could have great hope in God that enduring change would ultimately come about in counseling.[42] It is clear then that Adams believed the most basic counseling problem is sin, and the goal, by exhortation, was to see the counselee put away his sin.[43]

This reality leads to another key tenet of Adams's counseling system. If the basic problem that human beings have is sin, then their basic solution is found in the person of Jesus Christ and in his saving work of redemption. Adams said:

> How, then, shall we approach the Bible's teaching about salvation in its relationships to counseling? To begin with, it is important to restate the fact that salvation is what makes Christian counseling possible; it is the foundation (or basis) for all counseling. This is the positive side of the coin mentioned earlier about the impossibility of counseling unbelievers. When doing true counseling—i.e., working with saved persons to enable them to make changes, at a level of depth that pleases God—it is possible to solve any true counseling problem (i.e., any problem involving love for God and one's neighbor). Such assurance stems from the fact that all the resources necessary for change are available in the Word and by the Spirit. No counseling system that is based on some other foundation can begin to offer what Christian counseling offers. How tragic, then, to see purely human ideas and resources. They offer little hope and have no good reason to believe that they will succeed; yet (sadly) many Christians lap up (and follow) such advice.[44]

This quotation is worthy of careful analysis for several reasons. In the previous discussion regarding sin, reference was made to God's resources for change. Here, Adams made clear that *the* resource for change is the salvation that Jesus Christ accomplishes for his people and applies to them by his Spirit. Adams stated that counseling systems based on any other foundation offer "little hope" and have "no good reason to believe" that success will be the outcome of their efforts. Adams was clear that success in counseling (i.e., change) is possible only because of the saving work of Jesus Christ.

Adams did not believe that the transformation that the gospel brings happens in a mystical or instantaneous way. Rather, it occurs through a *process* of biblical change. Adams believed that change occurs in a two-part process of dehabituation and rehabituation. Adams grounded this teaching in passages such as Ephesians 4, with its exhortations to "put off" unrighteous behaviors (v. 22) and to "put on" righteous behaviors (v. 24). Adams illustrated this point with a dialogue:

Q. "When is a liar not a liar?"

A. "When he is something else."

Very good, but *what* else? When he *stops* lying, what must he *start* doing? With what does the Bible say that lying must be replaced? (That is the kind of question that counselors continually should be asking and answering.) Well, what does Paul say? Look at [Eph. 4:25]:

Therefore [he is now applying the principle of change] laying aside falsehood [putting off], speak truth, each one of you with his neighbor, for we are members of one another [putting on].

There you have it.

Q. "When is a liar not a liar?"

A. "When he has become a truth teller."

Unless he has been "reprogrammed" or rehabituated, when the chips are down, when he is tired, sick, or under great pressure, a counselee's good resolves and temporary cessation of lying will not last. He will revert to his former manner of life because he is still programmed to do so. The old sinful patterns have not been replaced by new ones. Until that occurs, he will remain vulnerable to sinful reversion. Dehabituation is possible only by achieving rehabituation. The counselee must be repackaged. New patterns of response must become dominant. It is to these instead that he must learn to turn habitually under life stresses.[45]

Adams's counseling model was not mystical but involved a process. This process was not passive but active, and it involved not only the task of putting a stop to sinful practices but also the task of beginning to practice righteous behaviors.

In Adams's system, God is the fundamental reality, sin is the fundamental problem, and redemption in Christ is the fundamental solution. Therefore, the Christian minister operating in the context of the local church is called to the task of helping people with their problems, of mediating God's truth to people, and of walking alongside them in the struggle to put off sin and put on obedience. Adams said:

> Counseling is a work that every minister may, indeed must, perform as a faithful shepherd of Jesus Christ. He must plan to do counseling, must learn how to do counseling and must make himself available for counseling. Referral, except to another faithful shepherd, is out of the question. Better than referral is personal growth on the part of the pastor through discovering and ministering God's answers to the problems encountered in pastoral counseling.[46]

Adams believed that all wise, growing Christians were *competent* to counsel,[47] but he also believed that the ordained Christian minister had the unique *mandate* to counsel.[48] Because of that conviction Adams railed against those mental health professionals outside the church who attempted to seize the counseling task of the church. He also railed against those inside the church who accepted the message, either referring to secular "experts" or joining them.[49] For Adams, the only place true counsel can be found is within the church. The Christian minister must counsel, not as an optional but an essential element of his ministry.

Adams's four major books on counseling were published between 1970 and 1979.[50] During that decade, Adams made a vigorous and thorough proposal for restoring theological reflection to the counseling task. As a result of Adams's ministry, much progress was made in recovering uniquely

Christian reflection on the counseling task. After the initial work of theological recovery, however, the task of theological development still lay ahead.

Theological Advancement

Adams continued to publish books throughout the 1980s but none were as seminal as his major works in the previous decade. He also continued his work of editing the *Journal of Pastoral Practice*. All this effort made Adams the uncontested leader of the biblical counseling movement. Indeed, his name was equated with the movement.

But by the late eighties and early nineties new leadership began to rise up, mostly out of one of the organizations founded by Adams, the Christian Counseling and Educational Foundation (CCEF). This new blood wanted to continue to think about conversational ministry that was theologically informed in the same tradition as Adams. The new blood consisted of men such as Ed Welch and Paul Tripp, but the clear leader was David Powlison.

Powlison had come to faith in Christ as an adult. He had majored in psychology at Harvard and had been working for several years in private psychiatric hospitals. Disillusionment with the mental-health system was a significant catalyst for his conversion. Even the elite level of psychiatric care had remarkably few resources to offer confused, hurting persons and no power to change people at a level of depth. Shortly after becoming a believer, he entered Westminster Theological Seminary to study biblical counseling. After graduation he became a faculty member at CCEF and later the editor of their journal, which he renamed the *Journal of Biblical Counseling*. He earned his PhD in the history of science and medicine from the University of Pennsylvania.

In his leadership roles as a faculty member, and ultimately as editor of the *Journal of Biblical Counseling*, Powlison was able to exert massive influence in directing the discussions that biblical counselors were having. It was ultimately under Powlison that biblical counselors began to reflect on their movement for the very first time. The foremost thinker in the movement had always been Jay Adams, but though he wrote voluminously over many years, he presented his thoughts with a certain finality and was never self-critical in print. A reader never gets the impression that there was an "early Adams" and a "late Adams." There was just "Adams, *period*." This is not to say that Adams did not broach new subjects or ever nuance his views (he did both). It is to say that before Powlison's leadership, there had never been a time of critically evaluating where the movement had been, considering some problems in the movement, and charting a positive way forward in the years ahead. Under Powlison the movement did all three.

Biblical counselors have followed Adams in almost every respect. There continues to be agreement that God in Christ is the fundamental reality behind all counseling. Biblical counselors have continued to believe that any positive change must flow from the power of Christ as he does his work in the believer through the power of the Holy Spirit. All biblical counselors continue to believe in the authority, wisdom, relevance, and sufficiency of the Bible to help people with any problem that requires counseling (see the appendix for more information about this). Having said that, the new group of biblical counselors, taking their cues from Powlison, have advanced the movement in several different ways.

First, there have been conceptual advancements. Counseling concepts are the fundamental set of beliefs that structure every counseling model. They are how counselors *think* about counseling. A counseling model answers questions such as: Who are we? What is wrong with us? How do we fix it? Who is God? *Is* there a God? What is the change process? All counseling systems answer such questions either overtly or covertly. Biblical counselors have advanced the theological reflection of Adams about how to do ministry, in two important ways. (1) They have brought about great development in an understanding of how to do ministry to people who are suffering as well as to people who are sinning. Adams did a great job of helping Christians know how to talk to and confront people who are caught in sin. It took some time and maturing for the movement to grow in wisdom concerning how to do ministry to those mired in suffering. (2) More contemporary biblical counselors have developed the movement with regard to motivational issues. When we talk about motivation, we are discussing the issue of why people do the things they do. Adams's answers to the issue of human motivation proved to be in need of change and development in order for the church to know how to help people in the wisest way possible.

Counseling methods are the second area where biblical counselors have advanced. Methodology refers to how counselors *do* counseling. What is the counselor's role in counseling? What is the role of the counselee? How does the change process transpire? Whether clearly stated or not, all approaches to counseling have a theory of how to proceed in the counseling relationship. For Adams, counseling was done in a very formal and authoritative way. Contemporary biblical counselors have sought to improve this approach based on the biblical teaching of loving, brotherly, one-anothering relationships.

The final area of advancement in theological reflection about counseling is apologetics. Apologetics has to do with how counselors *talk* to other, competing counseling systems. What is good in other counseling systems? What is not good? How much time will counselors spend investigating other systems? How will they use and interact with other systems? How can counselors advocate for the superiority of their own system? The existence of numerous, competing counseling systems necessitates that counselors seek to defend their own approach. Adams wanted to build a model, not engage with other models. Contemporary biblical counselors have seen the importance of talking with advocates of other models in a tone that is kind and gracious and less bombastic than Adams's.

Don't Misunderstand Me

This is a book about how biblical counselors have grown up and matured since the initial leadership of Jay Adams, but it is not a strike against Adams. To the contrary, the ministry of Jay Adams changed my life, and I love him. One of the great honors of my life has been to get to know him a bit over the last several years. I have spoken with him over the phone, talked for hours with him over pizza, and received great personal encouragement from him. He is one of the most gracious, godly, funny, and humble men I have ever met.

Beyond any personal connection, I believe Adams has been one of the most consequential men in church history in the last 150 years. His work revolutionized the way thousands of people do ministry. In the last forty years everyone who ministers the Scriptures or has had the Scriptures ministered to them according to the principles of biblical counseling has Jay Adams to thank. God has used him mightily to recalibrate the church's thinking about how to help hurting and struggling people. I have no interest in any sort of unkind or ungodly attack on a man to whom the church owes so much.

Having said that, Jay Adams's work was imperfect. This is, of course, a distinction his writing shares with every other Christian author whose work was not inspired by the Holy Spirit. Every great man in church history had imperfections in his work, whether it be Athanasius, Augustine, Calvin, or Edwards. God loves to raise up powerful though imperfect servants. Jay Adams is one of their number. Adams built a movement from scratch, almost alone, and was doing so against powerful forces opposed to his model. It is my goal to honor Dr. Adams by carefully considering his work and the context in which he built it and by highlighting the efforts of men laboring in the tradition he began, to improve upon the good work he started.

Because that is true, I want to be very careful in how I refer to Adams as well as to those who followed him in advancing the task he began. As I've mentioned, all biblical counselors are united around core principles of the sufficiency of Scripture, the necessity of the power of the gospel to bring about true and lasting change, progressive sanctification, the importance of the church, and concern over secular psychology. But because there has been advancement, I need a way to refer to those more contemporary biblical counselors who have attempted to advance his thought.

In this book I will refer to the leadership of Adams as the "first generation" of biblical counseling. I will refer to the leadership of Powlison and those who have followed him in improving Adams's thought as the "second generation." Such generational language captures the idea of change occurring but in the context of family union. This language also rightly captures the distinctions within the larger unity that have characterized biblical counselors.

So now we will turn to how the second generation of biblical counselors advanced the beliefs of the first generation. First we will look at how they advanced the movement conceptually, regarding how biblical counselors *think* about counseling. Second, we will look at how they advanced the movement methodologically, in how biblical counselors *do* counseling. And finally we will look at the way in which the movement developed apologetically, in how biblical counselors *talk* about counseling.

As we look at this together, please don't think that this is merely some book about a bunch of counselors. It really isn't. It's a book about how to do one-on-one ministry with people in a way that is theologically faithful. Specifically, it is about a group that has spent the last four decades trying to help the church figure out how to have conversations with troubled people in a way that is most faithful to the Scriptures and most honoring to Jesus Christ. Knowing their story will help you grow in faithfulness to Jesus, as well.

2

Advances in How Biblical Counselors Think about Counseling

Every counseling approach has a core set of beliefs, as was noted earlier. These core beliefs include understandings of the ideal of human functioning, understandings of what is wrong with human functioning, and theories about how to fix those things that go wrong. These concepts may be spoken or unspoken, right or wrong, and helpful or unhelpful; all approaches to counseling, however, operate from a conceptual core.

The biblical counseling movement from its inception has been united around several key concepts. These concepts include an understanding of the nature of man as created and dependent, an appreciation of the disastrous effects of sin in human living, a biblical view of progressive sanctification, the necessity of faith in Christ for true and lasting change, the importance of daily repentance and faith, which leads to love and obedience, and the necessity and sufficiency of God's inscripturated Word.[1] While there has been broad conceptual agreement, there have been two specific areas where the biblical counseling movement has advanced during the last twenty years. There has been conceptual advancement in the biblical counseling movement in the area of sin and suffering and in the area of human motivation.

Advancement Concerning Sin and Suffering

A crucial issue in proceeding through a counseling situation is the counselor's understanding of what is wrong with the counselee. Is the counselee beset by sin, by sickness and suffering, or by some combination of both? One of the main areas of advancement for the biblical counseling movement has been the degree to which a counselor should deal with counselees according to their sin, according to their suffering, or some combination. The model that Jay Adams developed included a heavy emphasis on confronting sin patterns observed in counseling. While the second generation has not abandoned the need to confront sin, it has sought to advance the movement by seeing the counselee in a more nuanced way as both a sinner and a sufferer. △ - suffering + sin

Adams's Focus on Sin

One virtue of the writing and teaching ministry of Jay Adams is that he is quite clear. From the very beginning of the movement he founded, Adams was clear that the foundational problem that people have is their sin. At the very beginning of *Competent to Counsel* Adams described his summer helping mental patients at two hospitals in Illinois. Adams was unambiguous as he described his opinion of what was wrong with those patients:

> Apart from those who had organic problems, like brain damage, the people I met in the two institutions in Illinois were there because of their own failure to meet life's problems. To put it simply, they were there because of their unforgiven and unaltered sinful behavior.[2]

Adams went on in that book to ground this idea in the ministry of the apostle Paul, saying, "Paul thought of bringing God's Word to bear upon people's lives in order to expose sinful patterns, to correct what is wrong, and to establish new ways of life of which God approves."[3]

In a chapter in the *Christian Counselor's Manual* entitled "Sin Is the Problem," Adams developed this point:

> Sin, then, in all of its dimensions, clearly is *the* problem with which the Christian counselor must grapple. It is the secondary dimensions—the variations on the common themes—that make counseling so difficult. While all men are born sinners and engage in the same sinful practices and dodges, each develops his own styles of sinning. The styles (combinations of sins and dodges) are peculiar to each individual; but beneath them are the common themes. It is the counselor's work to discover these commonalities beneath the individualities.[4]

Here Adams reiterated what had been observed but also developed it. Adams's belief that sin is the main problem in living was not simplistic. Rather, he explains here that sinful people display remarkable ingenuity in their ability to create new sinful patterns. Adams admitted that sorting this out in the individual cases is complex and difficult work.

One of the hallmarks of the thought of Adams in his discussions of sin is the analysis he provided of the mentally ill (an expression with which he generally took great exception). Adams understood the so-called mentally ill to have the same root problems as other people; namely, he believed such persons were primarily sinners in need of forgiveness. Adams had this understanding even with such extreme diagnoses as manic-depression and schizophrenia.[5] Adams concluded one discussion on this topic by saying:

> So whether the problem is chemical or moral, the answer to the question which heads this chapter (What's wrong with the "mentally ill"?) seems clear: there may be several things wrong with the so-called "mentally ill," but the one cause which must be excluded in most cases is mental illness itself.[6]

Adams strongly emphasized that people were hurting and in need of counseling precisely because they were sinful people living in a sinful world. This understanding is an unmistakable emphasis of his work. The reality of this fact, however, does not mean that Adams paid no attention to the reality of human suffering. He did indeed. In fact, in *A Theology of Christian Counseling*, Adams took great pains to correct his reputation for ignoring suffering. He said in one of the chapters about sin:

> Now, let me say one thing at the outset and be done with it. The notion that is so widely spread abroad (sometimes by those who ought to know better), that nouthetic counseling considers all human problems the direct result of actual sins of particular counselees, is a gross misrepresentation of the facts. From the beginning (cf. *Competent to Counsel*, 1970, pp. 108, 109) I have stated clearly that not all problems of counselees are due to their own sins. In *Competent*, I cited the cases of Job and the man born blind (John 9:1ff.). Those who persist in attributing to me views that I do not hold are culpable. Either they ought to know better before they speak and write (by reading the material available— nouthetic counseling has not been done in a corner!), or they should

have investigated on their own what they accepted as fact (but was actually only gossip).

While all human misery—disability, sickness, etc.—does go back to Adam's sin (and I would be quick to assert that biblical truth), that is not the same as saying that a *quid pro quo* relationship between each counselee's misery and his own personal sins exists. That I as quickly deny. It may be true in one given instance, but not in another. Neither is it true that all the suffering that some deserve they get in this life. Nor is true that all the suffering that others receive in this life they bring upon themselves. Suffering, in a world of sin, comes to all in one way or another in the providence of God, but before investigating each case, that is all that may be said about it.[7]

Adams did acknowledge suffering.[8] As with the other areas in Adams's thought, his mentioning of the issue is not the point. The topic at hand is the *degree to which* Adams addressed the issue and how his thought *stood in need of development*. There is good evidence that his thought did need to be developed in understanding and appreciating human suffering. Several facts prove this to be true.

First, Adams did not have a reputation for addressing suffering in his work. This reality is shown to be the case by the passage above. Why is it that both his opponents and his friends found Adams's treatment of suffering wanting?[9] There must be some reason. Indeed, in this reference, where he chided his critics for misunderstanding his position, he provided only two (very brief) references from a book written ten years before. His reference of such scant evidence seems to beg the question and point to at least some basis for the criticism.[10]

Second, in Adams's early work he made efforts to describe the various sources of people's problems in living. He did this twice, and in both places a biblical understanding of suffering was glanced over. In *Competent to Counsel* Adams said:

To put the issue simply: the Scriptures plainly speak of both organically based problems as well as those problems that stem from sinful attitudes and behavior; but where, in all of God's Word, is there so much as a trace of any third source of problems? . . . Until . . . a demonstration is forthcoming, the only safe course to follow is to declare with all of Scripture that the genesis of such human problems is twofold, not threefold.[11]

In this particular citation Adams was concerned to refute that mental illness is a legitimate cause of problems in living. In the process he described problems springing from two potential sources: biological problems and spiritual/sin problems. It is interesting that in a critical passage such as this one, Adams did not include various other sufferings. Significant issues such as betrayal at the hands of others, the intake of false values taught by a corrupt world, the experience of physical pains, death, dying, and many others are all important counseling concerns. They are not mentioned here.[12]

Adams made a similar argument in the *Manual*:

> There are, in the Scriptures, only three specified sources of personal problems in living: demonic activity (principally possession), personal sin, and organic illness. These three are interrelated. All options are covered under these heads, leaving no room for a fourth: non-organic mental illness.[13]

As above, Adams was here arguing against the category of mental illness. Once again he attempted to sketch out the biblical sources of problems over and against the supposed secular understanding. This reference shows some advancement in Adams's own thought. In the three years since his first work was published, Adams found room for a third biblical source of problems. Still missing in Adams's list, however, was a robust and nuanced appreciation of suffering and how to engage it in the life of the counselee. Adams believed that this kind of suffering exists.[14] Again, however, what Adams believed is not the issue. The concern here is the degree to which his teaching needed elaboration.

A third source of evidence regards Adams's treatment of suffering on those occasions when he did address it. Adams has published over one hundred books.[15] Those books include Bible commentaries and many that cover counseling topics, Christian living, and pastoral ministry. But none of these books unfolds a philosophy of suffering, captures the experience of suffering, or discusses at length how to counsel suffering people.[16] When, however, Adams did engage suffering, he did it in a way that did not fully appreciate the dynamics and complexities of suffering people. It is not possible to examine all the examples of this; one representative example will suffice. In *Counsel from Psalm 119*, Adams addressed Psalm 119:67, which says, "Before I was afflicted I went astray, but now I keep your word." This passage provides a clear opportunity for Adams to engage the problem of human suffering:

> Here is a verse that sings the praises of affliction! It is not often that you hear counselees join in the chorus. But it is a song that every counselor must teach his counselees to sing. Affliction may come in order to purify. It may be sent in order to turn one back to the proper pathway. When we go astray (and we all do from time to time) we often need affliction to wake us up to what we have done and where we have gone. Affliction is to the erring Christian as an alarm clock is to one who is apt to oversleep. Moreover, in addition to awakening us to our sinful ways, it often stops us and provides time for thought. When one is engaged in the hustle-bustle of life, he may take little time to think about this life. When he is stopped in his tracks by the loss of a job, by the onset of a debilitating illness, and the like, it can be a blessing to give him time to think seriously about his ways. There are many ways in which afflictions of all sorts may become a blessing by returning a counselee to the Word. This is, therefore, a key verse in the Psalm for every counselor. He should remember it and use it often. It is the answer to much of the whining that he hears. "What have you learned from God's Word during this time of trouble?" is a first class question for you to ask of those who complain.[17]

This represents a typical way Adams handled the issue of suffering and affliction. There are three things to mention about it.

First, Adams moved straight to a discussion of the benefits of suffering without considering—in dynamic and detailed ways—the personal pain and turmoil of those experiencing difficulty. Adams was, of course, correct that there is a benefit to suffering. The Bible is clear about this truth. However the Bible is also clear that affliction is difficult, hurting those to whom it comes, and that is a frequent topic of biblical counsel. Though the psalms expand upon this (try reading Pss. 119:22, 23, 25, 28, 42, 50, 61, 69, 71, 78, 85, 86, 87, 92, 95, 107, 110, 115, 120, 134, 141, 143, 147, 150, 153, 157, 161), Adams never did.

Second, Adams majored on the moral labor of turning to the Word. Obviously, it is important to turn to the Scripture in times of difficulty, since it is the only thing that can reorient hurting people to God's gaze. However, when the counsel is "Turn to the Word" before the counselor has appreciated the extent of the counselee's pain—when this exhortation comes as a mere moral imperative disconnected from the tender promises of grace from a God who cares and desires to minister help—then it will not be comforting. It will seem legalistic, rote, unhelpful, and perhaps even cruel.

Third, Adams referred to those struggling under the weight of pain as "whiners" and "complainers." Is it possible for sinful people to turn their suffering into a sinful pursuit of pity? Absolutely. This passage of Scripture, however, is not about whiners, and it is wrong to label strugglers as whiners in general. This talk represents an unbiblical harshness and insensitivity that critics have been right to condemn and that the second generation of biblical counselors has sought to correct.

The final and perhaps clearest evidence of Adams's inattention to the themes of suffering is his own words on the topic. In his book *Compassionate Counseling* Adams observed:

> Because so little has been written about compassion in counseling, I have undertaken to fill the gap. Since compassion is an essential component of all truly biblical counseling, it is essential to understand its nature, place, and effects upon counselees, counselors, and the counseling that they engage in.[18]

In a footnote to this passage Adams stated, "You can read through the indices of book after book—even those about biblical counseling—and find no reference to compassion."[19] This is a revealing admission. No person alive has written on, spoken about, or otherwise addressed biblical counseling themes more or longer than Jay Adams. Yet, by his own admission, the theme of compassion is one that has hardly been touched in counseling circles. It is not going too far to say that Adams himself bears some responsibility for this lack.[20]

After making such observations, it is important to note that Adams had a good reason to focus on sin the way he did. He was writing in a counseling context that had wholly been given over to secularism. The specific counseling models that Adams critiqued all located the cause of personal problems outside the person's responsibility. Adams was deeply concerned to restore an approach of personal responsibility to counseling that the secular psychologies had removed. For example, Adams argued regarding Freud:

> His views have encouraged irresponsible people to persist in and expand their irresponsibility. He has sanctioned irresponsible behavior and made it respectable. His views are iatrogenic (or treatment-engendering) only in that they can cause secondary complications. Freud has not made people irresponsible; but he has provided a philosophical and pseudoscientific rationale for irresponsible people to use to justify themselves.[21]

In light of this problem Adams made clear the responsibility of Christian counselors:

> It is difficult for some to acknowledge personal sin as the root and cause of most of the day-by-day counseling problems that arise. This is particularly true in an age deeply steeped in Freudianism. As Rogerianism has taught us to put feeling first, so Freudianism has declared blame-shifting legitimate. More recently, Skinnerianism has gone on record as opposing the very concept of responsibility *per se*. If, therefore, in ordinary activities it is hard for some to see the place of personal responsibility, this becomes still harder for them whenever they consider special cases. The Christian counselor must be firm at this point about his insistence upon human responsibility.[22]

Adams believed that it was critical to restore a sense of responsibility to the counseling task.

Seeing this evidence shows that Adams was writing not as a man who did not understand human suffering, still less as a man who did not understand the Bible's teaching on human suffering. Adams was writing as a man in a specific historical context that had overthrown personal responsibility in the counseling context. Adams was concerned to restore a biblical sense of responsibility to the counseling room, and nothing accomplished such a restoration like a focus on sin. Here was the ground on which Adams needed to fight, because a focus on sin highlighted the importance not only of responsibility but also of God and his Word, all of which had been discarded by secular approaches to talking about the problems people have. It was Adams's attention to sin and responsibility that was one of the main elements separating his project from every other counseling model. Adams's work made it possible for others to build on what he had started.

The Second Generation on Sin and Suffering

And it was necessary to build. Adams's work on sin was a critical first step, but it had become important to do more work in the area of suffering, for several reasons. First, paying proper attention to suffering in the counseling context is biblical. The biblical understanding of suffering is equally as profound as the biblical understanding of sin.[23] Counselors will be less than biblical if they avoid paying attention to the multitude of ways in which people (even sinful people) experience suffering.

Second, paying proper attention to suffering will make for counselors that are demonstrably more loving. It is loving for counselors to listen carefully to the problems of their counselees and develop nuanced ways of helping them. Whether Freudian erotic and aggressive drives,[24] Skinnerian behaviorism,[25] or Adlerian inferiority complexes,[26] it is secularists who artificially reduce the problems of people. Biblical counselors can distinguish themselves by their ability to minister in multifaceted ways to people as both fallen and frail.

Finally, paying proper attention to suffering will allow for counseling that is most effective. The problems and struggles of people are not limited to sin alone. On the one hand, if the biblical counselor truly desires to help those to whom he ministers, he must understand what the Bible says about both sin and suffering, which requires developing a model of each. On the other hand, if a counselor wants to earn the trust and respect of a counselee, he must earn credibility by dealing with all of the relevant issues. Facility in dealing with sin and suffering will allow for greater counseling instruction and a better response from counselees.

Perhaps it was similar observations that led Powlison to make a case for such development in his article "Crucial Issues in Contemporary Biblical Counseling." Powlison states, "The relationship between human responsibility and human suffering needs a great deal of clarification." He continues:

> [This issue] . . . challenges us to rethink our vision of the counselee and the counselee's situation. How do we see and understand the people whom we counsel? What kind of attention do we pay to the kind of world

the counselee inhabits? How important are the counselee's past and present circumstances?[27]

Powlison justifies this rethinking, saying:

> There is a *biblical* view of man as a sufferer. We can say it even more plainly: There is a biblical view of man as a victim. Biblical counseling has been repeatedly misunderstood to say that all problems are a result of personal sin. Why this misunderstanding? . . . Some of the misunderstanding of biblical counseling is caricature, from people who know all too well that "man is responsible" would undermine their whole counseling theory and practice. . . . But other misunderstanding highlights a problem, a crucial issue for contemporary biblical counseling. Our treatment of the victim side of the biblical portrayal of man has been anecdotal and occasional, not systematic.[28]

Powlison sees an oversight here in the biblical counseling movement. It is important to note, however, that while Powlison sees the importance of expanding and developing the thought in the biblical counseling movement, he is not seeking to separate from the thinking that has come before. Instead, Powlison is trying to strengthen the movement by advancing the previous thinking. He says:

> Biblically comprehending man-as-sufferer is never meant to answer "Why do I sin?" It does answer "When? Where? With whom? Under whose influence?" It describes the situation in which one is tempted and tried. With new eyes, the situation of suffering becomes the "when, where, with whom and against what" within which he will learn faith and obedience. We have said loudly, "responsible!" The biblical balance, "responsible amid hardship," has been more understated and assumed.[29]

Powlison wanted to advance the biblical counseling movement by adding to the focus on sin and responsibility a focus on suffering and understanding. His desire was to have counselors that understood the situation of the counselee as much as they understood the culpability of the counselee. Powlison developed this idea a bit more in a chapter in *Suffering and the Sovereignty of God* entitled "God's Grace and Your Sufferings." There Powlison says:

Often the biggest problem for any sufferer is not "the problem." It is the spiritual challenge the problem presents: "How are you doing in the midst of what you are going through? What are you learning? Will you learn to live well and wisely within pain, limitation, weakness, and loss? Will suffering define you? Will faith and love grow, or will you shrivel up?" These are life-and-death issues—more important than "the problem" in the final analysis. They take asking, thinking, listening, responding. They take time. Other people are often clumsy and uncomprehending about the most important things, while pouring energy and love into solving what is often insoluble.[30]

Here Powlison begins to do what he urges in the "Crucial Issues" article and looks at the situation of a suffering person.

Powlison is not alone in this effort, however. Following his lead others expressed a desire to correct the overemphasis on sin. One such example is Edward Welch in his article, "Exalting Pain? Ignoring Pain? What Do We Do with Suffering?" Welch observes the dilemma:

Human life entails misery and woe. Broken relationships, agonizing illness, the prospect of one's own death, depression, injustice and atrocity, quiet yet paralyzing fear, memories of sexual victimization, the death of a child, and many other painful problems leave none unscathed. It would be impossible to minimize the breadth and depth of suffering both in the church and the world. But this proposition sits at a juncture where Christians are pulled in one of two directions. Some exalt pain, others deny pain. Some are bleeding hearts, others are stoics. Some are "pain counselors," others are "sin counselors." Pain counselors are expert at having people feel understood; sin counselors are expert at understanding the call to obedience even when there is pain. Pain counselors run the risk of overemphasizing pain to where the alleviation of suffering becomes the thing of first importance. Sin counselors run the risk of rendering personal pain of little or no importance. Pain counselors can be slow to lead sufferers in responding to the gospel of Christ in faith and obedience. Sin counselors can run the danger of breeding stoics whose response of obedience is unaware of God's great compassion. Pain counselors might provide a context that enhances blame-shifting and counselee's sense of innocent victimization. Sin counselors may be so concerned about blame-shifting that they have a poorly developed theology of suffering. There are pitfalls of each.[31]

Welch understands the problem well, and, while he does not name names in his article, he actually references a significant area of development in the biblical counseling movement. The so-called "pain counselors" are the ones that Adams had spent decades trying to defeat. Likewise the "sin counselors," as it were, are people like Adams himself. Adams devoted his ministry to correcting the error of the "pain counselors," but Welch wants to provide a corrective for the Adams model:

> Those who lean in the direction of minimizing pain, or calling for a stoic acceptance of it, are often more precise in their theological formulations. But they may be guilty of ignoring important biblical themes and thus do not offer the full counsel of God to those who suffer. For example, if suffering is a result of being sinned against by another, those who minimize suffering might immediately think about the call to forgive the perpetrator. This theme is critical, so it certainly is no mistake to make forgiveness part of the counseling agenda. Yet it is a problem when forgiveness is made the only counseling agenda. Too often, the first and last advice given to a severely victimized woman is to forgive the perpetrator.[32]

It is clear then that the second generation of biblical counselors was aware of a need to balance the attention given to sin with a focus on suffering. How, though, would this balance be established? In answering this question it is possible to isolate three sources of development. First, biblical counselors have systematized suffering. Second, biblical counselors have enriched an understanding of the sources of problems with which people struggle. Finally, biblical counselors have demonstrated how to work out the more robust understanding of suffering in the context of actual counseling.

Systematizing Suffering

Saying that biblical counselors have "systematized suffering" can sound a bit sterile and inorganic and like something that is a little undesirable. That is not what I mean. Instead, I'm trying to show that more contemporary biblical counselors have worked so that an understanding and appreciation of suffering will be a standard part of counseling. In their book *How People Change*, Timothy S. Lane and Paul David Tripp seek to provide a systematic theology of biblical counseling. Their work lays out a systematic and practical theology of the change process. In their treatment, the practical process of change contains four parts. Three of their elements are identical to the teaching of Adams: Lane and Tripp offer a theology of ungodly behaviors and heart dispositions on the part of individual sinners;[33] they describe the presence and power of Christ as making it possible to change such ungodly behavior and motivations;[34] and they work toward the godly behaviors and attitudes that flow out of an encounter with the grace of Jesus.[35] But their fourth element—and the first one addressed in the book—is a theology of suffering. Lane and Tripp refer to this as "heat." Heat is a person's life situation. It is the collection of sufferings and difficulties that people face. They describe the heat (i.e., the situational suffering of the counselee):

> On this side of heaven, we all live under the Heat of trial in some way. Mark has a boss who never seems satisfied. Anne's husband is more committed to fishing than [to] their marriage. Sarah endures chronic pain. Tim's teenage son has been in trouble since he turned thirteen. Rachel's church has been through a gut-wrenching split. Jerry struggles with the burdens that accompany his promotion. Brooke lost most of her retirement money in bad investments. Fred is battling heart disease. Jennifer can't control her weight. Bob longs for the simpler days before he got his inheritance. Jason does all he can to avoid his angry father. Old age has ravaged Alex's body.[36]

That sample of a dozen troubles has no parallel in Adams's work. Lane and Tripp comment further:

> You and I always react to things that happen around us. Whether it is the scorching heat of difficulty or the unexpected rain of blessing, you are always responding to whatever comes down on you. The Bible is honest about the things that happen here.[37]

The relevant thing to note is that Lane and Tripp make room up front in their systematic practical theology for the situation of the counselee. Counselees are responsible for how they respond to their situation; they are responsible to repent, trust Christ, and bear fruit in keeping with repentance. All of that was emphasized in the first generation of the biblical counseling movement—and even developed to a fuller extent. In the model presented by Lane and Tripp, however, there is an effort to understand carefully the context in which the counselee exists. In so doing, they systematize a doctrine of suffering in their theology of change and show how it fits together with other elements in the change/counseling dynamic.

Exploring the Sources of Difficulty

Biblical counselors, having placed suffering in a theological context that is both systematic and practical, also sought to think through the issue of suffering in yet other ways. In his work on the subject, Welch sought to provide a more nuanced understanding of the sources of difficulty in the Christian life than had previously been articulated in the biblical counseling movement.

In fact, Welch made a major contribution to the biblical counseling movement when he articulated five possible causes for suffering. The first source he addressed was other people: "We are sinned against by other people and it hurts deeply." Second, the individual struggler is a cause of suffering: "I suffer because I have sinned." Third, people suffer as a result of the presence of sin in the world due to the curse of Adam: "It was Adam himself who sinned and brought misery and death to all his progeny. Because of his sin we experience the curse on all of creation." Fourth, the work of Satan causes suffering in people's lives: "Satan is the appropriate, although elusive, target [of human suffering]."[38] Finally, we suffer at the hands of the sovereign God: "By the time suffering gets to us, it is God's will."[39]

Welch develops the biblical counseling movement by placing sufferers in a larger context. The biblical picture of people is more multifaceted than simply seeing sinners. Sinners are also sufferers. Welch's work does more than simply noting the *presence* of suffering. He goes on to identify the multiple sources of suffering in the lives of individual strugglers. Such work had never before been done in the counseling movement. When you consider the slim treatment that Adams gave to this issue, it becomes clear that Welch has made a critical addition to biblical counselors' understanding of the task of personal ministry.

Suffering and the Counseling Task

Tripp's book *Instruments in the Redeemer's Hands* provides yet another layer in the efforts of contemporary biblical counseling to develop a more robust understanding of suffering. In his work, Tripp acknowledges the danger of approaching personal ministry with a set of truths about sin and responsibility but with little apprehension of the situation of the counselee:

> It is wrong to approach a struggling brother or sister with a condemning, self-righteous spirit. This puts you in the way of what the Lord is doing in their lives. You must grant them the same grace and love that you received from the Lord.[40]

He develops an important theme when he says:

> If you are alive . . . you are a sufferer who has been called by God to minister to others in pain. Suffering is not only the common ground of human relationships, but one of God's most useful workrooms. As God's ambassadors, we need to learn to identify with those who suffer. We do this by learning from the example of the Wonderful Counselor. . . . We are with Christ in the family of those who suffer. We must not forget that we serve a suffering Savior. We do not seek help from someone who cannot understand our experience. Jesus is compassionate and understanding.[41]

Adams's emphasis on the authoritative counselor rarely expressed such identification between counselor and counselee. Tripp urges counselors to work to identify with a counselee's suffering and situation. He does this based on two critical realities. First, Jesus Christ was a suffering Savior. Second, Jesus relates to his people as sympathetic co-sufferer. Tripp therefore argues that an understanding of the counselee's situation is grounded in nothing less than the gospel activity of Jesus as discussed in Hebrews 2:10–12.[42] In this passage the brotherhood that exists between Christ and his people is founded on the sufferings they share together. Welch adds to this:

> A brief study of the compassion of Jesus is a profound rebuke to [the problem of ignoring suffering]. The incarnation itself was the dramatic example of God entering into the lives of His people. Jesus was characteristically moved with compassion for those who were leaderless, oppressed, destitute, or bereaved. As Jesus counsels us to mourn with those who mourn, he points us to His own life as the example. The stoic avoids or ignores these clear themes in Scripture.[43]

The second generation has consistently developed the biblical importance of understanding the counselee's situation. That raises another question as to how it thinks a counselor should balance the truths of the earlier and later generations of biblical counselors. The second generation has not abandoned the teachings of Adams regarding the responsibility of the counselee even as it has sought to apprehend the situation of the counselee. If the balanced truth is that the counselee is a sufferer who is responsible, what is the way to keep that in balance without favoring an understanding of one over the other? These are methodological questions of which Tripp also feels the weight:

> What does it mean to comfort those who suffer? How do we come alongside them with compassion? Often we are unsure of what to say. We struggle with how to comfort someone who has lost a loved one, or who faces past experiences that can never be undone. We do not want to communicate truths in ways that are cheap and platitudinous. We want to anchor the person in what is true as he deals with this suffering, but in a way that shows him that we understand the intensity of his trial. We want to show him that the truths we share are robust enough to carry him through. Most of all we want him to know that he is not alone, because Christ is present as his Helper in times of trouble. The question is, "How do we avoid these pitfalls and accomplish these goals?"[44]

Tripp understands the dilemma. He seeks to avoid the pitfalls. On the one hand, there is the desire to "communicate truths." On the other there is the desire to avoid doing that in ways that are "cheap and platitudinous." On one side there is the goal to "anchor a person in truth." On the other side is the goal of doing so in "a way that shows we understand the intensity of his trial." Tripp's answer to this dilemma is for counselors to tell personal stories about their own suffering and what they learned in the midst of it. Tripp grounds this in Paul's teaching in 2 Corinthians:

> In 2 Corinthians 1, Paul says that he does not want the Corinthians to be uninformed about his suffering in Asia. He wants his story to result in deeper hope, strengthened faith, and renewed worship among them. Paul's experiences put flesh and blood on the promises of God. In them you see God in action, doing exactly what he promised to do for his chil-

dren. As people see God in Paul's story, they are given eyes to see God in their own, and they are comforted by this. This is one of the most personal and powerful methodologies of offering comfort. It presents realities that are deeply theological in the context of circumstances familiar to anyone in a fallen world. Our stories take God's truth to the struggles of life and present strong reasons not to give up.[45]

It is stories, Tripp argues, that put "flesh and blood" on the bones of truth and bring personal comfort to struggling people. Telling stories presents the truth of God's Word in a context that is understandable and relevant to anyone. Telling stories of lessons God taught them in their own suffering allows counselors to communicate truth in a personal way that shows its effectiveness. Tripp's work keeps the idea of the "responsible sufferer" in balance by having the counselor identify with the suffering counselee in listening first to the counselee's story and then sharing his own story. Such a strategy balances the identification of suffering with responsibility and truth by relating the lessons learned from the counselor's struggle, a process which is grounded in Scripture. I refer to this as the principle of listen, share, teach. Tripp teaches the importance of listening to the counselee's struggle, sharing the counselor's struggle, and then teaching the truths of Scripture (responsibility, sovereignty, God's good and wise purposes, etc.) that the counselor learned in his or her own struggle.

This methodological strategy, as Tripp notes, is only one way of keeping the two truths in balance. Another option is to deal with the counselee in a "psalmic" way. After listening to the counselee, the counselor finds a psalm (or other passage of Scripture) that resonates with the counselee's struggle. They then work through the psalm to see how Scripture identifies with the struggle and to show a biblical way to respond to the suffering that honors God.

Psalm 55 is one that might be used. This psalm resonates with sufferers, because David has been wrongfully treated (Ps. 55:3, 10–15, 20–21), and he is in deep agony over it (Ps. 55:2, 4–8). This element underlines identification with suffering. In the psalm, however, David also cries out to God and begs him for help (Ps. 55:1–2, 16–19, 22–23). This element underlines the counselee's responsibility to turn to God for help in suffering and to honor him in pain. This element of the psalm serves as a springboard into many other rich truths in Scripture that can equip strugglers to deal with their sorrow.[46]

Adams's work underlined the important biblical truth of man as a responsible sinner. This truth is of critical importance in a counseling context that sought (and still generally seeks) to avoid assigning moral responsibility to the counselee for his or her problems.[47] That work needed balance, however. The new generation of biblical counselors seeks to provide that balance by applying the truth of responsibility to the lives of particular people who struggle, hurt, and suffer. They developed the movement in this way by systematizing suffering in the change process, by elaborating on the sources of suffering, and by giving a methodology of how to work this out in counseling. This more balanced perspective calls upon counselors to understand the biblical teaching on people and the context in which they live as they understand the truths of Scripture about individual responsibility for sin. This reality is where personal ministry lives; understanding Scripture not generally but specifically in the lives of particular people who are, of course, responsible but suffer as well.

In the counseling context, effective ministry of the Word means understanding the situation of the counselee. Understanding the situation requires a counselor who is willing to listen, ask, probe, and walk with counselees in their struggle. Effective counseling in this regard means seeking to understand what a counselee is experiencing so that the critical themes of sin and responsibility can be communicated with love, specificity, care, grace, and the utmost relevance. It is the understanding of the context of the counselee that makes themes of sin and responsibility come alive. Counseling in this way also facilitates those themes being taught with love, grace, care, sensitivity, and a sense of what a sufferer is going through.

Advancement Concerning Human Motivation

The relationship between sin and suffering is not the only area where the biblical counseling movement has experienced advancement in how it *thinks* about counseling. Another important area is the one of motivation. To discuss motivation is to discuss why people do the things they do. This area of thought has seen deep change, as the leadership of the biblical counseling movement has shifted from Adams to the second generation. This issue of motivation has received more attention than any other in biblical counseling theory, so it is critical to unpack with some detail.

Adams on Motivation

As we have seen, Adams believed that the primary reason people do what they do is sin. But Adams's view of the dynamic of sin is unusual. In fact, it is really a theological innovation that the second generation would eventually repudiate. According to Adams, living such a lifestyle of sin creates sinful *behavioral habit patterns* that are very important to understand. Adams says, "The place of habit in Christian thought and life is significant, and the Scriptures recognize this fact."[48] In Adams's model, habit is critical to understand, because it is behavioral habits that condition sinners to sin. Adams states:

> Sinners, perverted from birth, will begin to develop sinful response patterns from the beginning of their lives (they cannot do otherwise before regeneration). Because of the great importance of habit in our daily lives, these patterns set up formidable barriers to growth in Christian living, with which counselees struggle, and with which counselors must deal.[49]

For Adams, then, it is sinful habits formed over the course of a life lived apart from God that are the controlling factor in explaining why people sin.

In fact, Adams went further and argued that it is these sinful habit patterns that the authors of Scripture have in mind when they use the term "flesh":

> For years, theologians and exegetes have puzzled and argued over the sixth to eighth chapters of Romans. Numerous questions have been raised, among which is the meaning of the word flesh, which has a specialized use in this place. . . . I wish to try to contribute something (at least) to the discussion. Other passages—Romans 12, Galatians 5, Colossians 3, Ephesians 4—pertain to the question of flesh and habit in the sinner; Romans 6–8 must not be studied apart from them. In all of these places, Paul considers the problem of sinful habits (or behavior patterns) acquired by the response of our sinful natures to life situations, and the difficulties that these raise for regenerate persons who seek to serve God.[50]

We shouldn't think that Adams believed this process was disconnected from a biblical understanding of the gospel. He absolutely did not. In fact, Adams thought it was the process of sanctification—made possible by Christ and empowered by the Holy Spirit—that makes it possible for sinners to change from their previous life of the flesh to a new life in the Spirit. It is in the process of sanctification that the habits of sin—the flesh—are done away with and Christians, slowly and over time, begin to look increasingly like the Christ in whose righteousness they have been declared to stand. For Adams, this change from being motivated by the flesh to being motivated by the Spirit happens in a two-part process of dehabituation and rehabituation.

Adams grounded his teaching on dehabituation and rehabituation in the biblical instruction of "putting off" and "putting on." In Ephesians 4:17–24, Paul writes:

> Now this I say and testify in the Lord, that you must no longer walk as the Gentiles do, in the futility of their minds. They are darkened in their understanding, alienated from the life of God because of the ignorance that is in them, due to their hardness of heart. They have become calloused and have given themselves up to sensuality, greedy to practice every kind of impurity. But that is not the way you learned Christ!—assuming that you have heard about him and were taught in him, as the truth is in Jesus, to put off your old self, which belongs to your former manner of life and is corrupt through deceitful desires, and to be renewed in the spirit of your minds, and to put on the new self, created after the likeness of God in true righteousness and holiness. (Cf. Col. 3:1–17)

Both the processes of putting off and putting on are taught by Paul, and both are central to the change process. Adams says, "These two factors always must be present in order to effect genuine change. Putting off will not be permanent without putting on. Putting on is hypocritical as well as temporary, unless it is accompanied by putting off."[51] Adams continues:

> Unless [a sinner] has been "*reprogrammed*" or *rehabituated*, when the chips are down, when he is tired, sick, or under great pressure, a counselee's good resolves and temporary cessation of [sinning] will not last. He will revert to his former manner of life because he is still *programmed*

to do so. The old sinful habit patterns have not been replaced by new ones. Until that occurs, he will remain vulnerable to sinful reversion. Dehabituation is possible only by achieving rehabituation. The counselee must be *repackaged*. New patterns of response must become dominant. It is to these instead that *he must learn to turn habitually* under life stresses.[52]

What is perhaps most important to note about Adams's understanding in this regard is that the whole scheme had a very practical element for counseling. Adams believed that true change would never occur if people focus only on what they need to *stop* doing. There must also be a focus on replacing the bad behavior with a good behavior. In other words, liars must not only stop lying but also start telling the truth. Thieves must stop stealing but also start working and giving. This, for Adams, was the hard work of counseling—over time dehabituating the sin of lying, stealing, and a million others, and rehabituating truth-telling, hard work, and other righteous counterparts of behavior. This was all brought about through discipline and a process Adams referred to as "total structuring."[53]

Another element to notice about Adams's understanding is how focused on behavior it is. There is little discussion of what stands behind this behavior. There is hardly any focus given to asking the question of "why," which most people have in mind when they consider issues of motivation. This neglect of "why" with a focus on behavior was intentional for Adams and was done with a specific pastoral purpose in view. In *Competent to Counsel* Adams discusses the sin of the sons of Eli in 1 Samuel 2 and condemns Eli for two things. First, he argues that Eli was wrong to avoid confronting his sons earlier. Second, he laments that when Eli finally did approach his sons, he began with "the fatal word, 'Why.'"[54] Adams argues:

Eli's stress upon "why" may indicate one of his failures as a father. It was not his business to speculate about the causes of his sons' wicked deeds beyond the fact that he already knew—they were sinners. It was his task to stop them. Too great an emphasis upon "why" may indicate an attempt to find extenuating reasons for excusing conduct which otherwise must be described as sinful. . . . Eli would have done better to have emphasized the word "what" instead. If he had compared the behavior itself to God's standards, he might have been able to help his boys.[55]

Adams continues:

> Usual counseling methods recommend frequent long excursions back into the intricacies of the whys and wherefores of behavior. Instead, nouthetic counseling is largely committed to a discussion of what. All the why that a counselee needs to know can be clearly demonstrated in the what. What was done? What must be done to rectify it? What should future responses be? In nouthetic counseling the stress falls upon the "what" rather than the "why" because the "why" is already known before counseling begins. The reason why people get into trouble in their relationships to God and others is because of their sinful natures. Men are born sinners.[56]

For Adams, a focus on behavior is the most biblical and most practical approach. Adams thought that a hazy focus on *why* would lead away from taking responsibility. Such a consequence is unnecessary, given the fact that we already know the ultimate why: men are born sinners. Sinners sin because they *are* sinners. This fact was enough for Adams. But it turned out to be a problem for the second generation of biblical counselors seeking to advance the thinking of their movement.

The Second Generation on Motivation

With Powlison in 1988, the biblical counseling movement began to assess whether there had been enough attention given to motivational issues:

> Behavior flows "from within, out of men's hearts" (Mark 7:21). There is an internal cause of interpersonal conflict (James 4:1f); the varied works of the flesh express inner cravings (Galatians 5:15–21); every kind of evil roots in misplaced affections (1 Timothy 6:10). This we all know and affirm. But both our theory and practice have not given this area the attention it needs. We must become as familiar with the practical, everyday details of faith and idolatry as we are with the details of those acts of sin and righteousness which flow from our hearts. The changes for which biblical counseling must aim are both internal and external.[57]

Powlison made this assessment not because of any "fatal defect" within the movement, but because there was a need for increased "emphasis and articulation."[58] That is to say, as far as Powlison was concerned, the need to address motivational issues grew out of a desire to *advance* the biblical counseling movement, not to abandon the foundation. This advancement has occurred over the last twenty years in two principal ways. First, authors critiqued and modified Adams's views on motivation. Second, they attempted to articulate a more biblical understanding of motivation.

Critiquing Adams

The most open critique came out in two articles in the *Journal of Biblical Counseling*: "How Theology Shapes Ministry: Jay Adams's View of the Flesh and an Alternative," by Edward Welch, and "Critique of 'Habituation' as a Biblical Model of Change," by George M. Schwab.[59] Both Schwab and Welch demonstrate in their articles that Adams's understanding of the flesh is untenable given the understanding of the expression in the New Testament as well as the history of the term's interpretation. Welch states:

> Scripture consistently teaches that sin has its ultimate source in our heart, our "mindset," our spiritual substance, and it is expressed through the instrument of the body. . . . No text clearly teaches that the body of a sinful person is gradually programmed to sin to the point where the body can sin by itself, without the agency of the heart that is inclined to evil.[60]

Schwab agrees with Welch's view here but additionally shows that Adams's view of habituation was not developed from an exegesis of specific passages of Scripture:[61]

> Adams's theory that our moral habits (either faith or unbelief; either sins or love) operate according to habituation dynamics is not actually substantiated in any of his citations. One must assume such a phenomenon before one comes to the verse, and then read it accordingly.[62]

Schwab's statement that Adams's views did not come from Scripture is a strong charge. It raises questions regarding the true origins of Adams's motivational theory. In order to address these issues Schwab includes a discussion of where Adams's assumption was developed, arguing that it came from the influence of secular thinkers such as William Glasser and O. Hobart Mowrer:

> The stimulus for Jay Adams's theory of habit also came from outside the Bible. Adams admits that what radicalized him—what set him free from Rogers and Freud—was the influence of particular secular psychologists, O. Hobart Mowrer and William Glasser. However, Adams claims that the Bible is sufficient for counseling and that all so-called psychological insights must stand the test of Scripture. Yet, some of his "Bible-based" theories and emphases seem almost identical to those of his secular predecessors. Was part of the "grid" through which Adams reads the Bible supplied by these secularists?[63]

Schwab answers yes to his own question while being clear that—in an ultimate way—Adams found the models of Mowrer and Glasser "hopelessly inadequate because of their God-lessness."[64]

So then Schwab and Welch each agree that Adams's model of habituation is unbiblical. In addition to this, Schwab establishes that the origins of Adams's thinking were found in secular psychological theories, not in specific texts of Scripture. In other words, Schwab shows that the problem—cited by Welch—of Adams's understanding of the term *flesh* was imposed by Adams on the biblical text and actually derived from the influence of unbelieving people.

Having identified the biblical-theological problem of Adams's understanding, Welch points out the practical difficulty that this error has on the task of counseling. Welch states that Adams's habituation theology necessarily impacts his approach to counseling: "As with all theological commitments, Adams's view of the flesh is expressed in his counseling theory and practice." Welch then goes on to list twenty specific ways he thinks counseling will be impacted by an adoption of Adams's model.[65] It is not necessary to list all of those here, but three are of particular importance to this discussion on motivation. Welch observes:

> Counseling will be similar to a consultation with a behaviorist. It will be a step-by-step, somewhat mechanical process. It will be a problem-solving task. Motivations will not be the target for change; overt behaviors will. Adams has often been accused of sounding like a Christian behaviorist. His view of the flesh is one theological commitment that

leaves him vulnerable to such charges. The language of reprogramming, the emphasis on practice, the lack of a robust model of the inner life have analogies to present day behavioral and cognitive-behavioral approaches.

Without attentiveness to motives and the inner life, counselees might not feel understood. They will sometimes have a sense that a counselor did not go "deep" enough.

Counseling will not be alert to good behavior that has ungodly motivations because, since sin is embedded more in the body than in the heart, the model does not induce one to examine motivations. The body doesn't have motivational patterns: beliefs, desires, hopes, trusts, aspirations, anxieties, identities, etc.[66]

It is important to add at this point that Adams himself ferociously denied the charge of being a behaviorist.[67] In responding to Welch in particular, he wrote a letter to the editor of the *Journal of Biblical Counseling*. In the letter, Adams responded to each of Welch's counseling implications as an improper understanding of his view. The only available record of Adams's response had been a statement in the *Journal of Biblical Counseling*, saying, "Now, it is fortunate that Ed admits that I might 'disavow' some of his conclusions. I certainly do! In fact, I disavow most, if not every one, of them."[68] The full statement is now available in the appendix of this book.

In fact, it is not as though Adams never mentioned any realities behind human behavior. For example, in discussing habituation he said, "Do not fail to note how plainly Paul speaks of more than the cessation of some objectionable actions; he calls for a change in the 'manner of life.' Paul calls for genuine change; change in the person. Not merely in his actions."[69] A bit later he argued:

All of the stress that the Bible puts upon human effort must not be misunderstood; we are talking about grace-motivated effort, not the work of the flesh. It is not effort apart from the Holy Spirit that produces godliness. Rather, it is through the power of the Holy Spirit alone that one can endure. Of his own effort, a man may persist in learning to skate, but he will not persist in the pursuit of godliness. A Christian does good works because the Spirit first works in him.[70]

These are examples of Adams's early writing that demonstrate that he was certainly not a bald behaviorist. Having said that, Adams did not do a very thorough job of incorporating these thoughts into his model. He never spoke of *details* in heart change. Adams himself noted:

> It is important to note that all those who think that they are pleasing God by keeping counseling assignments must be told to obey from the heart. It is not enough to line up the required actions and then do them *seriatim*. Neither is there merit in that alone, as some think. Rather, those who think that there is have the mind of the Pharisee at work within them. The Pharisee, Jesus said, washed the outside of the cup, but inside it was full of corruption. The Pharisee, He continued, was like a white-washed grave that looked good on the outside, but was full of death and corruption within. The Pharisee vainly tried to earn acceptance and approval by God through these outer works. In short, there must be reality, love, faith, and genuineness within, as well as proper action without. I have been accused of teaching behaviorism because in some of my earlier writings I did not explain this thoroughly enough. Wrongly, I expected the reader to know that when I spoke from the Bible about "action," I meant the one and only kind that God accepts—works motivated by faith and love. But some did not understand. Here, I want to make it explicit that the sort of action that [I am] talking about is action that not only conforms outwardly to God's commands, but conforms inwardly as well.[71]

Adams did two things here that are very important to this discussion. First, he noted that the heart—that is, the biblical seat of motivation—is important to behavior. He further indicated that a focus on behavior is ultimately insufficient without a focus on the motivations behind the behavior. Second—and more importantly—Adams admitted that this idea had been missing from his previous work. Somewhat ironically, he even described the motivation for not including it as a wrong assumption about what others would understand him to mean.

It is important to note this observation of Adams for two reasons. First, it does show the common cause that exists between the streams of counseling, whether of the first or the second generation. Second, it shows, by the admission of none other than Adams himself, that the movement he founded was in need of development and clarification. Missing in Adams's model was an elaboration of all that was included in the idea of heart motivation. It is this important work of elaboration that the recent leadership in the biblical counseling movement has tried to accomplish.

Constructing a More Thorough Understanding of Motivation

After raising the need for more focus on motivation in the "Crucial Issues" article, Powlison expands on his proposal in "Idols of the Heart and 'Vanity Fair.'" In this article, Powlison articulates motivational themes behind an individual's behavior in a fuller way than had ever been done in the counseling movement. At the beginning of his article he states the issue:

> Has something or someone besides Jesus Christ taken title to your heart's trust, preoccupation, loyalty, service, fear and delight? It is a question bearing on the immediate motivation for one's behavior, thoughts, and feelings. In the Bible's conceptualization, the motivation question is the lordship question. Who or what "rules" my behavior, the Lord or a substitute?[72]

For Powlison, the key that unlocks the door of motivation is worship. It is worship that motivates human activity. The central feature here is not *whether* there is worship, but instead *what* is being worshiped. According to Powlison, there are two options: the living God in Christ or a substitute. In articulating what this substitute may be, Powlison describes heart idols:

> "Idolatry" is the characteristic and summary Old Testament word for our drift from God. . . . Interestingly (and unsurprisingly) the New Testament merges the concept of idolatry and the concept of inordinate, life-ruling desires. Idolatry becomes a problem of the heart, a metaphor for human lust, craving yearning, and greedy demand.[73]

Powlison points away from idolatry as the worship of actual physical images and toward a more internal problem, with the support of Ezekiel 14:1–8:

> Son of man, these men have taken their idols into their hearts, and set the stumbling block of their iniquity before their faces. . . . Thus says the Lord GOD: Any one of the house of Israel who takes his idols into his heart and sets the stumbling block of his iniquity before his face, and yet comes to the prophet, I the LORD will answer him as he comes with the multitude of his idols, that I may lay hold of the hearts of the house of Israel, who are all estranged from me through their idols. (Ezek. 14:3–5)

Powlison goes on to contend that these heart idols originate from both within and without:

> Behavioral sins are always portrayed in the Bible as "motivated" or ruled by a "god" or "gods." The problem in human motivation—the question of practical covenantal allegiance, God or any of the substitutes—is frequently and usefully portrayed as the problem of idolatry. Idolatry is a problem both rooted deeply in the human heart and powerfully impinging on us from our social environment.[74]

Powlison's point is clear: human beings are worshiping beings whose actions are motivated by the true God or idols. These heart idols are generated from inside or learned from outside the heart of man and can include anything from the love of money, to sex and power.

It would be difficult to overstate the influence Powlison's contribution has had on biblical counselors. Indeed it could be fair to say that over the last twenty years the movement has been defined by the usage of Powlison's metaphor. The "idols of the heart" metaphor has been used extensively by any number of authors. Tedd Tripp has made great use of the metaphor for child-rearing:

> Since there is no such thing as a place of childhood neutrality, your children either worship God or idols. These idols are not small wooden or stone statuary. They are the subtle idols of the heart. The Bible describes such idols using terminology such as fear of man, evil desires, lusts, and pride. The idols include conformity to the world, embracing earthly mindsets, and "setting the affections on things below." What we have in view are any manner of motives, desires, wants, goals, hopes, and expectations that rule the heart of a child.[75]

Tripp's brother Paul David Tripp invokes the metaphor as a central understanding in counseling methodology. In commenting on the Israelites in Ezekiel 14 he says:

> God points out their idolatry, which is idolatry of a specific kind. They have *idols in their hearts*, a more personal and fundamental form of idolatry than ritual religious or cultural idolatry. An idol of the heart is *anything that rules me other than God*. As worshiping beings, human beings always worship someone or something. This is not a situation

where some people worship and some don't. If God isn't ruling my heart, someone or something else will. It is the way we were made.[76]

Edward Welch has also made use of the metaphor and has done so in strikingly diverse ways. In his book *When People Are Big and God Is Small*, Welch engages in a lengthy discussion of heart idolatry. He says:

> What is it that shame-fear and rejection-fear have in common? To use a biblical image, they both indicate that people are a person's favorite idol. We exalt them and their perceived power above God. We worship them as ones who have God-like exposing gazes (shame-fear) or God-like ability to "fill" us with esteem, love, admiration, acceptance, respect, and other psychological desires (rejection-fear). . . .
>
> When you think of it, idolatry is the age-old strategy of the human heart. The objects of worship may change over time, but the heart stays the same. What we do now is no different from what the Israelites did with the golden calf.[77]

Welch places his understanding of idols of the heart as a central element in his understanding of addictions:

> One of the most common portrayals of the human condition, and one which captures both the in-control and out-of-control experiences of addictions, is the theme of idolatry. From this perspective, the true nature of all addictions is that we have chosen to go outside the boundaries of the kingdom of God and look for blessing in the land of idols. In turning to idols, we are saying that we desire something in creation more than we desire the Creator.[78]

Three years later, writing on the topic of depression, Welch relates that topic to heart idols:

> At some level, all people know God (Rom. 1:21). We don't just have a fuzzy idea that there is a god, gods or "higher power" out there somewhere. Within the human heart, there is a personal knowledge of the God who is, and we are either trusting him or something else. To use more religious language, we are either worshiping him, or we are worshiping idols such as pleasure, money, success, and love. Ultimately the heart is either/or.[79]

In her book *Idols of the Heart* Elyse Fitzpatrick says, "Idols aren't just stone statues. No, idols are the thoughts, desires, longings, and expectations that we worship in place of the true God. Idols cause us to ignore the true God in search of what we think we need."[80]

It is apparent then that Powlison's theme of heart idolatry has earned a broad following in the biblical counseling movement. The notion of heart idolatry is one that addresses motivation and seeks to answer concretely the question "why" and explain the *because* of behavior. It attempts to describe the *because* of behavior by explaining the wrongly placed desires in the worship of things that are not God.

This motivational development brought critical change to the model first proposed by Adams. For starters, this teaching on motivation honors the biblical teaching that our behavior springs from motives in the heart. Jesus is quite clear in his teaching: "Do you not see that whatever goes into a person from outside cannot defile him, since it enters not his heart but his stomach, and is expelled?" (Thus he declared all foods clean.) And he said, "What comes out of a person is what defiles him. For from within, out of the heart of man, come evil thoughts, sexual immorality, theft, murder, adultery, coveting, wickedness, deceit, sensuality, envy, slander, pride, foolishness. All these evil things come from within, and they defile a person" (Mark 7:18–23).

This teaching from the lips of Jesus clearly instructs that all behavior that humans engage in, including their thinking (e.g., evil thoughts), springs from motives deep within the heart. In articulating this biblical truth, the contemporary biblical counseling movement has strengthened the theology undergirding their practice. When the Bible teaches that all behavior is grounded in the heart, and when this is affirmed in a confessional and practical way, it makes biblical counseling more *biblical*.

Another benefit of the "idols of the heart" metaphor is that it helps to understand people as worshiping beings. This is clearly at the center of Powlison's understanding of the expression. In Powlison's writings on what he calls "X-ray questions," he seeks to give counselors (and counselees) guidance about how to understand the motivational issues. He said:

[These questions] provide aid in discerning the patterns of a person's motivation. The questions aim to help people identify the ungodly masters that occupy positions of authority in their hearts. These questions reveal "functional gods," what or who actually controls their particular actions, thoughts, emotions, attitudes, memories, and anticipations. Note that "functional gods" in a particular situation often stand diametrically opposed to the "professed God." . . . As a Christian you profess that God controls all things, and works everything to his glory and your ultimate well being. . . . [When you sin] your functional god competes with your professed God. Unbelievers are wholly owned by ungodly motives— their functional gods. Yet true believers are often severely compromised, distracted, and divided by our functional gods as well. Thankfully, grace reorients us, purifies us, and turns us back to our Lord. Grace makes your professed God and functional God one and the same.[81]

Powlison is correct here in his understanding that human beings are fundamentally worshiping beings. The idols of the heart metaphor highlights this worshiping nature, as his X-ray question number thirty shows:

What are your idols or false gods? In what do you place your trust, or set your hopes? What do you turn to or seek? Where do you take refuge? Who is the savior, judge, controller, provider, [or] protector in your world? Whom do you serve? What "voice" controls you? This entire list of thirty-five questions pursues things that usurp God. Each of these can metaphorically be termed an "idol" to which you give loyalty. The voices you listen to mimic specific characteristics of God. Start to trace that out into the details of everyday life, and your ability to address the vertical dimension relevantly and specifically will mature.[82]

Finally, this emphasis on heart motivation, which is always worship oriented, has very practical benefits for counseling and addresses the concerns raised by Welch, above. When counseling is focused on the motivational issues behind behavior, it moves biblical counseling beyond behaviorism and into counseling that is truly biblical and deals with all the issues the Bible itself addresses. Also, a focus on motivation allows counselors and counselees to "go deep" together, thus bringing about the true understanding of behavior. Such depth allows for change—not only at the critical level of behavior but at the level of the heart where life is always lived *coram Deo*, before the face of God. Finally, a focus on motivational issues will be attentive to right behavior that is done for wrong reasons. This kind of counseling will be more equipped to root out pharisaism and legalism.

Adams would admit these benefits. In the earlier quote from *Critical Stages* (page 74), he conceded that the heart is important. The point here, however, is not to engage what Adams personally believed but to engage those elements of Adams's thought that he unpacked in his teaching. In this area, by Adams's own admission, his thought was in need of further development. Such development has occurred over the last twenty years in the areas of motivation, and that development has been positive.

Conclusion

The extensive ground covered in this chapter has been necessary because of the importance of theoretical concepts in any counseling model and because of the space these issues have received in the biblical counseling movement. With regard to understanding the counselee as sinner and sufferer, biblical counselors have taken significant steps developing the work of Adams. Rather than seeing counselees in a monolithic way as sinners, the second generation has sought to add texture by showing how counselees are both sinners and sufferers and need to be engaged as such in the context of counseling ministry.

Motivational issues have also been developed within the last twenty years of the biblical counseling movement. The movement has advanced from Adams's outward focus on behavior to a more inward focus on motivation. There has been development from a true, but often simplistic, understanding of motivation in human sinfulness to a more dynamic appreciation of all the factors in the human heart that motivate people to behave in various ways.

Each of these advancements has brought maturity to the church's wisdom about how to have theologically informed, ministry-driven conversations with struggling people.

3

Advances in How Biblical Counselors Do Counseling

When we talk about how counselors *do* counseling, we are talking about methodology. Methodology refers to the manner in which counseling proceeds.[1] A counseling methodology is a counselor's understanding of how to navigate the counseling process, and it contains any number of issues, including how the counselee relates to the counselor, how the counselee will collect data, how much personal information a counselor provides, how much time the counselor should talk, how much time the counselee should talk, how the counselees will implement what they learn from counseling, how long sessions will last, how many sessions there will be, and more. A methodology provides the contours for counseling technique.

All approaches to counseling have some kind of methodology, but biblical counselors approach methodological issues differently than secular counselors because they believe that the methodological commitments of the counselor are theological commitments growing out of the pages of Scripture. The reality is that God's Word provides us with the resources we need to construct a theology of counseling process. It is not necessary for Christians to listen to secular psychology to learn how to do counseling. Additionally, where counselors land with regard to the counseling process is the acid test of whether they are truly biblical. Jay Adams argued that a counselor's methodology reveals the true extent to which he is committed to the Bible:

> Methodology and practice plainly reveal what is truly central to a theory. The consideration of a counselor's or therapist's actual practice enables one most incisively to slice through the extraneous to the core material.

What is considered truly operative (regardless of rhetoric or theoretical trappings) will find its way into the basic everyday methodology of a practitioner. Other materials, though interesting, usually form a large residue of non-operative material. To say it the other way around, it is not in affirmations that one always may discover the fundamental presuppositions and foundational beliefs upon which a system is built; these may be dimly perceived, faultily stated, or even intentionally clouded. Again, what one does for his client in counseling or therapy most pointedly shows what he believes the client's real problem to be. Methodology then is where it's at. All sorts of people can agree upon noble goals, but when the question arises about how these goals may be attained, they soon begin to part company. Conflicts over methodology plainly expose the true differences between therapists and between counselors.[2]

Adams was clear that the ultimate test of a person's theory is found in his methodology. According to Adams, all counselors will ultimately reveal their true commitments at the level of methodology—that is, how they proceed in counseling. A biblical counselor will demonstrate his true commitment to the Bible when he engages with a counselee and seeks to help him. Methodology, then, is critical. All counselors (whether or not they are *biblical* counselors) possess it (and so have a theology that is either correct or aberrant), and it is *the* test of one's theoretical commitments.

Jay Adams's first written work about counseling, *Competent to Counsel*, was an initial effort at laying out the conceptual framework of biblical counseling. Three years later he followed that work with *The Christian Counselor's Manual*, which was meant to begin the work of constructing a biblical counseling methodology. In that work Adams argued, "I feel constrained to do something to meet the need (frequently expressed) for a 'how to' manual. . . . In *The Christian Counselor's Manual* I have tried to fill that need to some extent."[3] Biblical counselors have been concerned with the development of their methodology ever since.

Areas of Consistency in Counseling Methodology

This chapter explains how the biblical counseling movement has advanced its methodology during the leadership of the second generation of biblical counselors. Before engaging in a discussion of methodological advancement, however, it is necessary to outline those areas where the biblical counseling movement has remained constant. Without proper care, a project like this one can create the appearance that the differences in the movement are more apparent than the areas of agreement. Such is not the case. Indeed, the biblical counseling movement has much on which to agree in the area of methodology. Three specific areas of consistency can be discussed.

1) Consistency in Information Gathering

From the founding of the movement to the present, biblical counselors are unanimous in their understanding of the importance of gathering good and accurate information about the counselee's problems.[4] Biblical counselors think that listening to the counselee is important for at least three reasons.

First, it is biblical to listen to and learn from counselees about their problems. Proverbs 18:2 says, "A fool takes no pleasure in understanding, but only in expressing his opinion." Likewise James 1:19 says, "Be quick to hear, slow to speak." The biblical model for interpersonal engagement is to listen first and speak last. This is true for anyone but especially for the counselor, who is charged with ministering to people in the midst of their difficulty. Paul Tripp grounds the importance of data gathering in the ministry of Jesus. After discussing the reality of Jesus's sympathizing with the weaknesses of his people, from Hebrews 4:14–16, he says:

> Since Christ is our model for personal ministry, we too want to understand people so that we can serve him in their lives. We too must be committed to entering their worlds. We can begin by taking the time to ask good questions and listen well. Our hope is that others would seek us out and share more of their true struggles, so that they may find, through us, the Lord himself. Entering a person's world enables us to apply the truths of the gospel in a way that is situation- and person-specific.[5]

Second, listening and learning are important for the counselor. There is a reason why it is biblical to listen before speaking. The reality is that a person (counselor or otherwise) needs information before he or she is equipped to say anything helpful (Prov. 18:13). Words spoken before a matter is understood will not be truly helpful. Wayne Mack discusses the disastrous counsel that Job received and identifies the problem as a failure to understand the situation:

We must be careful that we do not make this mistake in our counseling. If we attempt to interpret people's problems before we gather adequate data, we will only add to their difficulty rather than relieve it. . . . The wise person seeks and acquires knowledge—not assumptions, speculations, or imaginations. And knowledge has to do with facts.[6]

If counselors are to be helpful, they must know what is going on with their counselees, and this requires information about their problems.

Third, listening and learning are important for the counselee. In *Speaking Truth in Love* David Powlison discusses two kinds of questions that counselors should always ask. First, Powlison says that counselors should ask questions about the situation the counselee is facing. Second, Powlison urges counselors to ask questions concerning what God has to say about the situation the counselee is facing. He justifies these questions, saying:

Both questions help us to work on the things that count. Ministry is always helping people make connections they haven't been making. It's always reinterpreting what's going on, identifying redemptive opportunities in what seem like the same old ruts. It traces out previously unseen practical implications of life in Christ. It's always remaking minds, hearts, and lifestyles that are still misshapen. These questions will help you to say the timely, significant, and appropriate words that encourage such a disciplining of lives.[7]

Counselees are usually quite aware of the *what*—the brute facts of their situation. They are, however, usually very poor interpreters of the *why*—the reasons behind their behavior, the significance (from God's point of view) of what is going on, the purposes and promises of God's redemptive intervention. Listening and learning are important for the biblical counselor because they allow him to reinterpret the experience of the counselee in a way that makes biblical and therefore better situational sense. Without a thorough process of listening to and learning from counselees, biblical counselors may be able to help them understand the Bible, but they will not be able to help them see their life as God would have them see it. In short, the biblical counseling movement has consistently seen the methodological importance of getting good information about counselees' problems.

2) Consistency in Counseling Instruction

Another area in which those in the biblical counseling community have consistently agreed is the methodological importance of instruction. Adams wrote that biblical counseling is the "bringing of God's Word to bear upon people's lives in order to expose sinful patterns, to correct what is wrong, and to establish new ways of life of which God approves."[8] Adams believed this exposition of sinful patterns and establishment of new patterns came about through a process of teaching. He describes a critical element of biblical counseling, saying, "Problems are solved nouthetically by *verbal* means."[9]

Indeed the emphasis on counseling instruction is, historically, very significant in the biblical counseling movement. When Adams first appeared on the scene, the chief influence on the task of helping people with their problems was the person-centered therapy of Carl Rogers.[10] Rogers believed a counselor should never advise, teach, or direct but should only elicit healing forces from within the counselee. Adams was interested in challenging Rogers's notion of a passive therapist in favor of an activist one. Adams argued:

> Quite contrary to the idea of the necessity of the expert, Rogers would contend that there is no need for an expert at all. . . . Rogerian theory (and therapy) is based upon the idea that all men have adequate knowledge and resources to handle their problems. . . . The therapist (or counselor) shares time with a client in order to help him to help himself. The therapist is a catalyst. . . . The counselee, by the process, himself is able to come up with the answers. . . . The counselor, therefore, becomes a wall or mirror off of which the counselee's own resources are bounced or reflected back to himself.[11]

Adams truly detested Rogers's understanding. It was fundamentally at odds with his understanding of the sinfulness of mankind and of the importance of Christians to walk together and instruct one another.[12]

Biblical counselors are no longer locked in a struggle against Rogerianism, but biblical counselors have continued to affirm the importance of instruction apart from situational concerns. Mack says:

> Scripture makes clear that instruction plays a necessary part in every person's spiritual growth and that it is indispensable in the process of solving

problems. So if we want to help people change, we must be skilled in biblical counseling instruction—and we must make it an important part of our counseling.[13]

Mack is clear then that instruction in counseling is not based on historical considerations but on biblical ones. Because instruction is prescribed in Scripture, it is an essential and enduring part of any biblical counseling ministry.

3) Consistency in Counseling Implementation

A final methodological area in which biblical counselors have been consistent is counseling implementation. Biblical counselors are concerned about far more than giving their counselees truth from Scripture—even when it is meaningfully connected to the details of their specific situation. Biblical counselors are concerned to make their instruction come alive and bear fruit in the daily lives of their counselees as they become more and more like Christ. Mack says:

> Biblical counselors want to promote biblical change as a life-style; they want to foster the implementation and integration of biblical principles into the lives of people so that they will become consistently Christ centered and Christ-like in every area of life including desires, thoughts, attitudes, feelings, and behavior.[14]

Because biblical counselors are concerned about this real-life-change dynamic, they are concerned about the implementation of principles embraced in counseling. Whether it has been called homework,[15] training,[16] doing,[17] or even dehabituation and rehabituation,[18] the biblical counseling movement has repeatedly and consistently emphasized the importance of counseling implementation. Counseling is not just talk or even insight; change always involves doing something different that expresses trust in God's mercies and love for God and neighbor. If counseling is the personal ministry of the Word, and preaching is the public ministry of the Word, then implementation is to counseling as application is to the sermon.

It is now time to turn to an examination of those areas where the biblical counseling movement has experienced advancement in how it does counseling. It is important to see, however, that the movement has a large amount of consistency with regard to its methodology. As advances are considered, it is critical to observe those areas that have remained constant.

Adams's Work and the Need for Methodological Development

As has been demonstrated, it was Adams who did the initial work in formulating a counseling methodology from Scripture. Because Adams was a pioneer doing work that no other person was doing, it is only natural that there were areas of his work that needed more attention. The most significant area of Adams's methodology that needed advancement was his understanding of the counseling relationship. Adams's approach to the relationship between counselee and counselor was relatively formal and authoritative in nature. For example, in *Shepherding God's Flock* Adams stated, "Counseling is best carried on in the study, not in the home. While the pastor must be flexible, and must be prepared to counsel anywhere, he will endeavor to restrict all intensive counseling to formal sessions in the study."[19] Later he added:

> The average pastor to whom I speak tells me that he does not counsel in a systematic and organized way. This is a mistake; sloppiness in counseling brings sloppy results. A pastor must help the counselee to recognize by his efficient, business-like, take-charge (though not officious) approach and by his demand for a commitment to counseling (as well as his own willingness to make it), that the counseling relationship into which they are entering is not a casual, take-it-or-leave-it matter.[20]

In a note on this passage Adams said, "Everything possible must be done to establish among Christians the truth of the fact that by God's ordination the pastor is the *professional counselor*."[21]

These ideas of counseling at a desk, having a counseling demeanor that is "business-like" and "take-charge," and assuming the role of the professional counselor all convey an approach to counseling that is overly formalized.[22] In reality, however, there is no evidence that any such approach is commended in Scripture. Adams has his reasons for making these suggestions,[23] but at this point, biblical counselors should follow Adams's own advice and be sure to make a careful distinction between the suggestion of the counselor and the commands of Scripture.[24]

Another signature of Adams's counseling methodology is its authoritative nature. Adams stated, "But notice that Christian counseling involved the use of authoritative instruction. 'Authoritative instruction' requires the use of directive, nouthetic techniques."[25] Writing in the Rogerian context, Adams was eager to restore a concept of authority to counseling. Because this was true, Adams was interested in inspiring in counselors an understanding of the authority that they possessed in the counseling context.[26]

There is, of course, an authoritative element in biblical counseling, as in all biblical ministries.[27] But Adams's emphasis on pastoral authority tended to obscure the importance of building loving relationships with counselees. In fact, some of Adams's emphases—beyond obscuring a loving relationship—actually seem to work against such a relationship:

> Probably the chief reason why nouthetic counselors fail is because they sometimes become too sympathetic to the complaints and excuses of the counselee. Frequently when a counselee tells a very pitiful tale, there is the temptation for a counselor to decide that this indeed is a special case.[28]

Adams's words seem to present a false dilemma. After all, there is no necessary link between careful, sensitive listening and counseling failure. Adams may realize this,[29] but his language does not seem to take seriously the plight of a struggling counselee.

We should not come down too hard on Adams, however. He commended his approach of authority and formality for at least two good reasons.[30] First, he believed that because biblical counselors base their counsel on Scripture, their words—when derived from the Bible—come with the authority of God:

> There is need for divine authority in counseling. Only biblical counseling possesses such authority. The counselor, as an ordained man of God, exercises the full authority for counseling that Christ gave to the organized church (1 Thessalonians 5:12, 13). To the extent that all Christians must counsel (Colossians 3:16; Romans 15:14), they exercise the authority that Christ has conferred upon them as saints.[31]

For Adams, whether a person is a pastor or a parishioner, he has authority in counseling that derives from the Word of God. Such authority is critical because of the counseling context that had removed authority from counseling in general while removing God's authority in particular.[32]

A second reason Adams had for emphasizing authority and formality in counseling was that without it the element of responsibility that Adams believed is so critical in a counseling situation is undermined:

> Counselors fail when they become too sympathetic toward excuses and do not hold counselees responsible for their behavior, but they can never fail when they become truly sympathetic toward them. Perhaps the first attitude may be called sympathy and the latter empathy. When counselors simply become softhearted, they are most unmerciful toward their counselees. The most kindly (empathetic) stance is to tell the truth, help the counselee to face up to his own sin, and encourage him to make the changes necessary to rectify the situation.[33]

In fact, there is no necessary connection between an honest, careful hearing of the concerns of a counselee and counsel that is devoid of authority and leads to an abdication of responsibility on the part of the counselee. The reality is that there can be an honest hearing, a deep and abiding relationship, *and* careful and confident teaching from the Scriptures. The Bible not only calls Christians to faithfulness in teaching but also to mutuality in their relationships.[34] The emphasis of Adams on a formal and authoritative style seems to miss this important element of biblical relationship.

In short, Adams was responsible for a strong emphasis on formality and authority in counseling. This emphasis was admirable, biblical, and historically necessary. Adams's neglect to build an understanding of the importance of engaging with the counselee in a caring relationship, however, meant that there was room for a second generation to advance the movement in this way.

Methodological Development

Powlison had these same concerns when he wrote his "Crucial Issues" article. He argues:

> There is a "danger to the left of us" in various secular constructions of the counselor-counselee relationship, which zealously avoid any overt

authority (covert authority is, of course, present in every counseling system). But there is also a danger to the other side. The biblical view of the counseling relationship has non-authoritative elements, in which the "counselee" sets the agenda, in which "the relationship" is central to constructive counseling taking place! The Scripture demands that we probe the interplay between authority and mutuality characteristic of healthy biblical relationships. We must mirror the variety of counselor-counselee configurations, which the Bible portrays as vehicles for the Lord's authority. . . . In fact, the authoritative shepherd who decisively intervenes is only one of the modes of biblical counseling. It is not even the primary mode. It is the backup mode for when the primary mode fails. The most characteristic biblical counseling relationship is a long-term friendship, consisting of mutually invited counseling and generating dependency on God as well as constructive interdependency on one another. The authoritative, short-term intervention is the emergency, life-saving measure.[35]

Powlison's words here point the way forward and are salient in analyzing where the movement has come and where it needs to go. Later, Powlison takes on Adams directly in a more critical way: "Adams tells me I need compassion, identification, and mutuality, but he teaches and models rebuke, proclamation, and authority. He calls me to balance, but doesn't teach me how."[36] Powlison made the initial call for methodological development in understanding and appreciating the relationship between counselor and counselee, but other biblical counselors would join with him in the actual work of doing this. Six specific areas of development may be isolated.

1) Counseling That Is Familial

Adams emphasized elements of authority/submission and shepherd/sheep in counseling, whereas more contemporary work in understanding counseling methodology has sought to emphasize the family relationship that exists between counselee and counselor. Both Powlison and Mack have done work in this regard. Powlison grounds his approach in 1 Thessalonians 5:14: "We urge you, brothers, admonish the idle, encourage the fainthearted, help the weak, be patient with them all." Powlison comments on this passage:

What paradigm for counseling relationships informs 1 Thessalonians 5:14? Who are these ["brothers"] called to patiently admonish, encourage, and help? And who are these recipients of care, described as the self-willed, the disheartened, or the disabled? As we listen to 1 Thessalonians as a whole, it becomes clear that the letter portrays—and calls for—a familial paradigm for understanding the 'counselor-counselee' relationship. Older children help younger. Because the needy ones come with different sorts of problems, the wiser ones must be highly adaptable in their love.[37]

Mack grounds his familial approach in 1 Timothy 5:1–2, "Do not rebuke an older man but encourage him as you would a father, younger men as brothers, older women as mothers, younger women as sisters, in all purity." Mack says:

Think of the counselee as a family member. . . . When I counsel, I deliberately try to imagine how I would treat one of my close relatives. I ask myself, how would I talk to them? How would I proceed if this were my mother or my father or my brother or my sister sitting across the desk from me? In reality, our counselees are our spiritual brothers and sisters, and our heavenly Father demands that they be treated as such.[38]

These comments of Powlison and Mack provide critical balance to the counseling methodology of Adams. The counselor does possess the authority of God when speaking from God's Word. When, however, the counselor speaks the Word to a counselee, he or she is speaking to a brother or sister in Christ. The counselor is still speaking authoritatively, but authority has a different tone when done in the context of a brother-sister relationship than when it is done in a general-corporal relationship.

2) Counseling That Demonstrates Affection

Counseling that is done in the context of family should demonstrate affection to the counselee. Powlison says:

Real understanding—accurate, concerned, merciful, probing, gentle, communicated—matters a great deal in counseling. When a counselee, a friend, a spouse, a child *knows*, "This person cares about me, this person knows me, and this person knows my world," good things tend to happen.[39]

Several things stand out about Powlison's comment here. First, Powlison talks about the importance of real understanding being communicated. It is not enough that a counselor *intends* to be understanding. Instead, a sense of understanding must be *apprehended* by the counselee. In this same vein, he describes a counselor appreciating the cares of the counselee. "People don't care how much you know until they know how much you care" is a cliché, but it seems to capture a biblical point that Powlison articulates about the importance of demonstrating affection to counselees.

Tripp also contributes to the need for genuine understanding:

> I am deeply persuaded that the foundation for people-transforming ministry is not sound theology; it is love. Without love, our theology is a boat without oars. Love is what drove God to send and sacrifice his Son. Love led Christ to subject himself to a sinful world and the horrors of the cross. Love is what causes him to seek and save the lost, and to persevere until each of his children is transformed into his image. His love will not rest until all of his children are at his side in glory. The hope of every sinner does not rest in theological answers but in the love of Christ for his own. Without it, we have no hope personally, relationally, or eternally.[40]

Tripp overstates the case here. There is no reason to drive a wedge between love and theology to make his point. Ironically, Tripp grounds his understanding of the primacy of love in a *theology* of incarnation, substitutionary atonement, justification, sanctification, and perseverance. Even more ironically, Tripp does this while articulating a *theology* of love. No, it is not necessary to drive a wedge between love and theology to appreciate the larger truth that Tripp discusses. Love is important in counseling. Love needs to be apparent if counseling instruction is to bear fruit.

Adams believed that his counseling approach was fundamentally loving. He believed it was loving to confront people with their sin and give them the resources to change. Adams is to be commended for this understanding. What he did not develop was the way to demonstrate care for the counselee so that the instruction he emphasized was most effective.

3) Counseling That Is Sacrificial

If counseling should be a demonstration of love to those in the context of familial relations, then a main way that a counselor can demonstrate this relational love is by investing sacrificially in the lives of his counselees. Tripp says:

> When we forget the call to incarnate the love of Christ, we take our relationships as our own. Soon they are governed by our pleasure, comfort, and ease. We get irritated at people who interfere with these things, and much of our anger is due to the fact that we are relationship thieves. People do not belong to us; they belong to God! Relationships are not primarily for our fulfillment. On the contrary, relationships between sinners are messy, difficult, labor-intensive, and demanding, but in that, they are designed to result in God's glory and our good as he is worshiped and our hearts are changed. Effective personal ministry begins when we confess that we have taken relationships that belong to God and used them for our own selfish purposes.[41]

Tripp does something fascinating here in his conception of the counselee-counselor relationship in personal ministry. Clearly Tripp believes that counselors should invest in the lives of their counselees. Even more, he believes that they should invest in their counselees to the point of great personal sacrifice. His point is even more than that, however. Tripp goes so far as to say that people who do not invest sacrificially in those to whom they minister are "selfish" and "thieves."

This idea of sacrificial investment captures perfectly the Pauline idea of ministry in 1 Thessalonians: "We were gentle among you, like a nursing mother taking care of her own children. So, being affectionately desirous of you, we were ready to share with you not only the gospel of God but also our own selves, because you had become very dear to us" (1 Thess. 2:7–8).

These ideas of being affectionately desirous and willing to share oneself are simply not addressed by Adams. The biblical counseling movement should be thankful for Adams's emphasis on truth in counseling and even for his practical approach to counseling in a handful of sessions.[42] The counseling movement should also be thankful for the advances that have added to all of this a biblical necessity of sacrificial investment in other people.

4) Counseling That Is Person-Oriented

As has been pointed out, when Adams founded the biblical counseling movement he did so in the context of a counseling environment that had embraced a Rogerian notion of person-centered counseling. Adams's counseling model sought, in contrast, to emphasize the elements of counseling that dealt with sin in an authoritative way and that stood on the truthfulness of God's Word. In the process of developing such a model he tended to focus on problems above people. Contemporary biblical counselors seeking to move beyond this limitation have developed the model in a way that avoids the excesses of Rogerian counseling but still deals with people in an appropriate biblical way. It is not person-*centered*, but it is person-*oriented*.

Mack addresses the issue as frankly as anyone when he specifically engages Adams. He writes, "Biblical counseling is about solving people's problems. It is about discovering the causes of their problems and then applying biblical principles to those causes. Sometimes, even well-intentioned counselors err, however, by counseling without cultivating the key element of involvement." Mack goes on to give an example from Jay Adams's *The Christian Counselor's Casebook*:[43]

Clara comes to you stating that she has filed for divorce on the grounds of mental and bodily cruelty. Clara returns for the third session. "I tried to get him here but he had other things to do," she begins. "You know what his other things are, of course. I told you all of them."

"I don't want to hear such charges behind Marty's back," you respond. "This continuing hostility toward him, even though you told him you forgave him, seems to indicate that you made little or no attempt to bury the issue and start afresh. I don't think that you understand forgiveness. You . . . "

"Forgive him! You know there is a limit. After he has beat me, and his drinking away our money maybe, but when I came home and found him in my bed with that woman, I can never bury that! He is just an immature, immoral, animalistic pig," she declares.

You tell her that it will be necessary for her to change her language about her husband and that you are here to help but not to salve her self-righteous attitude and listen to her ever-increasing charges against her husband.

"Why are you siding with him? I'm the one that belongs to this church!" She breaks into tears.

Why did that session deteriorate into near hopelessness before it had hardly begun? Although most of what the counselor said was probably true, the session turned sour because the counselor took, what I call, the auto mechanic approach to counseling. When someone leaves a car for repair, the mechanic pulls out the shop manual, puts the car through various diagnostic tests, then repairs the problem according to the manual. Some counselors, I fear, treat people this way. They are interested only in finding out what the problem is and what the book says to do about it. Then they immediately try to fix the problem with little regard to their relationship with the counselee.[44]

The example of counseling that Adams provided in this passage is cruel. Some important elements of counseling are clear (e.g., unchecked anger, unforgiven sin, etc.), but other important elements are completely passed over, for example, issues of suffering and struggle in the life of the counselee. Because of these missing elements, the counsel offered is ultimately harsh, even when it addresses some true things. This one-sided approach to counseling that only addresses sins and transgressions of the counselee ultimately fails the law of love and so fails at offering counsel that is truly helpful. Tripp adds to this:

We can focus on the problems and miss the person in the middle of it. Biblical personal ministry certainly includes problem solving, but it must be person-focused. God's work of change certainly involves changes in situation and relationship, but it has radical personal transformation as its goal. When we have a problem focus as we listen to people, we will be like someone at the shooting gallery at the county fair. We will be hunting for problems like they are plastic ducks floating by, and when we hear them, our goal will be to shoot them down. We will listen for a problem word (adultery, doubt, fear, lust, stealing, greed, envy, conflict) and then fire away until we have said everything we know about the Bible's views on the topic. Not only does this do violence to the way God wants his Word to be used, it completely misses the heart struggles of the person with the problem.[45]

Tripp and Mack commend an approach to counseling that deals with problems by engaging the counselee. They recognize that counseling deals with persons experiencing problems and not just with problems alone. They point out that counseling must not only address sin but also engage with suffering persons. They understand that the Bible mandates not only the truthful content of speech but also the loving context of speech (Eph. 4:15). They emphasize dealing with counselees who experience problems rather than with problems articulated by counselees. They also provide some direction on how to do this.

5) Counseling That Sees the Counselor as a Fellow Sinner and Sufferer

Adams's counseling methodology, which focused on authority in counseling, did not address how to engage the counselee as a fellow sinner and sufferer in need of mutual grace. Powlison said, "Adams rarely adopts the stance of fellow sufferer and fellow sinner in need of identical mercy and grace."[46] Counselees can find in Adams a counselor who understands the biblical theme of sin and who knows how to rebuke, confront, exhort, and point the way forward to biblical change. Not so apparent in Adams's style is a counselor who can identify with the sins and struggles of the counselee.[47] Not so apparent is the approach commended by Mack:

> When we become aware of sin in the counselee's life, we must always remember that we are not immune to sin ourselves; we can fall into it just as easily as anyone else. No one has done anything that we could not do, but for the grace of God. If we keep this in mind we will avoid becoming self-righteous or condescending toward those who sin. Instead, we will reach out to them in compassion.[48]

Here, Mack urges humility on the part of the counselor. He reminds that no sin has befallen the counselee except that which is common to counselors (1 Cor. 10:13). He reminds of the prideful spirit of the Pharisee that can fall on the counselor who loses sight of this reality. Tripp expands upon the idea:

> Our service must not have an "I stand above you as one who has arrived" character. It flows out of a humble recognition that we share an identity with those we serve. God has not completed his work in me, either. We are brothers and sisters in the middle of God's lifelong process of change. I am not anyone's guru. Change will not happen simply because someone is exposed to my wisdom and experience. We share identity, we share experience, and we are of the same family.[49]

Tripp and Mack each call counselors to humility in the counseling task, urging against the notion that they are somehow above their counselees. Whereas Mack points out the negative reality of not identifying with the counselee, Tripp points out the positive benefits of doing so. In fact Tripp argues that this kind of humble-identifying approach is essential to the counseling task for at least three reasons.

First, it appreciates that counselors are being changed through the process of sanctification just as much as are counselees. Second, this approach protects against an enmeshment on the part of the counselee in which they begin to see the counselor as their source of help instead of God in Christ. Humbly identifying with their sin and suffering will demonstrate that counselors are "works in progress" just as the counselees are.[50] Third, identifying with sin and struggle helps the counselor be an example in the life of the counselee. As long as counselees place counselors on pedestals, they will be wary of believing that they can do what counselors do. When, however, they see that counselors are sinners and strugglers in need of the same grace, counselees can have hope in the power of God to work in their lives as well.[51]

Apart from the practical benefits that Tripp mentions, such an approach to counseling methodology also has the benefit of being biblical. Paul says, "Brothers, if anyone is caught in any transgression, you who are spiritual should restore him in a spirit of gentleness. Keep watch on yourself, lest you too be tempted" (Gal. 6:1). Such a passage underlines the common sinfulness and tendency toward temptation that unites all people, regardless of whether they occupy the role of counselor or counselee in personal ministry.

6) Counseling That Addresses Suffering before Sin

The work done by the second generation of biblical counselors in understanding and identifying with the situation of the counselee has led to a very practical methodological strategy of personal ministry to those who are hurting and struggling. The strategy is to identify and engage the sufferings of counselees before engaging their sin. Mack says:

> Consider again the case of Clara. She quickly concluded that her counselor was not sympathetic with her. All she sensed from him was con-

demnation. He needed to listen to her complaints and concerns before he tried to understand how she felt. Before responding, he could have asked himself, "What would it be like for me to come home to a wife who was wasting all of our money on alcohol? What would it be like to have a wife calling me names, scratching me, and throwing things at me? What would it be like to have a wife who didn't care about what I thought or what I said? What would it be like for me to come home and find my wife in my bed with another man? How would I feel? What emotions would I be experiencing?" This is where the counseling must start. And although the sin problems must be addressed and solved, in most cases, effective counseling cannot occur until the counselor has shown the counselee the compassion of Christ by identifying with his or her struggles.[52]

Writing in this same vein, Tripp discusses the idea of "entry gates."[53] Entry gates are the doors to a deeper level of ministry, and they consist of the counselee's current struggles. In the midst of this discussion, Tripp poses the counseling problem of a woman who awakens in the night to find her husband gone. He has taken most of their possessions and cleared out the bank account. Tripp considers what the greatest struggle is for such a woman and concludes that it is fear:

> Fear is the most significant heart issue at this moment. It is where the war is taking place and where your ministry begins. This woman would not be helped by a recap of all the Bible has to say about marriage and divorce. If that's all you offer, you will likely lose future opportunity to help her. . . . Helping her face her fears gives you a wonderful opportunity to show love and build a ministry relationship. When we speak to people's real struggles, they respond, *this* person has heard me. This person understands me. I want more of this kind of help. This is the power of a loving relationship.[54]

Tripp's point here is that counselors will not be effective ministers of the Word until they engage their counselees in their struggles before engaging their sin. It is this approach that will gain respect and trust, will prove love, and will earn the opportunity of a further hearing.

Conclusion

In sum, the second generation of biblical counselors urges those who practice personal ministry to avoid the error of Job's counselors, who had a monolithic view of Job as a sinner. They ministered to Job in a static and ultimately unhelpful way. Their counsel failed because they did not identify with Job as a sufferer or seek to minister to him accordingly.

The counseling methodology of Adams provided necessary correction to the counseling models that were dominant at the time. As true as that is, Adams's model needed to be advanced and developed to include a more biblical understanding of the counseling relationship. This advancement has occurred in the work of biblical counselors over the last twenty years.

Such development has been critical. Early in this chapter Adams was quoted as saying:

> Methodology and practice plainly reveal what is truly central to a theory. . . . What is considered truly operative (regardless of rhetoric or theoretical trappings) will find its way into the basic everyday methodology of a practitioner. . . . What one does for his client in counseling or therapy most pointedly shows what he believes the client's real problem to be. Methodology then is where it's at.[55]

Adams's statement is true. There is also something relevant to learn from it concerning Adams's own counseling. Adams's lack of development in understanding the situation of the counselee (how he *did* counseling) had implications in Adams's treatment of counselees. Adams's counseling methodology was in need of development because Adams's understanding of counseling concepts was in need of development. Counseling concepts always affect counseling methodology, and the biblical counseling movement can be thankful for Adams's work in the creation of counseling concepts and methodology as they seek to advance them to be more biblical.

4

Advances in How Biblical Counselors Talk about Counseling

The discipline of apologetics is a varied but indispensable field. It has mainly to do with making an argument for one's own position and defending it against attack from the positions of others. Apologetics is necessary in philosophy and Christian theology, and, as shall be seen, in counseling. The biblical counseling movement does not exist in a vacuum but instead in the context of numerous other models for understanding people and helping to solve their problems. It is just as necessary for biblical counselors to articulate and defend their model in a marketplace of other counseling options as it is for Christians generally to defend their faith in a religiously syncretistic society. David Powlison says:

> A model gives a standpoint from which to interact with others. We make the case for what we believe is true and good. We subject competing models to systematic questioning. We defend our own model against critics. We develop our model under the stimulus of criticisms by others. We seek to win others.[1]

Powlison is talking about the nature and necessity of apologetics in the biblical counseling movement. He is discussing how biblical counselors talk *about* biblical counseling and how they talk *to* other models. But there has been a problem. The biblical counseling movement has been a relatively insular movement. Biblical counselors have articulated a model, to be sure. They have also engaged in substantial critiques of competing models.[2] The problem is that, for the most part, as biblical counselors have engaged in this work of articulation, defense, and critique they have been largely speaking to themselves in their books, journals, and conferences. In what follows, it will be important to observe the biblical counseling movement's effort at apologetic engagement and to see how that engagement has developed from the work of Jay Adams to the present day.

Eight Apologetic Moments

It is possible to discuss eight apologetic moments in the life of the biblical counseling movement. This work will consider only those published efforts in which biblical counselors have sought to defend their model and critique other models by engaging those with whom they disagree.[3] In order to examine those times when biblical counselors have interacted beyond the borders of their movement, we need to look at times when such interaction has been recorded. Has a biblical counselor at Master's Seminary had a conversation with a psychologist at UCLA? I hope so, but I don't know about it. I only know about what has been recorded and published, so that is what will be discussed here. As has been the case with every area examined, this apologetic work began with Adams's efforts but has developed beyond his initial work. As this development is examined, the great need for more work in the area of apologetic engagement will become clear.

Beginning the Apologetic Task

Adams began the *Christian Counselor's Manual* saying:

> If . . . I should at places seem brash or appear to take too much for granted it is probably because I have tried to use bold strokes and vivid colors. After all, I am writing this book for my friends; for those who so enthusiastically responded to my previous efforts. I am not trying to sell anyone here; this is an instruction manual intended principally for those who have already bought the product and wish to make the most effective use of it. The apologetic and polemic notes, therefore, largely will be absent.[4]

Those words were penned specifically to introduce Adams's work on methodology, but there is something about them that rings true for Adams's entire ministry. Adams was mainly concerned to talk to those with whom he agreed. He was trying to build a model and pass it to those who would use it in local churches. He was not, primarily, trying to defend that model. Powlison observed this point when he said, "Another noteworthy feature [of the counseling model founded by Adams] is that little direct confrontation occurred between Adams and those theoreticians and institutions he opposed."[5]

This reality does not mean that Adams never engaged those outside his own movement.[6] Indeed he did. In fact, the first five moments of apologetic engagement examined here involve Adams. We will turn to those now.

1) *The airport meeting.* The movement's first recorded effort to talk to others happened between a small group of integrationists and Adams.[7] The meeting took place at the International Airport Motel in Philadelphia on March 20–21, 1969.[8] The National Liberty Foundation had given Adams funds toward the completion of *Competent to Counsel* and was interested in sponsoring a meeting with others for the purpose of evaluating Adams's work. Bruce Narramore from the Narramore Christian Foundation and Donald Tweedie from Fuller Theological Seminary's Graduate School of Psychology were among those present to review Adams's work.[9] The participants had been issued copies of the rough draft and presented their reactions to the book at the gathering. Though the participants at the meeting commended Adams for his attempt to construct an orthodox model of counseling growing out of Scripture, the response to his work was generally negative. Powlison records:

> They charged him with diverse and serious failings. His version of presuppositional biblical counseling tended to be "biblicistic," and failed various particular tests of both Scripture and science. His model was superficial and simplistic in addressing the complexities of both the human psyche and the counseling task. They thought Adams guilty of at least an incipient legalism-moralism [that] compromised the graciousness of God's acceptance of people. He neglected motivational issues in the interests of stressing behavioral change. His ideal counselor projected an aggressive, impatient, and business-like stance towards counselees, rather than communicating a caring patient presence. His discussion failed to comprehend other theoretical positions, and so misrepresented those he attacked. He failed to recognize the extent of Mowrer's heritage implicit in nouthetic counseling. His arguments were framed too polemically, and he had oversold the success of nouthetic counseling making unsubstantiated claims.[10]

In spite of such withering criticism, the meeting encouraged Adams, because his central thesis that the Bible was sufficient for counseling had not been shaken. The first effort at engagement by a biblical counselor resulted in a generally critical view of the movement from outsiders but served to hearten Adams nonetheless.

2) *The Krisheim symposium.* Almost exactly ten years after the airport meeting, Adams met again with leaders in the integration movement.[11] John Bettler, Adams's close friend and co-laborer at CCEF, arranged the meeting. Bettler was concerned that in the intervening decade a failure of the two groups to engage with one another was resulting in a failure of the groups to understand one another. Bettler was also concerned that apart from engaging other views, the nouthetic movement would be marginalized and have no platform from which to engage the broader evangelical and academic community. Bettler hoped that the March 1979 meeting, at which participants were to debate "What Is Biblical Counseling?," would be an attempt at bridge building.

Adams and Henry Brandt represented biblical counseling at the symposium. Bruce Narramore, John Carter, Gary Collins, and Larry Crabb—all significant leaders in their movement—represented the integration position. Debate at the conference quickly coalesced around three issues. The first issue concerned the nature of sin, the second concerned the authority of Scripture and its relationship to secular psychology, and the third regarded the nature of the counseling relationship. The participants managed to reach broad agreement on the first issue and were divided about the other two.

What is important to understand here, however, is not the details of the debate but the result of the Krisheim symposium.[12] The result of the Krisheim symposium was not the hoped-for bridge building but rather more sustained division. The integrationists were deeply put off by Adams's vociferous tone during the debate. Carter, Narramore, and Crabb each expressed their total unwillingness to speak to Adams again because of his "irascible and sectarian" tone. [13]

Adams, for his part, was also disgusted by the event and had no desire to speak again to the integrationists. Powlison captures the division when he writes:

Bettler had come with high hopes. But his hope for a nouthetic counseling come into its intellectual maturity, engaging the wider evangelical counseling world, a party in significant dialogue, able to be both sharpened and to sharpen others, was dashed. Adams was a proclaimer of truth who endured but did not enjoy forums such as Krisheim. He was one to convert others, not one to converse with them. He was not one to listen quietly to those he suspected of using Bible words to pull secular wool over the eyes of the church. The Krisheim conference confirmed in Adams's mind that the evangelical psychologists promoted serious conceptual, methodological, and institutional errors dressed up in Bible words. He had come to Krisheim at Bettler's urging, having previously stated that he was not interested in dialogue with "the self-styled 'professionals.'" . . . [After Krisheim], he would never again dialogue with them.[14]

The Krisheim symposium had a devastating effect on the efforts of leaders both in and out of the biblical counseling movement to talk to one another. An interpersonal rift divided the leaders of the biblical counseling movement from the integrationists. Even with the extreme difficulty flowing from Krisheim, Adams would still have one more opportunity to address integrationists directly.

3) *The Congress on Christian Counseling.* In November of 1988, Gary Collins arranged a gathering of thousands of integrationists in Atlanta, Georgia. This gathering presented Adams with a plaque for his "pioneering" work in Christian counseling. In accepting the plaque, Adams gave remarks that he made clear were to provide an explanation as well as offering an invitation:

First, the explanation. Contrary to what you may think, I have not spent the last fifteen to twenty years trying to refute (or even irritate) so called Christian professionals (psychiatrists, psychologists, sociologists) like yourselves. Had I intended to do so, I assure you I would have done a better job of it! No, I have not had you in mind. My efforts solely have been to help pastors who, according to 2 Timothy 3:17, are God's professionals. That's why the approaches and arguments in my writings are not tailored to you. Rather I designed them to expose to pastors the futility and dangers of attempting to integrate pagan thought and biblical truth. Moreover, while these negative measures are necessary to alert and inform pastors, my work is fundamentally positive.[15]

Adams thus made it clear that his effort was not fundamentally an apologetic one at all. He was not trying to reach out to those with whom he disagreed. His goal, as we noted earlier, was to develop a model that could be given to the pastors of local churches. He further indicated here that he was not trying to tear down the integration movement but was attempting to build the biblical counseling movement. He would go on to state that, when he offered criticism, he was critiquing ideas and not persons.[16] Adams continued:

So much for the explanation; now, the invitation. With all that is within me I urge you to give up the fruitless task to which I alluded: the attempt to integrate pagan thought and biblical truth. In his latest book Gary Collins admits, "It's too early to answer decisively if psychology and Christianity can be integrated." Too early? Think of the millions of hours, the more than one generation of lives, already spent on this hopeless task! Why are there no results? I'll tell you why: because it just can't be done.

Remember God's words: "My thoughts are not your thoughts, neither are your ways my ways" (Isaiah 55:8). What does God tell us to do to resolve this radical antithesis? Integrate? No! In that passage He commands us to forsake our thoughts and our ways and turn to His Word, which He promises will not return void.

Counseling has to do with changing people. But, you see, that's God's business. There are only two ways to change people: God's way and all others.

You simply can't build a Christian counseling system on a pagan base; nor can you incorporate pagan teachings and methods into Christian counseling. Pagan thoughts and ways are at odds with God's. God proposes to produce fruit (love, joy, peace, self-control, etc.) by means of His Spirit through His Word. Then others come along and claim they can produce love, joy, and peace apart from the Spirit and the Word. The two proposals and the methods that go with them are essentially competitive. That's why they can't be integrated. If the Old Testament teaches anything, it's this: God doesn't bless His competition. That's why integration won't work.

I invite you to abandon this useless endeavor. Instead, come join the growing number of those who are discovering that the way to construct a truly Christian counseling system is to begin with the biblical blueprints, use biblical brick and mortar, and find Christian workmen to construct it from the ground up. Steer clear of the "me too" approaches of those Christians who emulate the world. Rather get out in front of the pack, showing the world what God by biblical counseling can do![17]

In the same address Adams, ironically, managed to say it was not his business to do apologetics, while engaging a body of adversaries in language that was overly aggressive. Adams's language at the congress would serve only to exacerbate his reputation for being contentious with Christians outside of the biblical counseling movement. It would be twelve years before any more engagement would take place between biblical counseling and integrationists. Adams, however, would never interact with them again. Such bombast characterized Adams's engagement with Christian psychological professionals. Adams's efforts at apologetic engagement, however, were not limited to integrationists alone. Adams made a few efforts at engaging the secular world as well.

4) *The Christian approach to schizophrenia.* In 1976 Adams was asked to contribute to a book entitled *The Construction of Madness: Emerging Conceptions and Interventions into the Psychotic Process.* Edited by Peter Magaro, the book included the views of contributors attempting to express various conceptualizations of schizophrenia. That Adams's work was included in a secular book was a strong indication of the massive influence he had exerted on the counseling community. In introducing Adams's chapter Magaro said:

> The positions expressed are not common themes in the current therapeutic discourse, but they stem from a focus of interest which has wielded a powerful influence throughout time—that of morality. . . . Making the spiritual explicit and bringing it into a relationship between treater and treatee is [Adams's] vision of the answer of what is commonly thought of as pathology. . . . [Adams's sincerity of belief] and his efforts to incorporate those beliefs into the usual conception of therapy deserves serious attention.[18]

Adams was asked to explain schizophrenia according to a Christian understanding, which he did in "The Christian Approach to Schizophrenia." In his contribution to this volume Adams demonstrated his usual clarity:

> The truth of the matter seems to be that the word "schizophrenia" has become a non-specific wastebasket term covering a multitude of prob-

lems (and often covering up a vast amount of ignorance) all of which appear to have but one common denominator: the inability of the counselee to function meaningfully in society because of bizarre behavior.[19]

Adams then went on to give the Christian understanding for this bizarre behavior, saying, "As Christians look at it, the [schizophrenic] is a sinner, who, according to the Bible, has been subjected by God to vanity because of his rebellion against his Creator. Sin, the violation of God's law, has both direct and indirect consequences that account for all of the bizarre behavior of schizophrenics."[20] Adams laid out how Christians should deal with schizophrenics:

> The Christian counselor seeks to deal with schizophrenia in the same manner as he would in confronting those who have other problems occasioned by sinful living patterns. In this large measure of responsibility lies hope. What is due [to] sin can be changed; there is no such certainty if, as some think, schizophrenia is largely due to other factors.[21]

Adams clearly stated his usual themes here. Even "extreme" cases like schizophrenia traffic in the same themes of sin and responsibility that were the staples of Adams's biblical model. Adams thus gave a faithful presentation of his counseling model in a secular context but with one major change —the edge was gone. The brisk edginess that characterized his engagement with integrationists was not present. Adams's tone was much more patient and winsome. Adams would repeat this style in his other recorded engagement with secular psychologists.

5) *Address to the University Psychiatric Clinic*. In 1977 Adams was invited to address the faculty and students at the University Psychiatric Clinic in Vienna, Austria. In a sense, Adams's audience could not have been more unfriendly. He was an American conservative Protestant who believed that the secular mental-health field was bankrupt in its ability to give ultimate help to people's problems. His audience was the secular mental-health establishment that he opposed. In this context, Adams's rhetorical strategy to his audience is fascinating. There are at least three things to observe.

First, Adams began by creating a sense of doubt in hearers. Did secular mental-health professionals truly have the resources to help hurting people with their problems? He raised three issues in order to suggest that they possibly did not: the vast number of different and competing personality theories, embarrassing "therapeutic failures," and the need for a standard.[22] Adams spent the most time addressing this last point:

> Asking the question why there has been no consensus, particularly in this field in which people are trying to change the lives of other persons, many of us came to the conclusion that it was because there has been no standard by which this was attempted. You may say that society is the standard, or you may say pragmatically that what works is the standard, or that the counselee is the standard; but when you finally boil it all down and strip off the external, what you have left is this: the individual psychotherapist determines the standard. The problem of subjectivity is enormous. Something from outside of the counselor and counselee is needed; something far more solidly grounded than any limited and biased individual is required. Otherwise, the kind of splits and divisions that occurred at the very beginning right here with Freud are inevitable. . . . Why do we need a standard, a yardstick, a rule? Because we are dealing with the problem of changing human lives. What man has the right or the ability to say to another, "I know how you shall live"? What man will take it upon himself to say, "This is wrong in your life, this is right in your life, and this is how I want to change you"? Some think they can divorce themselves from the ethical issues. They think that values can be cast aside. But you can't; you continually get involved in the realm of values when you deal with people and their lives.[23]

Second, Adams described to them the elements of his biblical counseling model. He described Jesus Christ as the standard that is absent from other approaches to people helping. Additionally, he presented three key tenets of his model, including the responsibility of counselees, the verbal confrontation necessary to engage them, and the counselors' concern for the counselees' well-being.[24]

A final element to observe about Adams's speech was the careful and patient way he stated his remarks and asked his audience to consider them. Adams said:

> I want to do one thing here tonight. As an advocate (a very strong advocate) of this viewpoint, I have something to give to each one of you, and

I hope you'll take it. I'm here to hand out some candy to each of you. This candy is not soft enough to swallow all at once, nor is it so brittle that you can bite down on it and crack it readily. I hope that it will be like good hard candy that you take into your mouth and that you'll suck on it for a while when you leave.[25]

Adams thus eloquently and graphically asked them to consider his opinion in a prudent and patient manner. Adams concluded his remarks:

That is a glimpse of nouthetic counseling. Doubtless some of you have spit the candy out already. Some of the rest of you are having a little difficulty with it sticking to your teeth. Nevertheless, I hope that you will continue to suck on it because when you deal with that question of the standard, you're dealing with the fundamental issue in counseling. Only their Creator and Savior can resolve problems that have to do with people ultimately.

If you think seriously at all, after you've talked about everything else you will come back again and again to the issue of the standard. I ask you not to close the door on this matter too quickly. Until it is resolved you can do nothing. You are planning to help people; fine. But that means changing them. The question is not only how, but, most basically, into what? The Christian replies, "Into the likeness of Jesus Christ." Is there any other answer?

Thank you so much. You've been a deeply attentive group, and I appreciate it.[26]

Adams's words here and in his contribution to thinking on schizophrenia demonstrate a much milder, more irenic tone than he displayed in his interactions with integrationists. What was the difference? Why the harshness with integrationists and the patience with secularists? The obvious answer is that, as a Reformed evangelical, Adams did not expect unregenerate persons to believe the Bible's teaching on how to counsel in a gospel-centered way. On the other hand, he had very little time for Christians who should know better than to incorporate secular teaching into the church's approach to ministry and so detract from Christ. It is this understanding that accounts for Adams's increased ire toward the Christian psychology professionals.

I arranged these five moments of engagement by Adams thematically. First we considered Adams's apologetic engagement with integrationists and then his engagement with secular thinkers. Looked at chronologically, Adams engaged a small group of integrationists near the founding of his movement in 1969 at the airport meeting. He interacted with secular thinkers toward the end of the 1970s. In 1979, he once again attempted dialogue with integrationists during the fateful meeting at Krisheim. Finally, Adams delivered his firm remarks at the Congress on Christian Counseling in 1988.

Developing the Apologetic Task

Now it is important to turn to the second generation of the biblical counseling movement and see how they have tried to engage other approaches to counseling. In his "Crucial Issues" article, Powlison urged biblical counselors to broaden the horizons of those to whom they spoke. He said, "Biblical counseling must cultivate other audiences. We need to do so for our own edification as a truly biblical movement. We need to do so in order to edify others with what God has given us."[27]

The more recent leadership in the biblical counseling movement has tried to follow this advice. Just as five published efforts at engagement with those outside the movement by Adams were isolated, it is possible to note three efforts by the second generation of biblical counselors.

6) *Address at Hahnemann University.* In 1995 the *Journal of Biblical Counseling* published the address of Edward Welch to doctoral students in clinical psychology at Hahnemann University. This opportunity, like Adams's address in Vienna, was an occasion to speak directly to those in the secular mental-health community. Also, like Adams's engagement with secular psychologists, Welch's words in this address were a demonstration of gracious candor. There was no bombast in Welch's statement, but there was a demonstration of frankness.

Welch asked his hearers to consider four propositions regarding their discipline. First, Welch argued that psychologists are essentially clergy doing pastoral work from a secular worldview. Second, Welch said that psychological professionals do their work based on a worldview that is theoretical and, therefore, not verifiable. Their discipline is more one of faith, he argued, than purely scientific. Third, Welch stated that secular mental-health positions most typically adopt their worldview (or faith) commitments in an uncritical way. Finally, Welch urged, psychotherapists are looking to win converts as they engage in the work of helping people with their problems. Welch ended his address by stating that though the Christian worldview begins with and takes God into consideration, it still speaks with profundity to issues of concern to modern psychology. Indeed, he argued that Christianity makes better sense of the psychological than secularist material does and that psychological realities ultimately are nonsensical apart from Christian thought.[28]

As has been observed, Welch spoke respectfully to his audience at Hahnemann. And yet, as true as that is, Welch's remarks in many ways were more stringent and confrontational than Adams's remarks in a similar context. The clearest example of this is that where Adams asked his audience to mull and consider his claims—as with a piece of hard candy, Welch ended his address by calling his audience to repentance:

> This seems like a strange way to end a somewhat academic discussion. What began as some simple propositions led to something interpersonal. Abstract questions about knowledge have led to the very concrete. Essentially, the question throughout has been, "In whom will you trust?" It is inescapable. Our knowledge is ultimately a very personal knowledge. Will you trust in the God who has spoken, or will you trust in yourself and some of the cultural icons that provide little scraps of meaning?[29]

Welch and Adams then share a lot in common regarding their styles of engagement with secular psychologists. They are each kind, winsome, and respectful. Both are also firm believers in the truthfulness of the biblical counseling movement and in the futility of secular approaches. Advancement does still take place from Adams to Welch, but the advance is chiefly historical. By the time Welch's address was published, it had been eighteen years since biblical counselors went on record engaging in face-to-face discussions with secular thinkers. Welch's address demonstrates that the biblical counseling movement was, once again, willing to take up the challenge of talking with and to those with whom they disagreed.

7) *The four views book.* In 2000 Eric Johnson and Stanton Jones edited *Psychology and Christianity*, which examined four Christian approaches to psychology.[30] David G. Myers represented the levels-of-explanation approach, Gary Collins represented integration, Robert Roberts repre-

sented Christian psychology, and David Powlison represented the biblical counseling movement. There had been no record of such an interaction since the Krisheim symposium ended in a bitter stalemate in 1979. Each representative contributed a chapter outlining his own view and then issued responses to the chapters of the other authors.

Powlison's presentation of the biblical counseling movement articulated the kind of frankness that Adams and Welch had previously demonstrated. Powlison candidly stated:

> We Christians have a distinctive and comprehensive point of view about our souls and the cure for what ails us. God's view of our psychology and his call to psychotherapeutic intervention differ essentially and pervasively from both the theories and therapies that have dominated psychological discourse and practice in the twentieth century.[31]

Powlison's conviction regarding the sufficiency of Scripture and the fallacy of secular models comes out on nearly every page of his essay. There is no effort on Powlison's part to equivocate on his convictions or hedge on the issues at stake. Powlison even issues a call to repentance, saying, "When the Faith meets the psychologies, we must lead with our own psychology, calling all others to repentance."[32]

In his responses to the other presenters, Powlison offers candid critique. He also, however, is kind and gracious, freely admitting the strengths of other views. Powlison also expresses common cause with the contributors in a number of areas. Finally, he is able frankly to admit weaknesses in his own model.[33] The balanced approach presented by Powlison fiercely contends for the truthfulness and accuracy of his own view without being triumphalistic, divisive, and unkind.

Likewise as the other contributors interact with Powlison's work, they find cause to commend him and—as must happen in multi-views books— to critique him as well.[34] Perhaps the most interesting pair of comments, however, comes from Myers and Collins. In responding to Powlison, Myers scolds:

> Whatever Powlison takes "secular psychology" to be, this much is clear: it is bad. He represents, I infer, what Gary Collins describes as the Jay Adams tradition of "vehement attacks on psychology." Psychology, we

are told, drains away the "lifeblood of humanness . . . leaving a figment, a beast, an automaton, a humanoid, a counterfeit, a corpse." For those of us who have not previously encountered the Jay Adams tradition, these "psychophobic" words (Collins's phrase) will be puzzling.[35]

A few pages later, however, Collins comments on Powlison:

> Not long ago I found myself seated next to David Powlison at a luncheon for Christian counselors. I was reminded again what a pleasant person he is—gracious and friendly. He and his associates represent a new generation that has come out of the nouthetic-counseling tradition. These are people who retain their strong and admirable commitment to the authority and inerrancy of Scripture but who are more gentle and less abrasive than some of their predecessors.[36]

For Myers, who had no exposure to Adams, Powlison's argument sounded ignorant, vehement, and psychophobic. For people with a basis for judgment, however, such as Collins (who had been present at Krisheim and the College of Christian Counselors), there had been a clear shift in the tone of biblical counselors toward outsiders. Indeed, a new day had dawned. There had been significant development concerning apologetic engagement of the biblical counseling movement. Disagreements aside, for the first time in nearly a quarter of a century, biblical counselors were talking to those in the larger Christian counseling world.

8) *McMinn and Phillips, Care for the Soul.* After a twenty-one-year gap in the counseling conversation between integrationists and biblical counselors, one year seemed a brief turnaround for another collaboration. That is how long it took, though, for Powlison to contribute to another counseling volume. In 2001 Mark R. McMinn and Timothy R. Phillips edited *Care for the Soul*, which was an attempt to explore the intersection of psychology and theology. In demonstrating the accomplishment of having a biblical counselor included in the book, the editors devoted the most space in the introduction to the rift between the movement they represent and biblical counseling. They write:

> As uncommon as it is to bring psychologists and theologians together for a book such as this, it is even less common to bring together biblical counselors and Christian psychologists. Since the publication of the seminal

works of Jay Adams on the one hand, and Gary Collins, John Carter and Bruce Narramore on the other, biblical counseling has stood apart from Christian psychology. Each approach has its own training institutions and regimens, leaders in the two fields have often been critical of one another (fairly and unfairly), and each group has sometimes resorted to hyperbole when describing the other. Some biblical counselors have misrepresented Christian psychologists by asserting that they uncritically accept the worldview assumptions implicit in contemporary psychological theories. Some Christian psychologists have misrepresented biblical counselors by accusing them of holding a simplistic view of sin. . . . Given this heritage of disagreement and conflict, it is a monumental step forward to have both groups represented among the contributors of this volume.[37]

In his chapter Powlison defends the biblical counseling movement and critiques those outside of it. In this sense he does—in a new and freshly relevant way—what his predecessors had done. Powlison, however, accomplishes more than mere engagement in his chapter. He also does something that had never been done before by those in the counseling movement—he provides priorities for engagement. It had been common for biblical counselors, while expressing the sufficiency of Scripture, to state that psychology still maintains *some* value.[38] Powlison was the first biblical counselor, however, to give definition to what this value might be. Powlison outlines three epistemological priorities—three guidelines for an understanding of the usefulness of secular psychology. The first priority Powlison describes as "articulating biblical truth and developing our systematic theology of care for the soul." The second priority is to engage in "exposing, debunking, and reinterpreting alternative models." Finally, Powlison says the third priority should be "learning what we can from other models."[39]

These priorities can be alliterated as construct, confront, and consider. According to Powlison, biblical counselors must be concerned in a primary way to *construct* a biblical model of helping people with their problems. This means that there is no principal necessity on the part of Christians to learn from or borrow from other, conflicting models of counseling theory. In a secondary way, biblical counselors should *confront* secular models of counseling. Because secular models ultimately fail to understand people, and they offer help that is devoid of Christ and his Word, they are fundamentally wrong. This means Christians have a responsibility to point out those areas where they are wrong and show a better way. In a tertiary way, biblical counselors should *consider* what there is to learn from alternative models. Because of the doctrine of common grace, unbelievers can comprehend true information, ask significant questions, and critique (explicitly or implicitly) the church's failure.[40] Also, even the most incorrect secular theories understand some things correctly, giving them a ring of truth. Because of this reality, biblical counselors can listen to secularists and be provoked in their efforts to strengthen a biblical understanding of people.

Powlison's contribution is an important one because, as he is engaging in apologetics, he provides an apologetic approach;[41] that is, for the first time biblical counselors had been given a method with which to process and engage alternative models.

The Way Forward on Apologetic Engagement

Though there has been apologetic development, there is still room for more.[42] The biblical counseling movement continues to spend a great deal of time talking to itself. There may be legitimate reasons for this, but biblical counselors must be ever vigilant to develop ways to engage other counseling positions and, in the process, maintain their own as a viable intellectual movement. As the biblical counseling movement seeks to expand its frontiers, reach a lost world, and engage with other Christians who hold opposing counseling positions, there are two specific areas that must be considered: the professorate and the pastorate.

The Professorate

Powlison suggests that the biblical counseling movement address the academy:

> I would like to propose one particular audience into which biblical counseling must be contextualized. We need to speak with Christian academics. We have barely begun to generate meaningful dialogue with faculty and students in Christian colleges and seminaries.[43]

Powlison is correct, and his call has been heeded to a certain extent. During the first twenty years of the biblical counseling movement, the only institution that had an explicit commitment to biblical counseling was Westminster Theological Seminary. During these last twenty years ground has been taken. A number of institutions, including The Master's Seminary, Southeastern Baptist Theological Seminary, Southwestern Baptist Theological Seminary, and The Southern Baptist Theological Seminary, now have full-time faculty teaching biblical counseling courses. Such advances are important, since professors at those (and other) institutions provide an intellectual foundation for biblical counseling and, perhaps most importantly, train the pastors that go out to the churches.

If the biblical counseling movement is to expand, it will be necessary for those in the movement called to the academy to make—as part of their calling—the effort to engage with those who hold different views on counseling. This can be done through scholarship, as counseling professors contribute to journals and conferences and write books that show the intellectual foundation of a movement committed to the sufficiency of Scripture. This engagement can also happen through relationship as biblical counselors build friendships with those who hold other counseling positions.

I have had conversations with biblical counselors who agree with Adams and say that such apologetic interaction is not useful. They say it is a waste of time because engaging those with whom we disagree won't change anybody. To such an argument, I respond that engagement is important for at least four reasons.

First, biblical counselors need to engage other counseling positions so that they will have a voice with persons who are yet undecided and trying to determine the counseling approach they will adopt. I teach counseling to graduate students, undergraduate students, pastors, and laypeople, and I can personally testify to the importance of students' seeing biblical counselors engage other counseling approaches. How do biblical counselors respond to the criticisms of other models? How do biblical counselors articulate the weaknesses of other models? If those trying to evaluate different positions can't see biblical counselors engaging these issues, it will make it more difficult to embrace biblical counseling as credible.

Second, biblical counselors should not assume that people who are committed to opposing counseling models cannot change. The facts tell a different story. I know many people who have turned from other positions to embrace biblical counseling. Additionally, there is a trend in integration counseling literature of moving in a more biblical direction. I don't want to be triumphalistic about this. There is much work to do. I do believe, however, that it is possible to demonstrate that as integrationists, for example, have interacted with biblical counselors they have moved in a more biblical direction. The reality is that as long as any Christian is committed to the authority of the Scriptures above his own model, there is hope for change.

Third, biblical counselors don't have everything figured out. As biblical counselors engage with other models, we can be provoked to consider areas we have overlooked, things we have paid attention to that need more careful development and articulation, and things we have done that are wrong and unwise. None of these things have to do with moving away from Scripture but are about becoming more biblical as we learn from the insights of others and so become more authentically scriptural in our thinking.

Fourth, there is an important relational element that is impacting engagement. Biblical counselors should love their brothers and sisters in Christ with whom they disagree on counseling matters. Powlison made a striking comment about the division that occurred at Krisheim, when he said, "The intellectual and institutional rift had been ratified interpersonally."[44] Biblical counselors—especially those in the academy—should increasingly seek to practice what they preach regarding their theology of relationships (see chapter 2) by engaging in loving relationships with those to their theological left in counseling.

The Pastorate

Meanwhile, those called to the pastoral ministry must continue to heed the call that they are competent to counsel. They must counsel, and they must lead, train, and exhort their flocks to counsel.[45] Pastoral ministry in the local church is the front line of biblical personal ministry. People who come for biblical counseling ultimately do not care what the arguments for sufficiency are or whether a biblical counselor utilizes proper epistemological categories. People care whether the counselor in the room can help them with their problems. If pastors can attain and impart increased facility in counseling, there will be no more effective means to spread a biblical counseling vision.

One excellent example of this is the biblical counseling ministry of Faith Baptist Church in Lafayette, Indiana.[46] Begun by William Goode and Bob Smith and continuing under the current leadership of Steve Viars, Faith Baptist Church is an example of how effective a biblical counseling ministry can be in reaching a community for Christ. Leaders in the church have counseled thousands in the community during their weekly ministry. They are establishing counseling outreach centers at Purdue University, opening up new ministry centers for use by the community in Lafayette, and building facilities to contain men's, women's, and foster-child counseling ministries. Their program of ministry has been so effective that secular mental health practitioners now regularly refer hurting persons to this Baptist church because they know they will be helped! Such is the power of a biblical counseling ministry that is matched with effective leadership and engagement with the environing culture.

Another option for engagement that should be considered by local churches is the sending of counseling missionaries into secular mental-health facilities. Those called and gifted with sufficient skills in biblical counseling can pursue secular education and credentials under the spiritual direction of pastors in their local church. Involving the leadership of the church is important for at least two reasons. First, it is the responsibility of the church to ordain and call out its ministers. Those interested in counseling (i.e., personal ministry of the Word) must not think that they have a unilateral right to determine their own giftedness and calling. They must understand that when they engage in counseling, they are doing so as an arm of the body of Christ.[47] A second reason church oversight is important is the danger inherent in purely secular education. Ministers in training to be counseling missionaries should not be left to navigate the complexities of secular training (or practice) independently. They must be accountable to spiritual leadership that will be equipped to help them stay oriented to proper biblical principles of engagement. Such a plan, though in need of elaboration, provides another means of engagement for biblical counselors.

Conclusion

The biblical counseling movement has experienced advancement in how we talk to others about counseling. Adams made several attempts at this task before ultimately concluding that it was not to be a part of his ministry. The more recent leadership of the biblical counseling movement has demonstrated a desire to reengage the counseling world with which it differs.

It must be said, however, that this field of engagement is the one where biblical counselors have the farthest to go. Though the biblical counseling movement has demonstrated a desire to engage, there is much work to do to make this desire a full-scale project that actually does what it hopes to do.

It is also worth noting that this effort at engagement may continue to be the hardest area for biblical counselors to develop. There are at least two reasons for this. First, the sharp dividing lines between the movements make conversation difficult. Biblical counseling is distinguished from every other approach to counseling (secular or Christian) by its firm belief that Scripture alone is sufficient to help people with their counseling problems. This one is a nonnegotiable truth for biblical counselors and a nonnegotiable fallacy for everyone else. Such firm divisions make compromise difficult. Second, most biblical counselors simply are not willing to devote their ministries to intellectual defenses of the movement. Biblical counselors are typically those whom God has called into hands-on pastoral ministry, and they desire to help people with their problems as a demonstration of faithfulness to that call. Apparently there is little interest in wading into the theory that supports biblical counseling and defending it to those advancing other models.[48]

As true as this is, the biblical counseling movement has a responsibility to engage an atheistic society and the surrounding counseling culture. Nothing less than the Great Commission (Matt. 28:18–20) summons biblical counselors to faithfulness in engaging lost and hurting people in the personal ministry of the Word. Additionally, the Pauline call to speak the truth in love mandates that biblical counselors talk to those counselors with whom they disagree so that all might be more like Christ (Eph. 4:15). It is both evangelism and discipleship that support the call for biblical counselors to be increasingly diligent in their efforts at apologetic engagement.

5

Advances in How Biblical Counselors Think about the Bible?

This chapter is very different from all the preceding chapters in this book. In earlier chapters we considered where and how biblical counselors have advanced in their understandings from a first generation led by Jay Adams to a second generation characterized by more contemporary leadership. In this chapter we are going to consider one area where no advancement has taken place. This topic is important, because some scholars have stated that there has been change and advancement in the biblical counseling movement in areas where in fact there has been none.

One area where some have argued seeing advancement is in a gospel-centered approach to ministry. Some accuse Adams of being less committed to a gospel-saturated approach than those in the second generation of biblical counseling. I think such claims are not found in the evidence. Adams typically began his books with a chapter about the Holy Spirit and the necessity of his work to apply the truth of the gospel and bring about change in the counselee. Adams was the first biblical counselor ever to state that true and lasting change requires the power of Christ. Adams believed what was fundamentally wrong with every other approach to counseling was that it did not lay hold of core truths about the gospel of Christ to help people change.

Adams was gospel-centered. In fact, if we're going to give credit where it is due, he was the first authentically gospel-centered counselor in over one hundred years. The reason for objections in this regard has to do with many of Adams's practical exhortations that he gave to counselees to help them "put off" sinful behaviors and "put on" righteous ones. When such instructions are viewed in an isolated way, they can sound moralistic. The antidote to this problem is to read Adams in a Pauline way. Paul wrote his epistles beginning with gospel statements about who believers are in Christ and ending with ethical exhortations about how believers are to behave in Christ. Paul never intended for Colossians 3 and 4 to be read without an understanding of Colossians 1 and 2. He didn't start Romans at chapter 12. The same is true with Adams. His strong ethical statements should not be disconnected from his strong statements grounding those ethics in the gospel of Jesus.

This is just one example, however, and as important as it is, that is not what this chapter is about. It is about the extent to which second-generation biblical counselors are believed to be less committed to the sufficiency of Scripture than the first generation was.

Outside of this book, there has been only one other evaluation of how the biblical counseling movement has advanced. In *Foundations for Soul Care: A Christian Psychology Proposal*, Eric Johnson includes an assessment that is both similar to and different from the assessment made here. Johnson is an experienced counselor who has tried to read the biblical counseling movement in a way that is much more careful than others have done. In spite of this, he still finds much in the movement to question. Johnson's criticisms of the biblical counseling movement are substantial, and a careful response by those in the biblical counseling movement is necessary. But the purpose for our consideration is something else. We want to see that Johnson does something that no other has done: he both recognizes and seeks to evaluate the advancement within the movement of biblical counseling. Johnson's view of advancement, however, differs from what we have been considering thus far.

Johnson's View of Advancement

In seeking to understand the biblical counseling movement, Johnson makes a distinction between two schools of thought.[1] Johnson refers to the first school of thought as traditional biblical counseling (TBC). Johnson calls TBC the "dominant model in the movement," the members of which "adhere very closely to the emphases of Jay Adams."[2] Johnson mentions

John Broger, Wayne Mack, John MacArthur, Ed Buckley, and of course, Jay Adams as being leaders in TBC. He also lists organizations such as the National Association of Nouthetic Counselors (NANC), the Biblical Counseling Foundation, The Master's College, and the International Association of Biblical Counselors as being institutions committed to a TBC approach.[3]

According to Johnson, the signature trait of TBC is its commitment to the sufficiency of Scripture. Johnson variously calls TBC's position on sufficiency "absolute sufficiency,"[4] "extreme sufficiency,"[5] "a well-intentioned but unnecessarily restrictive doctrine of sufficiency,"[6] and even "scriptural positivism."[7] Johnson states:

> TBC proponents teach that Christian soul care must be based exclusively on what the Bible teaches and have suggested it is heterodox to make positive reference to contemporary psychological research and theory and argued that it compromises the adequacy of God's revelation in the Bible.[8]

Johnson looks mostly to Mack to support his argument.[9] He quotes Mack: "Because of our finiteness and sinfulness, our understanding of man and his problems can be trusted only when our thoughts and insights reflect the teaching of Holy Scripture. We simply are not able to ascertain truth apart from divine revelation."[10] Later Johnson says:

> Mack . . . has written, "Everything we need to know to live success-fully is found within the pages of God's Word." He . . . believes that "we do not need any extrabiblical resources to understand people and their problems and help them to develop the qualities, attitudes, desires, values, feelings, and behavior that are proper for relating to living before God in a way that pleases and honors Him." . . . He concludes: "Secular psychology has nothing to offer for understanding or provid-ing solutions to the non-physical problems of people. When it comes to counseling people, we have no reason to depend on the insights of finite and fallen men."[11]

Later, Johnson quotes Mack disapprovingly for saying that the Bible contains "a comprehensive system of theoretical commitments, principles, insights, goals, and appropriate methods for understanding and resolving the non-physical problems of people. When it comes to counseling people, we have no reason to depend on the insights of finite and fallen men."[12] Johnson takes strong exception to the sufficiency belief of what he calls TBC. He believes TBCs have overreached and gone beyond Scripture, claiming more than is appropriate.[13] He refers to the position represented by Mack as "an egregious misunderstanding . . . of the form of the Bible."[14] He says that TBCs have "overreached."[15] He likens the error to the one concerning Copernican theory,[16] and he insinuates that the position is arrogant.[17]

Johnson has much kinder words for the second school of thought, which he calls progressive biblical counseling (PBC). According to Johnson, PBCs are known by their "willingness to move beyond Adams's nouthetic model in certain respects."[18] Johnson lists David Powlison, Edward Welch, Michael Emlet, and Paul David Tripp as PBC leaders. He also notes Westminster Theological Seminary and the Christian Counseling and Education Foundation as institutions that embody a progressive approach, as well as the *Journal of Biblical Counseling*.[19]

Johnson mentions four specific areas where PBCs have developed beyond TBCs: (1) a focus on being rather than on doing; (2) a more balanced perspective on sin and suffering; (3) relationships in counseling; and (4) the more irenic nature of PBC discourse.[20] Johnson finds several areas of distinction between PBCs and TBCs, but where he draws a firm line between them is on the issue of the sufficiency of Scripture. Johnson says, "Progressives . . . have recognized the inadequacy of this [extreme sufficiency] position." He quotes Powlison:

> Do secular disciplines have anything to offer to the *methodology* of Biblical counseling? The answer is a flat no. Scripture provides the *system* for Biblical counseling. Other disciplines—history, anthropology, literature, sociology, psychology, biology, business, political science—*may be useful in a variety of secondary ways* to the pastor and the biblical counselor, but *such disciplines can never provide a system* for understanding and counseling people.[21]

Johnson laments Powlison's "strident" tone but generally commends his sentiment. According to Johnson, Powlison is correct here in seeing the limitations of Scripture's resources and the beneficial nature of other resources. Johnson says, "[Powlison] allows for a role for extrabiblical literature, and he recognizes that the Bible cannot be understood as 'an encyclopedia of proof texts containing all facts about people and the diversity of problems in living.'"[22] As he continues his analysis of Powlison's position, Johnson states, "PBC proponents believe that the Bible does not provide an exhaustive discussion of Christian soul care, but it is *comprehensive in scope*."[23]

For Johnson, the difference between PBCs and TBCs lies at the level of Scripture's sufficiency. TBCs have a commitment to the exclusive sufficiency of Scripture in counseling. They are "Bible only." PBCs, to the contrary, have a more nuanced perspective on the issue, allowing other sources of information to contribute to the Bible's teaching. They allow the usage of other sources of information. The question that must be asked and answered, however, is whether Johnson is correct in his analysis.

Advancement Concerning Sufficiency?

In fact, it appears that such a division of the biblical counseling movement into two groups regarding the sufficiency of Scripture is unwarranted. Positions that articulate such a division seem to miss key emphases of the positions of those in the biblical counseling movement. Such an oversight is applicable both for those labeled progressive as well as traditional.

The So-Called Progressives on Sufficiency

According to Johnson, Powlison's view on sufficiency is much more moderate and nuanced than that of those who articulate an "extreme sufficiency" position. Has Johnson correctly understood Powlison? It is necessary to look at statements from Powlison other than just the one that Johnson quotes in order to answer.

In "The Sufficiency of Scripture to Diagnose and Cure Souls," Powlison engages in a substantial defense of Scripture's sufficiency regarding problems in human living.[24] Powlison makes the case that the issues that concern God in the Bible are the same issues that are addressed in any counseling experience. Powlison is careful to make the point that people must read the Bible as those seeking to learn God's language for understanding people and their problems. One must not think that it will be fruitful to look up the term *schizophrenia* (for example) in the concordance of a Bible, however. Powlison's point here—as it is in other places—is that the Bible is about what counseling is about.[25] Even the title of his article, it seems, would be sufficient evidence to prove the point, and yet Powlison makes a number of strong claims concerning Scripture:

> The conviction? Scripture is about understanding and helping people. The scope of Scripture's sufficiency includes those face-to-face relationships that our culture labels "counseling" or "psychotherapy." The content? The problems, needs, and struggles of real people—right down to the details—must be rationally explained by the categories, which the Bible teaches us to understand human life.[26]

In this passage, Powlison argues that a core conviction concerning Scripture is that it is sufficient for counseling. He further argues that counselors must explain the problems, needs, and struggles of people in biblical categories if they are to offer real help.

Those words are strong on their own and yet, Powlison continues:

> What is a genuinely biblical view of the problems of the human soul and the procedures of ministering grace? Such a view must establish a number of things. First, we must ask, does Scripture give us the materials and call to construct something that might fairly be called "systematic biblical counseling"? In fact, we do have the goods for a coherent and comprehensive practical theology of face-to-face ministry. Scripture is dense with explanations, with instructions, with implications. We have much work to do to understand and to articulate the biblical "model." But we don't have to make it up or borrow from models that others have made up as ways to explain people.[27]

Powlison makes the strong claim here that, in Scripture, the Christian community has a coherent and comprehensive guide for systematic biblical counseling so that there is no need to borrow from any other model to understand, explain, and help people. He describes this understanding as a genuinely biblical view of the problems of the human soul.

These are two examples from one article by Powlison,[28] but these statements are representative of what others in the second generation of biblical counselors (or, what Johnson calls PBC) believe. Welch is another example:

> Biblical Counseling is built on a simple, enduring principle: the triune God has spoken to us through the Scripture. Furthermore, through biblical history, doctrine, law codes, poetry, and songs, God has revealed to us everything we *need* to know about Him, about ourselves and about the world around us (2 Pet. 1:3).
>
> This fundamental promise—"God has spoken"—has been the long-standing confession of the church. Every church attendee would agree. Brows might furrow, however, at the phrase "everything we need." We sense that the Bible talks about many important things, but there are complex life situations where we would like more specific direction, extra information, or novel counseling techniques. Yet the reality is that we have access to everything that Jesus had: "Everything that I learned from my father I have made known to you" (John 15:15). God has not held anything back from us. What Jesus knew from His Father, we too can know.
>
> Given the degree to which God has revealed Himself and ourselves, we can assume that the Bible's counsel speaks with great breadth, addressing the gamut of problems in living. It is certainly able to speak to the common problems we all encounter, such as relationship conflicts, financial pressures, our responses to physical health or illness, parenting questions, and loneliness. But it also speaks to distinctly modern problems such as depression, anxiety, mania, schizophrenia and attention deficit disorder, just to name a few.
>
> Of course, the Bible doesn't speak to each of these problems as would an encyclopedia. It doesn't offer techniques for change that look like they came out of a cookbook. But through prayerful meditation on Scripture and a willingness to receive theological guidance from each other, we find that the biblical teaching on creation, the fall, and redemption, provide specific, useful insight into all the issues of life.[29]

Welch's words demonstrate that progressives are just as committed to sufficiency as their forebears. The conviction articulated by Welch has been embraced, debated, and maligned since the founding of the biblical counseling movement. Some people will love it; others will think it is silly. But it is this belief that characterizes all those committed to the biblical counseling movement.

The So-Called Traditionalists on Science

So those in the biblical counseling movement labeled "progressive" have maintained their commitment to the sufficiency of Scripture. This reality raises questions about so-called traditionalists. Has their position on this issue been misunderstood as well? Is it true that TBCs are guilty of holding to a harsh and untenable position of extreme sufficiency and are unwilling to receive helpful information outside of Scripture? Does the evidence that is available to us support such a claim? Indeed, Jay Adams, the founder of the contemporary biblical counseling movement and *the* exemplar of TBC, strongly affirms the scientific value of secular psychology. In the opening pages of his very first book on counseling, Adams had this to say:

> I do not wish to disregard science, but rather I welcome it as a useful adjunct for the purposes of illustrating, filling in generalizations with specifics, and challenging wrong human interpretations of Scripture, thereby forcing the student to restudy the Scriptures. However, in the area of psychiatry, science largely has given way to humanistic philosophy and gross speculation.[30]

Adams made a similar observation several years later:

> Do you think that you can learn something helpful from psychologists? Yes, we can learn a lot; I certainly have. That answer surprised you, didn't it? If it did you have been led to believe, no doubt, that nouthetic counselors are obscurantists who see no good in psychology. . . . I do not object to psychology or psychologists as such. . . . That I deplore psychology's venture into the realms of value, behavior and attitudinal change because it is an intrusion upon the work of the minister, in no way lessens my interest, support, and encouragement of the legitimate work of psychology."[31]

In other words, Adams valued psychological science and affirmed its use. He urged caution, however, when practitioners begin to have worldview commitments that drive them away from that which is specifically scientific and more worldview dependent. These statements from Adams come very early—within the first few years of the founding of the biblical counseling movement. The earliest available evidence therefore shows that Adams, in fact, never held an unnecessarily restrictive view on this issue.

According to Adams's own testimony, he has always found value in psychological science and does not believe this endangers his own strong view of the sufficiency of Scripture. But what about Mack, whose work features prominently in Johnson's book? Johnson uses Mack to argue that TBCs have adopted an approach to the sufficiency of Scripture that is as extreme as it is unbiblical. Johnson quotes from two articles to critique Mack in particular and TBCs in general. Johnson's harshest criticism for Mack, however, comes in his interaction with a quotation from "What Is Biblical Counseling?." Mack's quotation was cited earlier but is repeated here with Johnson's criticism included. Johnson says:

> Mack goes even further: "Because of our finiteness and sinfulness, our understanding of man and his problems can be trusted only when our thoughts and insights reflect the teaching of Holy Scripture. We simply are not able to ascertain truth apart from divine revelation." Unless it is just carelessly worded, this is an example of "scriptural positivism," and it would seem to necessitate the rejection of all information not found in Scripture (for example, information about anorexia nervosa, neurotrans- mitters, and personality traits). Such extreme pessimism about human reason, however, is foreign to the greatest thinkers of the Christian tradition. Calvin, for example, recognized both sin's mental distortions as well as the preserving, blessed effects of God's common grace on non-Christian thought.[32]

Is this criticism correct? Is Mack a "scriptural positivist" who rejects the classic Christian doctrine of God's common grace and the classic Christian practice of ascribing value to extrabiblical information? To answer, it is important to understand Mack's article in the larger context of his life and ministry. Mack has devoted his life to the pastoral task of helping struggling people with their problems and training pastors for that same task. He has produced scores of materials to help people change and grow in Christ and has written dozens of books and articles to explain what biblical counseling is and how to do it.[33] In his writings, Mack never functions as a philosopher explaining theological epistemology but rather as a pastor attempting to explain how to help people according to a biblical counseling framework.

"What Is Biblical Counseling?" is just such an article. In it Mack explains and defends the nature of biblical counseling. The article is not about the nature of knowledge. In fact, the statement quoted by Johnson appears in a very specific context. As the article title indicates, Mack intends to answer a question regarding the nature of biblical counseling. Mack grounds his work in the Chicago Statement on Biblical Inerrancy, and he is clear on multiple occasions in his article that his goal is to help people with their nonmedical problems in living in a counseling context.[34] It would be too much to examine the many examples demonstrating this, but one will suffice. At the end of the article, Mack summarizes his argument this way:

> Because the Bible asserts its own *sufficiency for counseling-related issues, secular psychology has nothing to offer for understanding or providing solutions to the non-physical problems of people.* When it comes to *counseling people*, we have no reason to depend on the insights of finite and fallen men. Rather, we have every reason to place our confidence in the sure, dependable, and entirely trustworthy revelation of God given to us in Holy Scripture because it contains a God-ordained, sufficient, comprehensive system of theoretical commitments, principles, insights, goals, and appropriate methods for understanding and resolving *the non-physical problems of people.* It provides for us a model that needs no supplement. God, the expert on helping people, has given us in Scripture *counseling perspectives and methodology that are wholly adequate for resolving our sin-related problems.*[35]

Mack's work is clearly not in the field of epistemology but has to do with biblical Christian ministry. Furthermore, this passage articulates that, in helping people, he is talking about counseling with regard to nonphysical problems that stem from sin and other interpersonal issues. The charge that Mack is a "scriptural positivist" based on one quotation from this article does not seem to correspond to his larger body of work. It appears, instead, that there is a better way to read Mack. It is essential to understand Mack's context in writing in order to avoid unnecessary critique.

Finally, Mack states that psychology can have a limited usefulness:

> Secular psychology may play an *illustrative* (providing examples and details that, when carefully and radically reinterpreted, illustrate the biblical model) or *provocative* (challenging us to study the Scriptures more thoroughly to develop our model in areas we have not thought about or

have neglected or misconstrued) function, but, because of man's finite-ness and fallenness, the insights, methodologies, and practices of secular psychology are in many instances dangerously unbiblical, dishonoring to God, and harmful to people. Other aspects of secular psychology are at best neutral and therefore unnecessary.[36]

This statement is very carefully worded. Mack is clear that psychology can play a role in helping people with their problems. Psychology can have an illustrative and provocative purpose in the counseling task. Mack is also clear, however, that there is danger in psychology so that its findings must be reinterpreted and that it is *ultimately* unnecessary. Mack may be wrong in his position, as he articulates it in the passage above, but his views on the relationship between Scripture and psychology are no different from the ones advocated by Adams, Powlison, and all those in both first and second generations of the biblical counseling movement.

Do Traditionalists Disagree with Progressives?

Johnson looks at the movement from the outside and sees division con-cerning Scripture. What about those within the movement? Specifically, how does the first generation (Johnson's TBC) understand the position of the second generation (Johnson's PBC)? To understand the answer to this question, it is helpful to see how Mack cites Powlison in "What Is Biblical Counseling?" In fact, Mack quotes Powlison on two occasions. Each of these quotations is critical here. First Mack says:

> When he commented on the role that secular disciplines should play in biblical counseling, David Powlison vividly described the noetic impact of sin on man's thinking processes: "Secular disciplines may serve us well as they describe people . . . but they seriously mislead us when we take them at face value because they are secular. . . . Secular disciplines have made a systematic commitment to being wrong. This is not to deny that secular people are often brilliant observers of other human beings. They are often ingenious critics and theoreticians. But they also distort what they see and mislead by what they teach and do, because from God's point of view the wisdom of the world has fundamental folly written through it."[37]

In this section of his article Mack argues for the depravity of human nature and shows the impact this has on a Christian's ability to trust secular theories of helping people.[38] But Mack (a so-called TBC) agrees with Powlison's assessment about the descriptive and provocative value of secular thought. In another section, "The Need for Caution," Mack says:

> David Powlison has stated well the danger of including extrabiblical ideas in the counsel offered to or by Christians: "Do secular disciplines have anything to offer to the methodology of biblical counseling? The answer is a flat no. Scriptures provide the system for Biblical counseling. Other disciplines—history, anthropology, literature, sociology, psychology, biology, business, political science—may be useful in a variety of secondary ways to the pastor and the biblical counselor, but such disciplines can never provide a system for understanding and counseling people."[39]

Again, Mack's favorable quotation of Powlison shows that as far as he is concerned there is no disagreement. This passage is important for another reason, though. It is interesting here that this passage is the one quoted earlier by Johnson to show that—in his view—Powlison has taken the movement in a more nuanced and careful direction that is more inclusive of science.[40] But Mack himself reads the same words and concludes that he and Powlison have the same view of Scripture's sufficiency and the same nuanced concerns regarding psychology's utility and problems.

In fact, it is not too hard to see why Mack would come to such a conclusion. In the statement referred to here, Powlison articulates the standard sufficiency position that biblical counselors have always embraced. He answers a "flat no" to whether secular disciplines have anything *constitutive* or *fundamental* to offer a biblical approach to counseling. He says no other discipline can ever provide a *system* for understanding and counseling people. These italics are important because they show that Powlison's view sounds no less extreme than any TBC that could be referenced. Of course Powlison understands that other disciplines may be helpful in secondary ways, but his position is no different from the TBC position, as has been shown here.

Johnson seems to be aware of texture in the TBC approach to extrabiblical information on counseling and cites their willingness to use terminology from psychology. In a section entitled "The Actual Sufficiency Beliefs of the TBC," Johnson says:

> [The PBC] position legitimizes the use of valid terminology derived from extrabiblical sources. More surprising is the fact that even many Traditionalists are willing to use terms (with great misgivings) that are not found in the Bible, and many of which are derived from contemporary psychological discourse.[41]

Johnson describes a number of examples where he sees this, including the usage of *anorexia nervosa* by Elyse Fitzpatrick, *child development* and *blended families* by John Street, *dehabituation* and *emotion* by Jay Adams, *depression* by Wayne Mack, and the use of a plethora of psychological terms by the Ashers. Johnson then goes on to say:

> A careful examination of the above articles and books forces one to conclude that even some Traditionalists recognize some value in scientific labels not found in the Bible but developed in the twentieth century by secularists. . . . As a result, TBC itself appears to have benefited, to some extent, from the increased conceptual precision that has resulted from scientific research and theorizing in psychology.[42]

Johnson concedes that TBCs use psychological terms, but this is not new. As has been demonstrated, TBCs have always recognized that there is much to learn from sources outside the Bible and that this recognition and practice does not harm a strong notion of sufficiency. It could be incorrect to press a "Bible-only" position onto TBCs that they do not hold. The use of psychological terminology does not amount to inconsistency or contradiction on the part of "TBCs." Instead it shows that their position on sufficiencies is compatible with embracing information from other sources.

When all the evidence is examined, there is simply no reason to conclude anything other than that biblical counselors share a common view of the sufficiency of Scripture, and this view finds Scripture to be the sufficient source for developing a practical theology of counseling. However, this view of sufficiency also does not mean that biblical counselors exclude other sources of information as being helpful in a secondary or tertiary way. The statements of biblical counselors in their own words indicate this to be the case.

Do Progressives Disagree with Traditionalists?

As we have seen, Mack's use of Powlison's writing indicates he believes they are in agreement. In other words, TBCs think that PBCs agree with them. But what about PBCs? Do they think TBCs agree with them? A passage in one of Powlison's writings sheds light on the answer.

In an article entitled "Does the Shoe Fit?" Powlison engages various critics of the biblical counseling movement and assesses whether their criticism is founded or unfounded. James Beck's criticism of Powlison receives particular attention:

> Many of the old conceptual problems attendant to Adams and his thought remain. Their insistence that only the Bible should be used in our ministrations to the emotionally troubled is as rigid as ever. Their unrelenting dismissal of scientific, clinical, and counseling psychology is astounding. . . . This reductionism, in the name of faithfulness to the biblical record, winds up insulting the richness of scriptural thought and the complexity, which the authors of the Bible ascribed to the human experience.[43]

Beck is actually critiquing Powlison's contribution to *Psychology and Christianity: Four Views*, which was edited by Johnson.[44] According to Beck, Powlison is guilty of the same "extreme sufficiency" views of which Johnson accuses Mack and Adams. The point to notice, however, is that Powlison is incredulous at Beck's criticism. He responds:

> But what about his specific charges against *us*: biblicistic anti-science and a moralizing reductionism of the human condition? . . . Let me attempt a simple answer. I think that God intends Scripture to serve as the orienting and reorienting wellspring of all wisdom ("the Faith's psychology," we might call it). Scripture gives a vista, not a straitjacket. Other systems ("philosophies" in the Colossians 2:8 sense) give distorted lenses and compasses skewed away from North. They don't give us straight facts or a good sense of direction. God intends to teach us how to rightly understand and properly use anything in the whole world (without being misconverted). Everything is fair game: from your own life story to

today's weather; from something a counselee said yesterday to a research study of 829,000 students; *from a guru's comment* (Jay Adams favorably quoted Swami Akhilananda in the *Christian Counselor's Manual*) to war in the Middle East; from a hymn to Zeus (Acts 17:28) to observations of behaviors that never appear in Scripture. . . . All of this is a far cry both from biblicistic anti-science and from syncretistic integrationism. . . . The way James Beck puts it has the ring of his own prejudices. I hope we can replace the caricature with an accurate photograph. *He did not evaluate what was actually written in my articles or what has been written over the past 30 years.* In the *Four Views* book, *I openly criticized biblicism and distanced biblical counseling's epistemology from the notion that the Bible was intended or was to be treated as an exhaustive encyclopedia containing all truth. . . . I might be wrong in my view of the issues in question, and Beck might be right, but he savaged a view that I don't hold (and neither does Jay Adams).*[45]

This passage is fascinating. In responding to Beck's criticism of Powlison in particular, Powlison asks, "But what of his specific charges against *us?*," indicating that Powlison understands his position to be that of every other biblical counselor. Powlison refers to Adams's affirmation of extrabiblical information in *The Christian Counselor's Manual*.[46] He also notes that Beck cited no specific writings from the thirty years of the biblical counseling movement, which indicates that Powlison believes that nobody holds the view Beck creates. Finally Powlison says that Beck criticized a view (biblicistic, nonscientific) that neither he nor Jay Adams holds.

Powlison makes a similar point in another article:

Adams's formal epistemology is a rather typically reformed transformationist position toward the observations and ideas of secular disciplines. He denied their necessity for constructing a systematic pastoral theology, but affirmed their potential usefulness when appropriated through Christian eyes. Epistemologically, Adams is a radical Christianizer of secularity, not a biblicistic xenophobe. He is no triumphalist, believing that Christian faith has already arrived at the sum of all wisdom, but believes that secular disciplines can both challenge and inform us. But Adams was sharply against psychology when it came to dubious theoretical models and when it came to giving state-licensed, secularly-trained mental health professions the reins to the face-to-face care of souls.[47]

Powlison points out here that Adams was suspicious of secular psychology when it infringed on matters that belong uniquely to the Christian faith. Adams had further pointed out, however, that such secular disciplines could challenge and inform Christians even though they were not necessary. This is the exact point Powlison makes in his own work. In fact, Powlison says that Adams's position not only makes Adams a good biblical counselor but also makes him a good practitioner of Reformed epistemology. For Powlison then, Adams's project was not something strange but was identical to his own. All of this is clear evidence that Powlison sees no principled distinction between his view of sufficiency and the view of the so-called traditionalists.

Conclusion

What this all means is that no principal disagreement exists between TBCs and PBCs. Of course, there may be differences of emphasis, tone, and application, but all the people Johnson cites in his book, upon more careful examination, hold the same basic position on Scripture and the relevance of outside information for the counseling task. Every available piece of evidence indicates that all those who call themselves biblical counselors share a robust understanding of the sufficiency of Scripture and use Scripture as eyeglasses to see everything else in the world. The point of this project is not to debate whether the position on sufficiency is correct, although I think that biblical counselors are correct in the matter.[48] The important point here is to correct the misunderstanding that there is some kind of different view of sufficiency among those in the biblical counseling movement.

The development of the biblical counseling movement does not involve disagreements about the sufficiency of Scripture as some argue. More traditional biblical counselors are said to believe in the exclusive sufficiency of Scripture for counseling and are "Bible only." More progressive biblical counselors are said to adopt a nuanced view of sufficiency, recognizing the limitations of Scripture and allowing for other sources. This chapter has shown that distinctions between TBCs and PBCs over scripture do not exist. In fact, "traditionalists" are much more progressive and "progressives" are much more traditional than some believe. None of this is meant to indicate that there has been no advancement in the biblical counseling movement, which is what this book is about. The point is that there is no principal disjunction concerning scripture. Though some believe there has been disagreement among counselors concerning Scripture's sufficiency, in truth this is one of the main areas where there has been no change in the last twenty years. In the actual advancement of the biblical counseling movement, Scripture—far from being a source of division—is actually a source of unity.

6

An Area Still in Need of Advancement

The advancement of the biblical counseling movement regarding the issue of human motivation was analyzed in chapter 2. In this chapter we will consider where more advancement is needed in this regard. Because motivational issues in counseling are so critical, and because they have received so much attention, it is necessary to devote extra care in thinking through these aspects of biblical counseling.

Despite all the benefits of the "idols of the heart" language, there are also certain shortcomings.[1] Rather than undertaking a fundamental change of course, it is necessary to build upon the good work that has already been done by bringing increased theological precision to the language of motivation and idolatry. In the pages that follow, we will examine the biblical context of idolatry, showing how it functions to advance sinful self-interest in people's hearts. Understood in this sense, idolatry is a secondary problem flowing out of the primary problem, which is the sinful, self-exalting heart. It is necessary to make this important distinction at the outset and then to demonstrate why it is important. To do this, we will consider idolatry from both Old and New Testament perspectives and then examine the importance of these findings for understanding the human heart.

Idolatry in the Old Testament

The Israelites were incurably mired in the worship of the false gods of the nations. Israel was delivered out of Egypt by God and had received God's promises, witnessed his mighty acts, received his gracious gifts, and heard his authoritative voice through prophets. The fact that the Israelites repeatedly experienced all of these glorious things from God and then were able immediately to turn and worship a false god is unbelievable (see Exodus 32). The response of the prophets to such actions was shock, as is shown in Isaiah 44:9–20.

In this passage, Isaiah reflects at length on the utter absurdity of idolatry. The argument that Isaiah makes is that idols are "nothing" and "profitable for nothing" (vv. 9–10). In supporting this argument, Isaiah advances two lines of thought. First, Isaiah spends considerable time describing the labor of the human worker both in selecting the raw materials for the idol and in the work necessary to fashion such materials into an object of worship (vv. 12–14). Second, he shows that, after going to such effort to obtain the raw materials, the craftsman uses only part of the material for the idols, while the rest of the material is used for other things such as fuel for heating and cooking (vv. 15–17). Isaiah's clear point is that it makes no sense for a workman to worship an object of his own creation, a portion of which was also used for eating and keeping warm. Isaiah closes by saying: "They know not, nor do they discern, for he has shut their eyes, so that they cannot see, and their hearts, so that they cannot understand. . . . A deluded heart has led him astray, and he cannot deliver himself or say, 'Is there not a lie in my right hand?'" (vv. 18–20).

Such a portrayal of the futility of idolatry merely underlines the almost unbelievable nature of idolatry. How could clear-thinking people trade the glory of the infinite God for a statue that is not God? The importance of this question ought not to be missed. In speaking of idolatry in the Old Testament, counselors typically stop at the mere observation that God's people worshiped false gods. Rarely is there an investigation about the deeper motivations—the heart issues[2]—that would lead God's people to acts of such insanity. The Bible, however, does not leave the issue of the motivation for idolatry unaddressed. In fact, it is stated quite clearly. There are, perhaps, many texts that could be examined, but we will consider just two to demonstrate the issue: Jeremiah 44 and Hosea 2.[3]

In Jeremiah 44, the prophet excoriates the Israelites in Egypt for their worship of idols. Through Jeremiah God reminds the people of all the calamity he has brought to Jerusalem because of their idolatrous practices. God graphically promises to consume them with his wrath because of their idolatry. The response of the people to Jeremiah's message is the opposite of humble contrition. The Bible articulates the response of arrogant defiance from their lips:

As for the word that you have spoken to us in the name of the LORD, we will not listen to you. But we will do everything that we have vowed, make offerings to the queen of heaven and pour out drink offerings to her, as we did, both we and our fathers, our kings and our officials, in the cities of Judah and in the streets of Jerusalem. For then we had plenty of food, and prospered, and saw no disaster. But since we left off making offerings to the queen of heaven and pouring out drink offerings to her, we have lacked everything and have been consumed by the sword and by famine. (Jer. 44:16–18)

After hearing the starkest of warnings from God's anointed prophet, the people respond in abject defiance, saying they would not leave off the worship of their idols. In their rebellious articulation, the people were very clear about why they intended to persist: it was when they were worshiping their idols that they received all the things they wanted. It was after they quit worshiping their idols that bad things started to happen. This account from Jeremiah is very clear about what motivated the people to worship false gods: the idols gave them what they wanted.

Hosea 2 is another passage that gets at this same idea, but in a different way. Adultery is the graphic metaphor that pervades the book of Hosea. In forsaking the true God for idols, the people were committing acts of adultery against their husband, Yahweh. God had been a true and faithful husband to Israel, providing for her all the gifts that she had ever received, and yet Israel had painfully and persistently turned her back on her husband. Why has Israel behaved so shamefully? The prophet explains:

[Israel] has played the whore;
> she who conceived them has acted shamefully.
For she said, "I will go after my lovers,
> who give me my bread and my water,
> my wool and my flax, my oil and my drink." . . .
And she did not know
> that it was I who gave her the grain, the wine, and the oil,
and who lavished on her silver and gold, which they used for Baal.
Therefore I will take back
> my grain in its time,
> and my wine in its season,
and I will take away my wool and my flax,
> which were to cover her nakedness. . . .

And I will lay waste her vines and her fig trees, of which she said,
"These are my wages,
    which my lovers have given me."
I will make them a forest, and the beasts of the field shall devour
    them. (Hos. 2:5, 8–9, 12)

The Israelites turned their back on the true God because they did not see according to reality. The objects mentioned (bread, water, flax, and oil) were not luxuries but were essential for basic sustenance in the land. Without them, the people would die. The people believed that they had received these critical provisions from the hands of their lovers, the false gods. The people worshiped idols, again, because they perceived that the false gods gave them the things they desired.

These two texts conspire to demonstrate a fundamental reality of idolatrous worship: false gods in the ancient world were quite utilitarian. They were worshiped purely and exclusively for the benefits they were believed to convey. This is the point explained by Moshe Halbertal and Avishai Margalit in their book *Idolatry*. Halbertal and Margalit give a great deal of space to the metaphor of adultery, which is frequently applied to idol worship in Scripture. They say:

> The main function of the husband in [the] metaphor is the satisfaction of the wife's material needs. Extending the metaphor, it is God who satisfies Israel's needs. . . . [In spite of this], *Israel prefers other lovers because she thinks they satisfy her needs more successfully. . . .* The sin of idolatry is whoredom. *Israel gives her favors to whoever pays her the highest fee*, but idolatry is worse than ordinary prostitution because in this case the fee is always being paid with the husband's money, as he is the sustainer of the world. The sin of idolatry as whoredom is made even worse by the great gap between the husband's faithfulness and love for his wife, and the wife's faithless behavior. *For the wife sexual relations are based on pay, and she believes that the lover pays more. In theological terms, the Israelites relate to God as to a supplier of material goods, and when he seems to have disappointed them they turn to other gods.*[4]

The point advanced here is critical and has two elements that are necessary to understand. First, idols serve the very pragmatic function of meeting the needs and desires that God's people believe he has left unmet. Second, this reality gets to the deeper heart issues spoken of earlier. The

Israelites had a clear picture of what they needed and wanted. The problem with the Israelites is that they wanted to decide, unilaterally, what they needed and how they would get it. They did not seek to learn from God about their needs and trust him for his provision. Instead, they became gods unto themselves, worshiping themselves.

Idol worship, then, was a secondary problem flowing out of the primary problem of the worship of self. The reason the Israelites could switch back and forth between serving God and serving idols is that each was thought to serve the same function: Yahweh and Baal were both errand boys for Israel. The true Israelite god was the Israelite himself, pursuing his own ends by whatever means worked best. These two elements come together to teach that the problem of the Israelites was not idolatry per se but their effort to decide—unilaterally—what they wanted and how they would go about getting it. The problem for the Israelites was that of every man doing what was right in his own eyes (see Deut. 12:8; Judg. 17:6; 21:5; Prov. 12:15; 16:2; 21:2). Idolatry flowed out of this larger, deeper problem and was simply one way that the Israelites could attempt to manipulate the creation, bringing it into their service.

The Israelite problem was that they failed truly to worship the Lord as God. Instead, they worshiped themselves, focusing on their own desires, both good and sinful, to the exclusion of what seemed good to the Lord to provide. Their affections having been captured, they turned to any possible source to fulfill them. This indulgence in one's own desire rather than in delighting in God and his provision is the root sin of idolatry and, it will be argued, of every other sin.

Idolatry in the New Testament

It is not uncommon for commentators to note the relative absence of the theme of idolatry in the New Testament. When one grasps how idolatry functions in the Old Testament, however, it becomes clear that the fundamental biblical understanding of what is wrong with people has not changed, but only its manifestations. In other words, the New Testament picture of people's deep heart problems is the same as the Old Testament picture. Though outward acts of idolatry are more prevalent in the Old Testament, both Testaments present the same underlying heart problem.

Many texts could be cited to demonstrate this, but the clearest one is, perhaps, Matthew 22:37–40. This passage is Jesus's response to the pharisaic question of which commandment in the law is the greatest:

> You shall love the Lord your God with all your heart and with all your soul and with all your mind. This is the great and first commandment. And a second is like it: You shall love your neighbor as yourself. On these two commandments depend all the Law and the Prophets.

What makes Jesus's response so important is that in two sentences he reduces the entirety of God's perfect law into two axioms. With two brief statements, the Son of God describes the root behind every sin people commit. Every sin in the history of the human race shares in common a failure to love God and a failure to love one's neighbor.

Since Jesus sums up the totality of righteousness in love of God and neighbor and roots all sin in a failure to accomplish these two things, that means the hearts of sinful people are deeply committed to serving another. Who is it that sinful people seek to serve if not God and neighbor? The New Testament repeatedly teaches that the person sinners love above all others is the sinful self:

> But each person is tempted when he is lured and enticed by his own desire. Then desire when it has conceived gives birth to sin, and sin when it is fully grown brings forth death. (James 1:14–15)

James describes the process of temptation in a logical progression from desire to sin, and from sin to death. The Bible is clear elsewhere that the wages of sin is death (Rom. 6:23) but what precedes sin? The answer of James is that every sin happens when "each person . . . is lured and enticed by his own desire." This text is a perfect complement to Matthew 22:37–40. Just as it is true that every sin has its root in a failure to love God and neighbor, so it is true that every sin has its root in a pursuit of one's own desire above all other considerations.

The apostle Paul writes in a similar vein in Philippians 2:4–8:

> Let each of you look not only to his own interests, but also to the interests of others. Have this mind among yourselves, which is yours in Christ Jesus, who, though he was in the form of God, did not count equality with God a thing to be grasped, but emptied himself, by taking the form of a

servant, being born in the likeness of men. And being found in human form, he humbled himself by becoming obedient to the point of death, even death on a cross.

Paul's words could be considered the theme passage of Philippians, and it is relevant to the discussion here. If Matthew 22:37–40 describes the most basic command in God's kingdom, and if James 1:14–15 describes the most basic reality of the existence of sinful mankind, then Philippians 2:4–8 describes the ideal man whose life is completely conformed to God's Great Commandment and has rejected the sinful lifestyle of every other human being. In other words, Jesus Christ is *the* example of one who perfectly fulfilled the law of God and resisted wicked desire.

In the Philippians passage Paul gives the command that each person should look not only to his own interests but also to the interests of others; he then gives the example of Jesus as one who has done this perfectly.[5] Jesus makes himself nothing and serves his Father (first) and mankind (second) by his obedient death on the cross.[6] The most amazing aspect of this obedience is that Jesus "was in the form of God" and yet did not grasp it. Because of this reality, Jesus's selfless service to God and man is the highest and holiest example of self-denial that can be conceived.

Jesus perfectly kept the Great Commandment by doing everything his Father commanded him and by loving his people unto death. Jesus's righteousness is seen in the fact that he denied himself and sought no honor when, in fact, he deserved all honor. Fallen humanity is the opposite of Jesus in that it seeks all honor when, in fact, none is deserved. Instead of loving the Lord with all they have, humans yearn after equality with God, something that is not theirs by right, and seek to bring their neighbors into service to them instead of loving them. The root of every sin is fundamentally an unwarranted desire to exalt oneself above all other considerations (God or people). Mankind's most fundamental problem is the desire to grasp after divine status. All sinful people desire to manipulate others into service instead of seeking selflessly to serve them.

The problem with sinners is that instead of seeking to love God, they seek to put themselves in the place of God. All unrighteousness is grounded in the desire of the sinner to have equal status with God. This concept is, of course, consistent with what caused the human race to get into trouble in the first place. In Genesis 3, when the Serpent wanted Eve to taste the forbidden fruit, he appealed to the very deepest of heart issues, the desire for self-supremacy, when he said, "You will be like God" (v. 5). The temptation worked, as the next verse indicates: "So when the woman saw that the tree was good for food, and that it was a delight to the eyes, and that the tree was to be desired to make one wise, she took of its fruit and ate, and she also gave some to her husband who was with her, and he ate" (v. 6). All of this conspires to show that sinful mankind does not want to love God and neighbor; instead, the biblical description of mankind's most fundamental problem is its desire to be God. Apart from grace, sinners cannot stand to worship the God who alone sits on the throne in heaven. Instead, in a perpetual grasping after god-hood, they seek to become God themselves, reigning from his throne and bringing everything and everyone else into their service. The wickedness of humanity is seen in, more than anything else, its grasp after god-hood.

Self-Supremacy and Idols of the Heart

Whether it is called "pride," "hubris," "self-supremacy," "arrogance," "a desire to be like God," or a hundred other things, the most important consideration in the sinful human heart is oneself. Sinners exalt themselves above the true God, making their own rules and deciding on their own what is good for them. Sinners jockey for position with their neighbors and seek to be served rather than to serve. Our task is now to see how this understanding of the deepest problem in the human heart complements the teachings on the idols of the heart as developed by David Powlison and those following him.

Idols actually come at the end of a process that has its genesis in this evil disposition of the heart. The sinful, self-exalting heart produces lusts or evil desires that the New Testament discusses so frequently and that Powlison addresses in his "Idols of the Heart" article. These desires and lusts grow out of a heart that sees itself as supreme and as the greatest and sole determiner of what is best. The sinful heart lusts because it seeks sinful comfort instead of godly suffering; it seeks control instead of humble trust in the real God; and it seeks to be served instead of selflessly serving others. All the lusts and evil desires that the Bible mentions are a secondary problem that flows out of the primary problem, a heart that sees itself as supreme.

These lusts, however, do not occur in a vacuum but face strong influences. These influences are what the Bible defines as the world, the flesh, and the Devil (see Eph. 2:1–3).[7] These influences work powerfully to shape the lusts of sinful people so that no two people manifest their desire for self-supremacy in exactly the same way. Each sinner has his own peculiar interaction with the world (e.g., upbringing, role models, exposure to different cultures) so that each sinner exalts himself in ways he learns from the world.

But the world is only one influence. As sinners exist in their world, they are constantly rejecting and accepting the lusts that are presented to them. Each sinner has his own set of lusts that are uniquely appealing to his flesh. As Powlison says, the problems of sinful people do not only impinge from the social environment but are also rooted deeply in the human heart.[8]

Working in and through each of these is the dark power of the Devil. The battle for righteousness is a battle not only against the world and against one's own flesh but also against the principalities and powers. Dark and powerful forces exert influence in this sinful and fallen world to lead people away from the worship of the true God and toward the false worship of self.

Each of these influences—the world, the flesh, and the Devil—place objects of desire before the sinful heart to feed its lusts and to stoke its love of self. Such idols can be blocks of stone and wood; they can be sex, relationships, power, and a million other things. Idols are external elements that the world, the flesh, and the Devil use in influencing people to feed the lust of their self-exalting heart. Idols, then, are those outward things that the sinful heart fixates upon to fulfill its desires in its exercise of attempted self-sufficiency (see Figure 6.1).

Figure 6.1: Idolatry and the Self-Exalting Heart

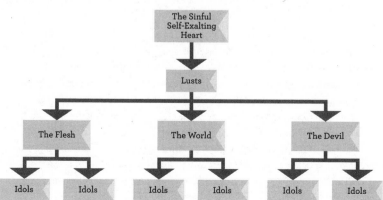

This is how idolatry functioned in the Old Testament. The fundamental problem with the Israelites in the Old Testament was that they reserved for themselves the prerogative to determine what they needed and when they needed it, instead of trusting the Lord. The self-oriented hearts of the Israelites then looked to the world (the neighbors in their midst) and followed their lead in bowing to gods that were not God in order to satisfy the lusts of their self-exalting hearts. When this is comprehended, it portrays a terrible irony of Israelite false worship. When the Israelites followed the lead of their neighbors and bowed before blocks of wood, that act of false worship underlined their desire for autonomy and, in an ironic way, was an exaltation of themselves even more than of the idol. The idol itself was incidental; (in our world today it could be a pornographic picture, a spouse as the particular object of codependency, or an overprotective mother's controlling fear attached specifically to her children) the self-exalting heart was the problem, which remains the same today.

The main problem sinful people have is not idols of the heart per se. The main problem certainly involves idols and is rooted in the heart, but the idols are manifestations of the deeper problem. The heart problem is self-exaltation, and idols are two or three steps removed. A self-exalting heart that grasps after autonomy is the Grand Unifying Theory (GUT) that unites all the idols. Even though idols change from culture to culture and from individual to individual within a culture, the fundamental problem of humanity has not changed since Genesis 3: sinful people want—more than anything in the whole world—to be like God.

A. W. Tozer observed the same thing when he wrote *The Knowledge of Holy*. He said:

> The natural man is a sinner because and only because he challenges God's selfhood in relation to his own. . . . Yet so subtle is self that scarcely anyone is conscious of its presence. Because man is born a rebel, he is unaware that he is one. His constant assertion of self, as far as he thinks of it at all, appears to him a perfectly normal thing. He is willing to share himself, sometimes even to sacrifice himself for a desired end, but never to dethrone himself. No matter how far down the scale of social acceptance he may slide, he is still in his own eyes a king on a throne, and no one, not even God, can take that throne from him. Sin has many manifestations but its essence is one. A moral being, created to worship before the throne of

God, sits on the throne of his own selfhood and from that elevated position declares, "I AM." That is sin in its concentrated essence.[9]

In his "Crucial Issues" article, Powlison makes this statement: "I am not saying that there is a fatal defect within existing biblical counseling. Our problem is a lack of emphasis and articulation."[10] This is precisely the point advanced in this chapter. The issue is not that the biblical counseling movement is fundamentally off the mark in their use of the "idols of the heart" language. In fact, Powlison gets at the idea in his article on heart idolatry, saying, "When a 'hunger drive' propels my life or a segment of my life, I am actually engaging in religious behavior. I—'the flesh'—have become my own god, and food has become the object of my will, desires, and fears."[11]

This corresponds perfectly with the understanding we are developing here. Later Powlison says: "We should not forget that the reductionism the Bible consistently offers is not a typology that distinguishes people from each other but is a summary comment that highlights our commonalities: all have turned aside from God, 'each to his own way,' 'doing what was right in his own eyes.'"[12]

This is another way of arguing for the root problem being sinful self-centeredness. Welch has also touched on this understanding in a few respects:

> The purpose of all idolatry is to manipulate the idol *for our own benefit.* This means that we don't want to be ruled by idols. Instead, we want to *use* them. For example, when Elijah confronted the Baal worshippers on Mount Carmel (1 Kings 18), the prophets of Baal slashed themselves and did everything they could to manipulate Baal to do their will. Idolaters want nothing above themselves, including idols. Their fabricated gods are intended to be mere puppet kings, means to an end.[13]

The point here is not that no one in the counseling movement has mentioned these concepts. The point is that they have not been developed as much as they should. The goal of this discussion is to evaluate what stands in need of further development. Because the issue of motivation has occupied such an important role in biblical counseling discourse and because of its crucial role in the ministry of counseling, these ideas need to be developed with an increased level of care.

Biblical counselors have tended not to develop the complex view of idolatry that has been presented here. Heart idolatry has more typically been discussed as a reality in and of itself rather than as something that points much deeper.[14] It has become slang. Indeed, Powlison makes the same point when he says:

> I would add something else that I think is very important, and often misunderstood by both biblical counselors and our critics. I don't see "idols of the heart" as the master, catch-all category and the key to all counseling. It's only one of many ways of describing "first great commandment defections." . . . I'm not hung up on the word "idols." I think it's overused among biblical counselors and has become a kind of jargon. People are often so captivated by its explanatory power that they go a bit overboard on it.[15]

Indeed this expression, "idols of the heart," is in keeping with Powlison's initial statements on the matter. In "Idols of the Heart and 'Vanity Fair,'" Powlison states, "'Idols of the heart' is only one of many metaphors which move the locus of God's concerns into the human heart, establishing an unbreakable bond between specifics of heart and specifics of behavior: hands, tongue, and all the other members."[16]

So Powlison seems to agree that there needs to be a kind of correction in the development of the movement regarding motivation and idolatry. It is always wise to strive for better, more faithful articulation of one's theological convictions. This is the very endeavor Powlison engaged in with his "Crucial Issues" article, and it should be continued. No movement has "arrived" and therefore should always be mindful of the need to be ever reforming. The understanding articulated here is a biblical elaboration of the problems of the human heart and how idolatry is a manifestation of that problem. The motivational distinction being made here between specific idols and the sinful self-exalting heart is in many ways subtle, but the distinction has great practical relevance for counseling, which is seen in at least seven ways.

1) A Better Understanding of Pride
A fuller articulation of motivation and idolatry honors the New Testament emphasis on pride and self-centeredness. It is true that the New Testa-

ment mentions idolatry a number of times (e.g., 1 Cor. 10:14; Eph. 5:5; Col. 3:5; 1 Thess. 1:9; 1 John 5:21). As has been argued, however, when the Bible refers to the central problem of humanity, it refers to the sinful penchant to honor and love self above other considerations (e.g., Matt. 22:37–40; John 3:30; Rom. 12:3, 16; 1 Cor. 10:33; 2 Cor. 5:15; Phil. 2:1–11; 3 John 9). This big problem is demonstrated in lusts of the flesh (Rom. 1:29ff.; Gal. 5:16ff.; Eph. 4:22; James 1:14–15). In other words, because the human focus on worship of self is wrong, human desires are wrong.

The Old Testament discusses idolatry at length. The New Testament mentions idolatry but goes deeper to the root of idolatry. The apostolic writings help Christians understand idolatry by getting behind it, explaining where it comes from, and showing the problem is worshiping the sinful self instead of the eternal God. The issue here is one of having a more consistent biblical theology. Just as the New Testament brought clarity to the Old Testament's understanding of the Trinity, so Jesus and the apostles elucidate the Hebrew understanding of idolatry.

2) A Better Understanding of People

A fuller articulation of motivation and idolatry goes as deep as the Bible in understanding people. The second generation of biblical counselors has looked at behavior and asked why. They answered that question with a very helpful metaphor of heart idols—humans seek pleasure in things that are not God. As the counseling movement moves into a third generation, it is necessary to look at idols and ask, clearly and with specificity, why. The answer is that humans long for the glory that is due to God. A heart that longs for this glory lusts after idols that provide it.

3) A Better Understanding of Sin

A fuller articulation of motivation and idolatry is more biblical in understanding the problems sinful people have. When sinners think they might not get the glory due to God alone, they fret and plot about how to get it (anxiety); when they are denied that glory they punish themselves by recoiling in despondency (anguish), punish others with wrathful outbursts or slow, plotting revenge (anger); or they slink off to a garden of secret delights where they are in control (avoidance). Fully articulating the motivation/idolatry dynamic shows us that the man who screams at his wife for denying him sex and then spends the evening indulging in pornography does not have two problems, but one. Of course he does need to work on his outbursts against his wife, and he needs to be equipped to deal with his pornography problem. But appreciating the argument here shows how those two very distinct problems all trace back to a man who wants the glory due to God more than he wants to serve his wife. His problem is definitely a worship problem—as all biblical counselors would admit. What needs to be clarified is that his worship problem is not between God and his desire for sex-on-demand. His worship problem is between God and the man *himself*. The idol of sex is present in large measure, but it points to the deeper problem of his sinful, self-exalting heart.

4) A Better Understanding of Repentance

A fuller articulation of motivation and idolatry is more biblical in understanding solutions to the problems, because it leads to repentance at a level of depth. It is one thing to repent of one specific idol of the heart (for example, yelling at one's wife). It is another thing to repent of a heart that desires the glory that is due to God alone and to confess that verbal abuse and a desire to control another person are but indicators that a man desires to determine for himself what he should and should not receive rather than to trust God and serve others. The reality is that, in the Christian life, detailed and specific repentance leads to change that lasts. Bringing about detailed and specific repentance will equip God's people to deal with their sin problems with more lasting change.

5) Compassionate Counseling

A fuller articulation of motivation and idolatry leads to compassion and understanding on the part of the counselor. How can counselors who have never taken drugs, been addicted to pornography, tried to commit suicide, or vomited after every meal identify with and help counselees who struggle with those things? The understanding of motivation and idolatry being developed here shows that there is a common theme running through all wrong behavior. The husband who grouses at his wife every evening before dinner and the teenage girl strung out on crystal meth have one thing in common: they are living for the worship, honor, and glorification of themselves. The angry husband and the teenage addict seek glory for themselves and will reserve for themselves the determination about how that glory will be pursued. The sinful self-exalting heart seeks to get the universe to orbit around itself: all sinners—counselees and counselors alike—have this in common, though they will seek different methods to bring it about.

This means a counselor can never listen to a serial adulterer and respond in shocked disgust and disbelief as though such a sin has nothing to do with the counselor's own life. In fact the monogamous counselor listening to such an account knows exactly what it is to want to exalt himself and to be desperate for things that God hates. The difference: the monogamous counselor uses different means—different idols—to get to the same goal—exaltation of self—than the adulterous counselee. The counselor's idols may be more "socially acceptable" but, insofar as they are sought to honor self above God, they are equally sinister in the sight of God.

6) Protection against "Idol Hunts"

A fuller articulation of motivation and idolatry will guard against a preoccupation with what might be called "idol hunts." An idol hunt is the counselor's search to find *the* idol that is plaguing a counselee at a particular point. There is no evidence that any leader in the biblical counseling movement advocates such a pursuit, but as the teachings of the leaders have been distilled to the lay level—and expanded to other movements—there is some evidence that this is happening. An example of this is the book *Breaking the Idols of Your Heart* by integrationist authors Dan Allender and Tremper Longman III.[17] Allender and Longman never credit Powlison for his work, but they do spend their entire book developing his idea. Allender and Longman propose seven heart idols: power, relationships, work and money, pleasure, wisdom, spirituality, and immorality. In their work they develop each of these and show the danger of trusting in them.

There are a number of problems with the work of Allender and Longman. First, their categories are confused. For example, they deal with the idol of control but do not consider the fact that, for many, being preoccupied with work or immorality is another effort at control and not separate from it. As another example, they deal with the idol of pleasure but do not address the reality that money and relationships can also be a conniving way to pursue pleasure. A second problem is that though they write an entire book about the way idols can dominate a life, they never explain specifically how someone might turn from idols through specific acts of repentance.

For the work here, however, the most significant problem for Allender and Longman is that they do not seem to recognize the danger of proposing a finite list of idols. Allender and Longman do not ever get behind idols to discover what is going on in every human heart, whether they are preoccupied with some, none, or all of the idols that they list in their book. This one is simply not a helpful development of the thinking of those in the contemporary biblical counseling movement. It would be more helpful to avoid compiling a master list of idols (thus contributing to an idol hunt) and instead show the commonality of all sinful pursuits in the sinful self-exalting heart. Once that common theme is understood, counselors can help themselves and others understand the specifics of their problem—not by compiling a master list—but by asking: What is this person using to honor and glorify himself? and, In what areas of her life is this person reserving for herself the right to do and not do?

7) Protection against Introspection

Finally, a fuller articulation of motivation and idolatry will guard against introspection on the part of the counselee. If the previous benefit targets counselors and protects them from an idol hunt with their counselees, then this benefit targets counselees and protects them from an overemphasis on self-analysis. Sometimes counselees can become preoccupied with identifying their specific idol. This particular goal makes true and lasting change dependent on the isolation of one specific thing. An understanding of the Bible's teaching on the sinful, self-exalting heart frees the counselee from this quest. The biblical understanding allows counselees to understand that the fundamental problem of self-exaltation will be manifested in a million specific concretizations. This understanding does not mean that counselees should not seek to repent of specific sins and idols. It does mean that it is unnecessary for a counselee to be preoccupied with introspection to do so.

Rather, counselees must be reminded of the gospel of grace, which frees sinners from self by a simple call of faith and obedience.

Conclusion

The second generation of the biblical counseling movement has been helpful in thinking through a biblical theology of motivation. The "idols of the heart" language developed by Powlison has been both enlightening and important. This metaphor rightly captures that sinful human beings are motivated to act by things that are not God. It has been necessary to further elaborate on this metaphor, however, showing that, biblically, idols do not exist in and of themselves but instead are concrete manifestations of every human's deep-seated desire for self-exaltation. There are many benefits of this biblical understanding that all organize every idol against which a person may struggle within a unified understanding of sinful self-righteousness.

Conclusion: Increasingly Competent to Counsel

At the end of the 1960s Jay Adams's proposal of biblical counseling was radical.[1] The approach to helping people with their problems in living had been defined exclusively by its secularity. The church, of all places, denied her own rich resources. It was the church that had totally adopted secular theories and therapies for helping hurting people. It was the church that was often guilty of baptizing those approaches in prayers and proof texts.

Adams's role was to initiate a recovery of Jesus, the Bible, and the church in helping people with their problems. Adams's goal was to awaken slumbering Christians to the wealth of rich resources that God has given them for counseling troubled people. Adams's context and goal created a twofold necessity for the founder of the biblical counseling movement.

The Founding of the Biblical Counseling Movement

On the one hand, Adams needed to build an entire movement from scratch. While previous generations of Christians had developed helpful resources that were relevant for their own times, there were no resources to address the unique challenges confronting counseling in the twentieth century from a distinctly Christian perspective. In the providence of God, the initial task of providing both vision and resources fell almost exclusively to Adams. Adams needed to construct, from the ground up, a theoretical understanding of counseling, an approach to the counseling process, and a strategy to engage other counseling practitioners and theoreticians—all of which would meet his goal of being based exclusively on the teachings of Scripture. Furthermore, Adams did not have the leisure of decades to accomplish this task. In a sense, he built it on the wing. Adams and John Bettler commented on this in an interview:

> Adams: It wasn't planned. It was a casual thing.
>
> Bettler: Nothing about the counseling and the counseling center was planned then. It was all by the seat of the pants. Jay would do something on Monday, make it up in the moment; then he'd teach it on Tuesday in class at Westminster.
>
> Adams: It wasn't quite that bad—more like the next week! I at least gave it a week's thought and study. It was on-the-job learning, on-the-job teaching, on-the-job training.[2]

Adams was responding to a critical need, which demanded that he produce the materials for his model immediately, almost spontaneously. Investing significant time was a luxury he could not afford. Adams needed to present his model in such a way that it gained a hearing. This need for a hearing goes a long way in explaining why Adams often spoke the way he did. The assertive tone so frequently employed by Adams was less an inherent character flaw than a strategy to drive his hearers toward making a decision. Powlison describes an interview in which Adams commented on this:

> Adams discussed his rhetorical strategy freely. Blunt overstatement sounds different when understood as a conscious strategy rather than as the summary of a person's position. In person he offered a rationale for conscious overstatement: as a populist strategy for engaging in turf warfare, it pushed people to decide either for or against. He then criticized scholarly understatement as ineffective strategically, and frequently pusillanimous.[3]

For Adams, bombast was a conscious tactic. Such an explanation does not excuse everything that Adams did or said. There are times when a deeper appreciation of the biblical call to speak the truth in love might have led to a different approach on Adams's part.[4] However, such an explanation does place Adams's tactics in the context of a larger strategy. It reminds us that the concerns facing Adams in the first generation were different from those facing the second generation. It reminds us that the second generation has been able to bring finesse to a movement born through the forcefulness of its founder.

Adams did the hard work of launching a movement, and he did so against great forces opposed to or unaware of the need for such a movement. In fact, the task of creating a movement was so great that one marvels that Adams was able to accomplish all that he did. Despite the difficulties, he established a beachhead and gained ground in the fight to construct a biblical counseling movement. But the movement he founded was in need of advancement.

The Theological Advancement of the Biblical Counseling Movement

As the movement founded by Adams moved from a first to a second generation, it changed and matured. There was conceptual advancement as the second generation pondered more carefully how to balance biblical notions of sin and suffering, how to think through motivational issues, and how to explain and address the causes of behavior. There was methodological development as biblical counselors learned from Scripture to be more caring, kind, and relational and less formal and authoritative in their approach to relationships. And there was apologetic development as the second generation learned from the failures and strengthened the successes of the first generation's approach to engagement with outsiders.

The publication of Powlison's "Crucial Issues in Contemporary Biblical Counseling" in 1988 was the movement's first effort at being self-critical and intentional about developing upon Adams. From that starting point the movement has continued to grow and develop over the last two decades. The movement is more thoughtful; it is more caring; it is learning to speak more wisely and loving to outsiders—the movement is more biblical.

That this advancement occurred did not come as a surprise to Adams. Advancement within the movement was anticipated in Adams's own work. He was clear on a number of occasions that his work was only a beginning, as he encouraged others to come behind him and do more work. For example, in *A Theology of Christian Counseling* Adams commented on the need for solid theology in counseling:

> Truly, the situation is complex (I almost wrote "horrendous"). You can understand, then, why I am begging for volumes to be written, and why I make no claims about doing more than making a beginning at discussing the many matters of anthropology that confront the Christian counselor who wants to be thoroughly biblical. It is hard enough to know where to begin my sketch, let alone to attempt anything more ambitious.[5]

Adams knew his work was only a beginning, even remarking that the need for theological reflection in counseling was so great that it was a struggle to know where to begin. Those, therefore, who have followed Adams and done more work are fulfilling Adams's mandate. Adams even warned:

> My foundation surely has planks that are rotten and some that are miss-ing. The reader must watch where he walks. There may be planks that have been nailed in backwards or upside down. But of one thing I am certain: there are a number of biblical planks that are solidly nailed down. At present I am measuring and sawing others. But in order to get them nailed all of the way across, other Christians must also lay hold of the hammers and nails and help.[6]

Adams was also clear that his work was imperfect and that there was a need for others to join in the project:

> The nouthetic counseling group differs significantly from the psycho-analytic coterie with which Freud surrounded himself. For them to dif-fer with the master was heresy and it was necessary either to recant of anti-Freudian dogma or be excommunicated. No such relationship exists among nouthetic thinkers, all of whom are thinkers and theologians in their own right. They are yes and no men; and I learn continually from their nos.[7]

Adams was clear here that the counseling movement he founded needed independent theologians and thinkers to come after him and evaluate his project. He further made clear that the nos of others in the movement were a source of great learning for him. He further stated that intentional critical reflection was one of the things that should mark biblical counseling as different from secular approaches to helping people.

Responding to Advancement

As the biblical counseling movement moves from a second to a *third* generation, how should contemporary biblical counselors evaluate the advancement that has taken place over the past two decades? Before answering this question, it will be helpful to state how biblical counselors should *not* evaluate this advancement. There are three wrong approaches.

First, biblical counselors should not minimize the work done by the first generation. Adams's task was to create, to launch, and to found. Every person committed to a uniquely biblical approach to helping people with their problems has Adams to thank for the movement that they call their own. The goal of this book has been to show carefully how the movement founded by Adams has developed, and such work is critical for assessing where the movement is and where it has come from. Every attempt has been made, however, to do this work in a manner that shows appreciation for the founding work of Adams. Pointing fingers or accusing would be inappropriate, since God used Adams—flaws and all—as a servant to call the church toward more faithfulness in the task of helping struggling people. It would be unwise, unloving, and ungodly for contemporary biblical counselors to stomp on the shoulders of the giants on which they stand.

Second, biblical counselors should not evaluate the advancement that has taken place by ignoring or discounting the work of the second generation. Disregarding the advancements of the second generation would be just as wrong as minimizing the work of the first. The biblical counseling movement has advanced in *biblical* ways. All biblical counselors can be thankful for the increased insight into human suffering and human motivation; for greater care in creating relationships of love, care, and concern; and for the increased efforts to spread a vision of biblical counseling to those outside the movement. The biblical counseling movement is stronger today than it was two decades ago because of the faithful work of those following Adams and working according to his same vision.

Finally, biblical counselors should not evaluate the advancements that have occurred by drawing a firm line between the first and second generations, as though they are not ultimately "familial" differences. In looking at how the biblical counseling movement has matured, there is a danger of making distinctions inside the movement that blur deep commonalities that unite. It is important to remember—as has been addressed elsewhere in this book—that far more unites the first and second generations than divides them. All biblical counselors are united by a desire to help struggling people and see them change, by a commitment to progressive sanctification, by skepticism regarding secular psychology's usurpation of the ministerial role, and by a commitment to the sufficiency of Christ, his Word, and his church. This unity holds the generations of biblical counseling together as family. It is critical that the movement stand together on this unity and avoid a factious spirit.

How then should biblical counselors evaluate the development of the last two decades? It seems that two responses are appropriate. First, biblical counselors should be thankful for the founding work of the first generation and thankful for the advancement of the second generation as well. Also, biblical counselors should be thankful for the unity that exists between all those who are committed to a uniquely biblical approach to helping people with their problems.

A second response appropriate for biblical counselors is diligence. Biblical counselors need to be diligent to continue the work that has been done in the spirit in which it has been done. Adams was a Berean. He looked out over the counseling landscape that existed and refused to accept what he saw. Instead, he demanded something more biblical, and he worked to create it for the good of the church and the honor of Christ. The same is true of the second generation of biblical counselors. They observed the initial work of Adams but did not accept it as it was. Instead, for the good of the church and the honor of Christ they sought to make it more biblical. Biblical counselors in the third, fourth, and fifth generations and onward will be like those in the first and second when they receive all that has been handed down with gratitude while, at the same time, striving to make the work conform more closely to God's Word.

Building an Airplane in the Air

The work of developing a practical theology of biblical counseling was a bit like building an airplane while it was flying in the air. The first generation provided the force needed to launch the project into the air. The first generation also provided the force that was needed to keep such a project in the air, defending it against dismissive attack. Thinking of the founding of the movement in this way explains the need for development. Adams's initial theological proposals were tantamount to strapping an engine onto the wing of an in-flight airplane: he simply did not have the luxury of doing finishing work in the cabin—or even affixing a windshield.

Just as Adams's work of force was necessary to launch the plane, the second generation's work of finesse was necessary to improve the quality of flight. Thoughtful reflection on the issues mentioned in this book has been made possible by the first generation's diligent labors. The labor of the second generation makes the quality of the plane much better, and therefore a plane that is a greater pleasure to fly in.

Adams's work was not perfect. Understood in his historical context, however, there is no way that it could have been. Adams brought the force of a founder—and the flaws that come with it. Adams was a Luther. What *should* be expected is the necessity of advancement. What *should* be expected is theological reflection and development that makes wise and loving Christians increasingly competent to counsel. This effort has been the work of the second generation of biblical counselors. It will continue to be the work of successive generations.

Appendix:
What Alternative?

*In chapter 2 we addressed the criticisms made against
Jay Adams's view of the flesh by the second generation.
These criticisms were stated in an article by Edward Welch,
"How Theology Shapes Ministry: Jay Adams's View of the
Flesh and an Alternative"* (Journal of Biblical Counseling 20,
*no. 3 [2002]: 16–25). Jay Adams strongly disagreed with the
conclusions of Welch's article and wrote a lengthy response.
The* Journal of Biblical Counseling *published only a few
sentences of that response, however (see Jay Adams,
"Letter to the Editor,"* Journal of Biblical Counseling 22,
*no. 3 [2003]: 66). This appendix in this volume is a copy of
Jay Adams's response in its entirety. It is printed here with
permission, without editing or commentary, to provide a
record of Adams's response.*

I wish to thank Ed Welch for his comments on my view of "flesh"
found in Paul's letter to the Roman church. It gives me the opportunity
to squelch some of the erroneous ideas that may be floating around. The
opportunity that a response provides is to clarify, extend, and state those
views with greater vigor and to do a bit of teaching as well.

    I shall begin by asking the question—unanswered in the *Journal* arti-
cle—"If sin in some way is physically 'in the members,' 'in the body' and
'in the flesh' (three ways of saying the same thing), as Paul plainly taught
that it is, then what does he mean; and how is this so?" Paul was no Gnostic;
he believed that the body God gave man, as such, is itself neither evil nor
the source of sin; sin is not inherent in it. Then, how does sin gain control
of the body, the flesh and of the members thereof? If he does not mean that

sin gains control of the believer's body as the result of programming by the sinful spirit of man in his unregenerate state, and then through habitual practice takes over, bringing these habits into the new regenerate life, how does it do so? Plainly, in Paul's analogy, it is the slave's body (not his soul) that is owned and used by sin. And his members are, as Paul says, used to further sin's purposes. In the same way he pictures the Spirit gaining control and use of these very members of the regenerate man's body instead (Romans 6:13, 19). The believer is to present (or yield) the members of his body to God rather than to sin. How does he do so, except by consecration leading to obedience to God?

No, the "alternative" view, mentioned but not fully subscribed to by Ed, is that "flesh" doesn't pertain to the physical body at all, but to a "flesh group!" These people supposedly are those who depend on the law for salvation—in short, they are Judaizers. They are "living under the old covenant and not indwelt by the Spirit," he says. This group participates in a "*sarx* life" (life lived by the flesh) but now Paul belongs to a different "community." This new group lives the "Spirit life." Paul, he says, was merely using a "Rhetorical" device when referring to himself rather than speaking of "his actual experience."

But Paul doesn't set forth the struggle of Romans 7:14–24 as vacillation that comes from living under two covenants rather than one. The idea that the passage is not autobiographical, but speaking in rhetorical terms, leads the reader to the strange belief that he meant that the group was suffering from "tensions in life under two covenants rather than within the individual." Now, Ed makes it clear that he isn't by any means sure of this construction of Paul's words: "I have not developed alternatives." For that, I can only be glad. Yet he "briefly highlights" this new view as an alternative to mine. Frankly, I was greatly disappointed in this aspect of Ed's article. I thought there would be something solid in the article to get my teeth into. Why is he concerned to refute one view when not sure of his own?

Now, how can the "alternative" viewpoint account for expressions like sin in the flesh, sin in the body and sin in the members? Really, I cannot see how it can. The new view does not seem compatible with Paul's words. There is no reason to expect that Paul is using an analogy here. The analogy in the passage has to do with slavery. To posit another analogy on top of that one seems a stretch. Other expressions also clash with the "alternative" view. How does one stop "yielding" his members to sin as a master and begin yielding them to God? Ed dances around passages, saying things here and there about them, but hardly comes up with anything certain. The title of the article doesn't compute with what Ed does. He seems more concerned to debunk my view than to present an "alternative." The latter is given so tentatively and in such short compass that it looks like it was merely tacked on to the article which really is an attempt to refute my view of flesh.

How Ed goes about this is interesting. There is no exegesis. There is really no argumentation. What we encounter, instead, is a list of dotted references that Ed thinks my view of flesh might possibly lead to. So, in order to respond, all I can do is address the matter found in the article's twenty dots. This I shall now do. For convenience, I shall number the dots as D1, D2, etc. In order to follow along in his article, I suggest that you also number the dots in your copy of the journal article.

Under D1 Ed claims that my view of flesh leads to making self-discipline "the central task." Of course, that isn't true of Nouthetic Counseling. There is nothing wrong with emphasizing self-discipline when necessary—the Bible does. But the "central task?" Hardly. Unintentionally (I am sure) Ed makes it sound like I am teaching self-help. But instead of this, we hold that the central task is to so minister the Scriptures that God, the Holy Spirit, will use His Word to change the counselee. This misunderstanding of the biblical system is buttressed in D2 by comparing training "in righteousness" from the Scriptures (2 Timothy 3:17) with "developing a tennis serve." His concern is repetition. But why? The Bible is highly repetitive. There must be a reason for this! Moreover God has made the same man who "develops" a tennis serve by repetition able to learn many other things that way. Why should we not expect Him to help people learn how to live according to the Scriptures in a similar fashion? Christians may "learn" many things by the same means, but the great difference about counseling is that God directs, motivates and enables us to make the behavioral changes addressed. Repetition of thought and action is but one element in the process of sanctification. Again in D2, D3 and D4 the intimation is that Nouthetic Counseling is nothing more than a refinement of Behaviorism. Not so!

In D4 motivation is said not to be the "target" for change. Here an erroneous either/or view of Nouthetic Counseling is conjured up. There is no denial of the importance of motivation in my view. In D5 Ed seems concerned about the relationship of the counselor to the counselee as a "means of God's grace to a counselee." But the "means of grace" which most theologians and exegetes accept do not include this. Where does Ed find this in the Scriptures? The counselor's task is not to get in the way of the message that he is explaining from the Bible, thus impeding the counselee's progress. When it comes to furthering relations that are gracious, it is the counselor's task to assure the counselee that he must have the proper relationship to God. This is what he does. After all, it is the Holy Spirit Who changes His people—not the counselor. I said this as far back as the publication of *Competent to Counsel.*

Even unbelieving counselors may be able to bring about changes in counselees (often by their relationships), but these changes will not please God (Romans 8:8). Any change that arises in counseling that, at bottom, is not brought about by the Spirit, is unacceptable. The counselor's task is to so minister the Word that the Spirit uses it to bring about change.

In D6 Ed is concerned to have counselors reveal that they and the counselees are in the same boat. In 2 Corinthians 1:4 Paul does speak about being able to counsel others from his own experience. But a close look at the passage makes it plain that he was not interested in matching people with similar problems. He says that this experience will enable him to counsel others with any sort of problem. How? The type of experience is not in focus; it is God's comforting solution to the problem that he is speaking about. Sympathy for others is not enough. A biblical sort of empathy is necessary: in it the counselor enters into his counselee's problem in such a way that the counselor sees more deeply than his counselee. He reaches so deeply that he not only sees and feels the dimensions of the problem as his counselee does, but beyond that he sees God's solution to it.

In D7 Ed expresses fear that counselees are not taught "to look to Jesus in the battle against sin." Nothing could be farther from the truth. Faith, which he mentions, is not "defined" by us as "establishing new habits." Faith is trust in God that takes Him at His Word. It is believing and acting upon that Word so as to make changes that will please His Lord. Faith rests not upon counselors nor upon their words (D6) but solely upon God and His promises.

In D9 "teaching" is equated with "rote memorization." I have never said or done anything of the sort! Again, a false antithesis is constructed in which thinking is set over against "growing in the knowledge of Christ." When I give thought to my spiritual growth, I recognize that I cannot grow as I should without learning (the other side of teaching)! Repentance, for instance, involves not only a change of action, but also a change of thought. Knowing Christ for counselees is not developing some mystical, extra-biblical relationship by which they come to "know" Him better. Teaching is often necessary in counseling—precisely to help counselees to come to know Christ better and to serve Him more faithfully. Sometimes, when necessary, teaching is "heavy," something Ed apparently deplores. But rote memorization? Where does that idea come from? Certainly not from my practice or writings!

Again, connecting some of Ed's dots, what I said before applies once more. There is no either/or in Nouthetic Counseling as Ed describes it in D10.

I would like to discuss D11 in more depth than I can here. Ed focuses upon motivation. It is important to remember that the Bible teaches that it is impossible to know another's heart. He cannot know the motivation of others. God, in contradistinction to man, is called the "Heart-Knower" (Acts 1:24; cf. 1 Samuel 16:7). The heart belongs to God alone. On the issue of "Idols of the heart" (D13) I reserve comment for another time and place. There is much to be said, since unbiblical exegesis and ideas have been taught under this rubric.

Who said the model "does not induce one to examine motivations"? My "model" urges counselees to do so. But, N.B., they are called upon to examine their own motives for themselves. Again, this discussion must be reserved for a later time and place when ideas in D13 are more fully examined elsewhere.

The statement in D15 fails to describe Nouthetic Counseling. One reason medications are often opposed is because they may be used to mask true problems and circumvent God's ways.

D17 seems to ignore the fact that what one has done in his past may not correspond to his inner life (what he habitually thinks and revels in).

Perhaps out of fear of consequences, previously, he has refrained from doing what he now indulges in. Peter writes about those who have hearts "trained" in greed (2 Peter 2:14). He speaks also about how their "eyes" continually "look for sin." Isn't this a matter of hearts having trained the "members" of the body?

D18 fails to understand that the invention of "new ways to sin" may, itself, be a habitual pattern!

D19 simply doesn't fairly represent Nouthetic Counseling.

D20 ignores material written and taught about "covert" patterns.

Now, it is fortunate that Ed admits that I might "disavow" some of his conclusions. I certainly do! In fact, I disavow most, if not every one of them.

I ask again, if not by a process of habituation, how does sin in the body, in the flesh and in the members come about? How is it put off and how are new ways put on, if this doesn't involve learning about these from Scripture, asking God to enable one to obediently do what is right—and then doing it? When Paul writes about that which he calls the "law in my members" (Romans 7:23) what does he have in mind? This "law" is a power that opposes the law of his mind. To the extent that it overpowers his better intentions ("the law of my mind") it takes him "captive." That is to say, he finds it difficult to overcome. What power can sin exert upon the body so as to set up a warfare within the Christian? Can you think of anything other than habit which clearly fits the bill?

Bibliography

Books

Adams, Jay. *I & II Corinthians*. The Christian Counselor's Commentary. Hackettstown, NJ: Timeless Texts, 1994.

———. *The Biblical View of Self-Esteem, Self-Love, Self-Image*. Eugene, OR: Harvest, 1986.

———. *The Big Umbrella and Other Essays and Addresses on Christian Counseling*. Phillipsburg, NJ: Presbyterian & Reformed, 1972.

———. *Christ and Your Problems*. Nutley, NJ: Presbyterian & Reformed, 1971.

———. *Christ and Your Problems*. Phillipsburg, NJ: P&R, 1999.

———. "The Christian Approach to Schizophrenia." In *The Construction of Madness: Emerging Conceptions and Interventions into the Psychotic Process*. Edited by Peter A. Magaro, 133–50. New York: Pergamon, 1976.

———. *The Christian Counselor's Manual*. Grand Rapids, MI: Zondervan, 1973.

———. *The Christian Counselor's New Testament: A New Translation in Everyday English with Notations*. Phillipsburg, NJ: Presbyterian & Reformed, 1977.

———. *The Christian Counselor's Wordbook: A Primer of Nouthetic Counseling*. Phillipsburg, NJ: Presbyterian & Reformed, 1981.

———. "Comments." In *Prophets of Psychoheresy I*. Edited by Martin Bobgan and Deidre Bobgan, 105–6. Santa Barbara, CA: Eastgate. 1989.

———. *Compassionate Counseling*. Woodruff, SC: Timeless Texts, 2007.

———. *Competent to Counsel*. Grand Rapids, MI: Zondervan, 1970.

————. *Coping with Counseling Crises: First Aid for Christian Counselors.* Phillipsburg, NJ: Presbyterian & Reformed, 1976.

————. *Counsel from Psalm 119.* Woodruff, SC: Timeless Texts, 1998.

————. *Counseling and the Five Points of Calvinism.* Phillipsburg, NJ: Presbyterian & Reformed, 1981.

————. *Counseling and the Sovereignty of God.* Philadelphia: Westminster Theological Seminary, 1975.

————. *Critical Stages of Biblical Counseling.* Stanley, NC: Timeless Texts, 2002.

————. *Four Weeks with God and Your Neighbor: A Devotional Workbook for Counselees and Others.* Phillipsburg, NJ: Presbyterian & Reformed, 1978.

————. *Hebrews, James, I & II Peter, and Jude.* The Christian Counselor's Commentary. Woodruff, SC: Timeless Texts, 1996.

————. *How to Handle Trouble.* Phillipsburg, NJ: P&R, 1992.

————. *How to Handle Trouble: God's Way.* Phillipsburg, NJ: Presbyterian & Reformed, 1982.

————. *How to Help People Change: The Four-Step Biblical Process.* Grand Rapids, MI: Zondervan, 1986.

————. *Insight and Creativity in Christian Counseling.* Woodruff, SC: Timeless Texts, 1982.

————. *The Language of Counseling.* Phillipsburg, NJ: Presbyterian & Reformed, 1981.

————. *Lectures on Counseling.* Grand Rapids, MI: Zondervan, 1977.

————. *The Power of Error: Demonstrated in an Actual Counseling Case.* Phillipsburg, NJ: Presbyterian & Reformed, 1978.

————. *Prayers for Troubled Times.* Grand Rapids, MI: Baker, 1979.

————. *Ready to Restore: The Layman's Guide to Christian Counseling.* Phillipsburg, NJ: Presbyterian & Reformed, 1981.

————. "Reflections on the History of Biblical Counseling." In *Practical Theology and the Ministry of the Church, 1952–1984: Essays in Honor of Edmund P. Clowney.* Edited by Harvie Conn, 203–17. Phillipsburg, NJ: Presbyterian & Reformed. 1990.

————. *Romans, Phillippians, and I & II Thessalonians.* Hackettstown, NJ: Timeless Texts, 1995.

————. *Shepherding God's Flock: A Handbook on Pastoral Ministry, Counseling, and Leadership.* Grand Rapids, MI: Zondervan, 1975.

————. *Solving Marriage Problems: Biblical Solutions for Christian Counselors.* Phillipsburg, NJ: Presbyterian & Reformed, 1983.

————. *Teaching to Observe.* Hackettstown, NJ: Timeless Texts, 1995.

————. *A Theology of Christian Counseling.* Grand Rapids, MI: Zondervan, 1979.

————. *What about Nouthetic Counseling?* Grand Rapids, MI: Baker, 1976.

————. *What Do You Do When Anger Gets the Upper Hand?* Phillipsburg, NJ: Presbyterian & Reformed, 1975.

————. *What Do You Do When Fear Overcomes You?* Phillipsburg, NJ: Presbyterian & Reformed, 1975.

————. *What Do You Do When You Become Depressed?* Phillipsburg, NJ: Presbyterian & Reformed, 1975.

————. *What Do You Do When You Know That You're Hooked?* Phillipsburg, NJ: Presbyterian & Reformed, 1975.

————. *What Do You Do When You Worry All the Time?* Phillipsburg, NJ: Presbyterian & Reformed, 1975.

————. *What Do You Do When Your Marriage Goes Sour?* Phillipsburg, NJ: Presbyterian & Reformed, 1975.

————. *What to Do about Worry.* Phillipsburg, NJ: Presbyterian & Reformed, 1980.

————. *Your Place in the Counseling Revolution.* Nutley, NJ: Presbyterian & Reformed, 1975.

Adler, Alfred. *Understanding Human Nature.* New York: Greenburg, 1946.

Allen, Leslie C. *Ezekiel.* Word Biblical Commentary, vol. 29. Dallas: Word, 1994.

Allender, Dan B., and Tremper Longman III. *Breaking the Idols of Your Heart: How to Navigate the Temptations of Life.* Deerfield, IN: InterVarsity, 2007.

Baird, Samuel J. *A History of the New School, and of the Questions Involved in the Disruption of the Presbyterian Church in 1838.* Philadelphia: Claxton, Remsen & Haffelfinger, 1868.

Baxter, Richard. *A Christian Directory: The Practical Works of Richard Baxter.* Morgan, PA: Soli Deo Gloria, 2000.

Benner, David G. *Psychotherapy and the Spiritual Quest.* Grand Rapids, MI: Baker, 1988.

Bookman, Douglas. "The Scriptures and Biblical Counseling." In *Introduction to Biblical Counseling*, ed. John F. MacArthur and Wayne A. Mack, 63–97. Nashville: Thomas Nelson, 1994.

Boring, E. G. *A History of Experimental Psychology.* 2nd ed. New York: Appleton-Century Crofts, 1950.

Bridge, William. *A Lifting Up for the Downcast.* Carlisle, PA: Banner of Truth, 2001.

Brown, Kenneth O. *Holy Ground: A Study of the American Camp Meeting.* New York: Garland, 1992.

Calvin, John. *Epistle to the Romans.* Calvin's Commentaries, vol. 14. Grand Rapids, MI: Baker, 2003.

Capps, Donald. *Biblical Approaches to Pastoral Counseling.* Philadelphia: Westminster, 1981.

Carter, John D., and Bruce Narramore. *The Integration of Psychology and Theology.* Grand Rapids, MI: Zondervan, 1979.

Clinton, Tim, and George Ohlschlager. *Competent Christian Counseling: Pursuing and Practicing Compassionate Soul Care.* Colorado Springs, CO: Waterbrook, 2002.

Collins, Gary R. *The Biblical Basis of Christian Counseling for People Helpers.* Colorado Springs, CO: NavPress, 1993.

———. "An Integration Response." In *Psychology and Christianity: Four Views.* Edited by Eric L. Johnson and Stanton L. Jones, 232–37. Downers Grove, IL: InterVarsity, 2000.

———. *The Rebuilding of Psychology: An Integration of Psychology and Christianity.* Wheaton, IL: Tyndale, 1977.

Crabb, Larry. *Inside Out.* Colorado Springs, CO: NavPress, 1988.

———. *Understanding People.* Grand Rapids, MI: Zondervan, 1987.

Duguid, Iain M. *Ezekiel.* Vol. 23, NIV Application Commentary. Edited by Terry Muck. Grand Rapids, MI: Zondervan, 1999.

Edwards, Jonathan. *A Treatise Concerning the Religious Affections.* Sioux Falls, SD: NuVision, 2007.

Eyrich, Howard, ed. *What to Do When.* Phillipsburg, NJ: Presbyterian & Reformed, 1978.

Fosdick, Harry Emerson. *The Living of These Days.* New York: Harper & Row, 1956.

Freud, Sigmund. *Introductory Lectures on Psychoanalysis.* London: Lund Humphries, 1933.

———. *Psychoanalysis and Faith.* New York: Basic, 1964.

———. *The Question of Lay Analysis.* New York: Norton, 1950.

Ganz, Richard. *Psychobabble: The Failure of Modern Psychology and the Biblical Alternative.* Wheaton, IL: Crossway, 1993.

Gladden, Washington. *Ruling Ideas of the Present Age.* Boston: Houghton Mifflin, 1895.

Halbertal, Moshe, and Avishai Margalit. *Idolatry.* Cambridge, MA: Harvard University Press, 1992.

Higgens, Elford. *Hebrew Idolatry and Superstition.* Port Washington, NY: Kennikat, 1971.

Hiltner, Seward, and Lowell Colston. *The Context of Pastoral Counseling.* Nashville: Abingdon, 1961.

Hindson, Ed, and Howard Eyrich, eds. *Totally Sufficient.* Ross-shire: Christian Focus, 2004.

Hoekema, Anthony A. *Created in God's Image.* Grand Rapids, MI: Eerdmans, 1986.

Holifield, E. Brooks. *The History of Pastoral Care in America: From Salvation to Self-Realization.* Nashville: Abingdon, 1983.

Hunter, Rodney, ed. *Dictionary of Pastoral Care and Counseling.* Nashville: Abingdon, 2005.

Johnson, Eric L. *Foundations for Soul Care: A Christian Psychology Proposal.* Downers Grove, IL: IVP Academic, 2007.

Johnson, Eric L., and Stanton L. Jones, eds. *Psychology and Christianity: Four Views.* Downers Grove, IL: InterVarsity, 2000.

Jones, Stanton L. "An Apologetic Apologia for the Integration of Psychology and Theology." In *Care for the Soul*. Edited by Mark R. McMinn and Timothy R. Phillips, 62–77. Downers Grove, IL: InterVarsity, 2001.

Jones, Stanton L., and Richard E. Butman. *Modern Psychotherapies*. Downers Grove, IL: InterVarsity, 1991.

Lane, Timothy S., and Paul David Tripp. *How People Change*. Winston-Salem, NC: Punch, 2006.

MacArthur, John. *Counseling*. Nashville: Thomas Nelson, 2005.

Mack, Wayne A. "Developing a Helping Relationship with Counselees." In *Introduction to Biblical Counseling*. Edited by John F. MacArthur Jr. and Wayne A. Mack, 173–88. Nashville: W Publishing, 1994.

———. "Implementing Biblical Instruction." In *Introduction to Biblical Counseling*. Edited by John F. MacArthur Jr. and Wayne A. Mack, 284–300. Nashville: W Publishing, 2004.

———. "Providing Instruction through Biblical Counseling." In *Introduction to Biblical Counseling*. Edited by John F. MacArthur and Wayne A. Mack, 250–67. Nashville: W Publishing, 1994.

———. "Taking Counselee Inventory: Collecting Data." In *Introduction to Biblical Counseling*. Edited by John F. MacArthur and Wayne A. Mack, 210–30. Nashville: W Publishing, 1994.

———. "What Is Biblical Counseling?" In *Totally Sufficient*. Edited by Ed Hindson and Howard Eyrich, 25–52. Ross-shire: Christian Focus, 2004.

Mack, Wayne, and Joshua Mack. *God's Solutions to Life's Problems*. Tulsa, OK: Hensley, 2002.

Magaro, Peter A. *The Construction of Madness*. Elmsford, NY: Pergamon, 1976.

Marsden, George M. *Understanding Fundamentalism and Evangelicalism*. Grand Rapids, MI: Eerdmans, 1991.

McMinn, Mark R., and Timothy R. Phillips, eds. *Care for the Soul*. Downers Grove, IL: InterVarsity, 2001.

Moo, Douglas J. *The Epistle to the Romans*. Vol. 6, The New International Commentary on the New Testament. Grand Rapids, MI: Eerdmans, 1996.

Moore, Russell D. *Counseling and the Authority of Christ*. Louisville, KY: The Southern Baptist Theological Seminary, 2005.

Morris, Leon. *Epistle to the Romans*. Vol. 6, Pillar New Testament Commentary. Grand Rapids, MI: Eerdmans, 1988.

Murray, Iain H. *Revival and Revivalism*. Carlisle, PA: Banner of Truth, 1994.

Myers, David G. "A Levels-of-Explanation Response." In *Psychology and Christianity: Four Views*. Edited by Eric L. Johnson and Stanton L. Jones, 226–31. Downers Grove, IL: InterVarsity, 2000.

Narramore, Bruce. *No Condemnation: Rethinking Guilt Motivation in Counseling, Preaching, and Parenting*. Grand Rapids, MI: Zondervan, 1984.

Nash, Ronald H. *Great Divides: Understanding the Controversies That Come Between Christians*. Colorado Springs, CO: NavPress, 1993.

Odell, Margaret S. *Ezekiel*. Vol. 23, Smyth and Helwys Bible Commentary. Edited by R. Scott Nash. Macon, GA: Smyth and Helwys, 2005.

Ortlund, Raymond C., Jr. *God's Unfaithful Wife*. Downers Grove, IL: InterVarsity, 1996.

Owen, John. *The Mortification of Sin*. Carlisle, PA: Banner of Truth, 2004.

Phua, Richard Liong-Seng. *Idolatry and Authority*. London: T&T Clark, 2005.

Powlison, David. "A Biblical Counseling View." In *Psychology and Christianity: Four Views*. Edited by Eric L. Johnson and Stanton L. Jones, 196–224. Downers Grove, IL: InterVarsity, 2000.

————. *Competent to Counsel? The History of the Conservative Protestant Biblical Counseling Movement*. Glenside, PA: Christian Counseling and Educational Foundation, 1996.

————. "God's Grace and Your Sufferings." In *Suffering and the Sovereignty of God*. Edited by John Piper and Justin Taylor, 145–74. Wheaton, IL: Crossway, 2006.

———. "Integration or Inundation?" In *Power Religion*. Edited by Michael Horton, 191–218. Chicago: Moody. 1992.

———. *Power Encounters: Reclaiming Spiritual Warfare*. Grand Rapids, MI: Baker, 1995.

———. "Questions at the Crossroads: The Care of Souls and Modern Psychotherapies." In *Care for the Soul*. Edited by Mark R. McMinn and Timothy R. Phillips, 23–61. Downers Grove, IL: InterVarsity, 2001.

———. *Seeing with New Eyes*. Phillipsburg, NJ: P&R, 2003.

———. *Speaking Truth in Love*. Winston-Salem, NC: Punch, 2005.

Roberts, Robert. "A Christian Psychology Response." In *Psychology and Christianity: Four Views*. Edited by Eric L. Johnson and Stanton L. Jones, 238–42. Downers Grove, IL: InterVarsity, 2000.

Rogers, Carl. *Client-Centered Therapy: Its Current Practice, Implications, and Theory*. Boston: Houghton Mifflin, 1951.

———. *Counseling and Psychotherapy: Newer Concepts in Practice*. Boston: Houghton Mifflin, 1942.

Schreiner, Thomas. *Romans*. Vol. 6, Baker Exegetical Commentary on the New Testament. Grand Rapids, MI: Baker Academic, 1998.

Scipione, George C. *Timothy, Titus, and You: A Workbook for Church Leaders*. Phillipsburg, NJ: Pilgrim, 1975.

Shogren, Gary, and Edward Welch. *Running in Circles*. Grand Rapids, MI: Baker, 1995.

Skinner, B. F. *About Behaviorism*. New York: Knopf, 1974.

Smyth, Newman. *Christian Ethics*. New York: Charles Scribner's Sons, 1892.

Spencer, Ichabod. *A Pastor's Sketches*. Vestavia Hills, AL: Solid Ground, 2001.

Tripp, Paul David. *Instruments in the Redeemer's Hands*. Phillipsburg, NJ: P&R, 2002.

Tripp, Tedd. *Shepherding a Child's Heart*. Wapwollopen, PA: Shepherd, 1995.

Torrey, R. A., and A. C. Dixon, eds. *The Fundamentals*. Grand Rapids, MI: Baker, 1993.

Tozer, A. W. *The Knowledge of the Holy.* San Francisco: HarperCollins, 1961.

Warfield, B. B. *The Inspiration and Authority of the Bible.* Phillipsburg, NJ: Presbyterian & Reformed, 1948.

Welch, Edward T. *Addictions: A Banquet in the Grave.* Phillipsburg, NJ: P&R, 2001.

———. *Blame It on the Brain.* Phillipsburg, NJ: P&R, 1998.

———. *Depression: A Stubborn Darkness.* Greensboro, NC: New Growth, 2004.

———. *Running Scared.* Greensboro, NC: New Growth, 2007.

———. *When People Are Big and God Is Small.* Phillipsburg, NJ: P&R, 1997.

Wicks, Robert J., ed. *Clinical Handbook of Pastoral Counseling.* 2 vols. New York: Integration, 1993.

Wundt, Wilhelm. *Principles of Physiological Psychology.* Translated by Edward Bradford Titchener. New York: Macmillan, 1904.

Articles

Ackley, Tim. "Real Counsel for Real People." *Journal of Biblical Counseling* 21, no. 2 (2003): 37–44.

Acocella, Joan. "The Empty Couch." *Journal of Biblical Counseling* 19, no. 1 (2000): 49–55.

Adams, Jay E. "Balance in the Ministry of the Word." *Journal of Pastoral Practice* 6, no. 2 (1983): 1–2.

———. "Biblical Interpretation and Counseling." *Journal of Biblical Counseling* 16, no. 3 (1998): 5–9.

———. "Biblical Interpretation and Counseling, Part 2." *Journal of Biblical Counseling* 17, no. 1 (1998): 23–30.

———. "Change Them Into What?" *Journal of Biblical Counseling* 13, no. 2 (1995): 13–17.

———. "The Christian Approach to Schizophrenia." *Journal of Biblical Counseling* 14, no. 1 (1995): 27–33.

———. "Christian Counsel: An Interview with Jay Adams." *New Horizons in the Orthodox Presbyterian Church* 14, no. 3 (1993): 3–5.

―――. "Counseling and the Sovereignty of God." *Journal of Biblical Counseling* 11, no. 2 (1993): 4–9.

―――. "Editorial." *Journal of Pastoral Practice* 1, no. 1 (1977): 1–2.

―――. "Integration." *Journal of Pastoral Practice* 6, no. 1 (1982): 3–8.

―――. "The Key to the Casebook." *Journal of Pastoral Practice* 4, no. 3 (1980): 18–20.

―――. "The Key to the Christian Counselor's Casebook." *Journal of Pastoral Practice* 4, no. 4 (1980): 15–17.

―――. "The Key to the Casebook." *Journal of Pastoral Practice* 5, no. 1 (1981): 31–36.

―――. "The Key to the Casebook—'The Job Hunter.'" *Journal of Pastoral Practice* 5, no. 2 (1981): 12–14.

―――. "The Key to the Casebook." *Journal of Pastoral Practice* 5, no. 3 (1982): 42–46.

―――. "The Key to the Casebook." *Journal of Pastoral Practice* 5, no. 4 (1982): 83–86.

―――. "Key to the Casebook: Case No. 7." *Journal of Pastoral Practice* 6, no. 1 (1982): 43–44.

―――. "Key to the Casebook." *Journal of Pastoral Practice* 6, no. 2 (1983): 54–55.

―――. "Key to the Casebook." *Journal of Pastoral Practice* 6, no. 3 (1983): 59–60.

―――. "Key to the Casebook." *Journal of Pastoral Practice* 7, no. 1 (1984): 51–52.

―――. "Key to the Casebook." *Journal of Pastoral Practice* 7, no. 2 (1984): 62–63.

―――. "Key to the Casebook." *Journal of Pastoral Practice* 7, no. 3 (1984): 59–60.

―――. "Jay Adams's Response to the Congress on Christian Counseling." *Journal of Pastoral Practice* 10, no. 1 (1989): 2–4.

―――. "A Letter to the Editor." *Journal of Biblical Counseling* 22, no. 3 (2003): 66.

―――. "Looking Back." *Journal of Pastoral Practice* 9, no. 3 (1988): 3–4.

———. "The Motivation of Rejuvenation." *Journal of Pastoral Practice* 11, no. 1 (1992): 22–26.

———. "The Physician, The Pastor, Psychotherapy, and Counseling." *Journal of Biblical Ethics in Medicine* 3, no. 2 (1989): 21–26.

———. "Potential for Change." *Journal of Pastoral Practice* 8, no. 2 (1986): 13–14.

———. "Proper Use of Biblical Theology in Preaching." *Journal of Pastoral Practice* 9, no. 1 (1987): 47–49.

———. "A Reply to the Response." *Journal of Pastoral Practice* 9, no. 1 (1987): 1–5.

———. "What about Emotional Abuse?" *Journal of Pastoral Practice* 8, no. 3 (1986): 1–10.

———. "Why Is Biblical Counseling So Concerned about the Labels Used to Describe People's Problems?" *Journal of Biblical Counseling* 14, no. 2 (1996): 51–53.

Adams, Jay E., and David Powlison. "The Editor's Baton." *Journal of Pastoral Practice* 11, no. 1 (1992): 1–3.

Almy, Gary L. "Psychology." *Journal of Pastoral Practice* 9, no. 4 (1989): 8–11.

Babler, John. "A Biblical Critique of the DSM-IV." *Journal of Biblical Counseling* 18, no. 1 (1999): 25–29.

Beck, James. "Review of *Psychology and Christianity: Four Views*," *Denver Journal of Biblical and Theological Studies* 4 (2001).

Bettler, John F. "Biblical Counseling: The Next Generation." *Journal of Pastoral Practice* 8, no. 4 (1987): 3–10.

———. "CCEF: The Beginning." *Journal of Pastoral Practice* 9, no. 3 (1988): 45–51.

———. "Counseling and the Doctrine of Sin." *Journal of Biblical Counseling* 13, no. 1 (1994): 2–4.

———. "Counseling and the Problem of the Past." *Journal of Biblical Counseling* 12, no. 2 (1994): 5–23.

———. "Gaining an Accurate Self-Image, Part I." *Journal of Pastoral Practice* 6, no. 4 (1983): 46–52.

———. "Gaining an Accurate Self-Image, Part II." *Journal of Pastoral Practice* 7, no. 1 (1984): 41–50.

———. "Gaining an Accurate Self-Image, Part III." *Journal of Pastoral Practice* 7, no. 2 (1984): 52–61.

———. "Gaining an Accurate Self-Image, Part IV." *Journal of Pastoral Practice* 7, no. 3 (1984): 50–58.

———. "Gaining an Accurate Self-Image, Part V." *Journal of Pastoral Practice* 7, no. 4 (1985): 46–55.

———. "Gaining an Accurate Self-Image, Conclusion." *Journal of Pastoral Practice* 8, no. 2 (1987): 24–26.

———. "Jesus Our Wisdom." *The Journal of Biblical Counseling* 19, no. 2 (2001): 20–23.

———. "Keep the Truth Alive." *Journal of Biblical Counseling* 15, no. 2 (1997): 2–5.

———. "Make Every Effort: Ephesians 4:1–5:2." *The Journal of Biblical Counseling* 17, no. 2 (1999): 38–41.

———. "Sometimes You Get It Right." *Journal of Biblical Counseling* 15, no. 2 (1997): 44–47.

———. "When the Problem Is Sexual Sin: A Counseling Model." *Journal of Biblical Counseling* 13, no. 3 (1995): 16–18.

Bjornstad, James. "The Deprogramming and Rehabituation of Modern Cult Members." *Journal of Pastoral Practice* 2, no. 1 (1978): 113–28.

Black, Jeffrey S. "Making Sense of the Suicide of a Christian." *Journal of Biblical Counseling* 18, no. 3 (2000): 11–20.

Boswell, Andrew. "The Counselor and Pride." *Journal of Pastoral Practice* 4, no. 1 (1980): 11–15.

Boyd, Jeffrey H. "An Insider's Effort to Blow Up Psychiatry." *Journal of Biblical Counseling* 15, no. 3 (1997): 21–31.

Brand, Henry. "How to Deal with Anger." *Journal of Biblical Counseling* 16, no. 1 (1997): 28–31.

Bryant, Timothy A. "How to Live by Truth (Not Feelings)." *Journal of Biblical Counseling* 18, no. 3 (2000): 50–53.

Carter, John. "Adams' Theory of Nouthetic Counseling." *Journal of Psychology and Theology* 3 (1975): 143–55.

———. "Nouthetic Counseling Defended: A Reply to Ganz." *Journal of Psychology and Theology* 4 (1976): 206–16.

Cole, Steven J. "How John Calvin Led Me to Repent of Christian Psychology." *Journal of Biblical Counseling* 20, no. 2 (2002): 31–39.

————."An Integration View." In *Christianity and Psychology*. Edited by Eric L. Johnson and Stanton L. Jones, 102–29. Downers Grove, IL: InterVarsity, 2000.

Davis, Marc. "*Listening to Prozac* by Peter Kramer." *Journal of Biblical Counseling* 18, no. 3 (2000): 58–60.

Dial, Howard E. "'Sufferology': Counseling Toward Adjustment in Suffering." *Journal of Pastoral Practice* 3, no. 2 (1979): 19–24.

Emlet, Michael R. "Understanding the Influences on the Human Heart." *Journal of Biblical Counseling* 20, no. 2 (2001): 47–52.

Eyrich, Howard A. "Practice What You Preach and Counsel." *Journal of Biblical Counseling* 17, no. 3 (1999): 25–26.

————."Some Thoughts on the Tongue and Counseling." *Journal of Pastoral Practice* 8, no. 1 (1985): 16–21.

————. "Why Should Pastors Do the Time-Consuming Work of Counseling?" *Journal of Biblical Counseling* 14, no. 1 (1995): 65–66.

Fisher, Dick. "Anorexia—What?" *Journal of Pastoral Practice* 4, no. 4 (1980): 10–14.

Forrey, Jeffrey. "The Concept of 'Glory' as It Relates to Criticism." *Journal of Pastoral Practice* 10, no. 4 (1992): 26–49.

Ganz, Richard. "Confession of a Psychological Heretic." *Journal of Biblical Counseling* 13, no. 2 (1995): 18–22.

Gavrilides, Gregory. "Secular Psychologies and the Christian Perspective." *Journal of Pastoral Practice* 3, no. 4 (1979): 5–10.

Going, Lou. "Modern Idolatry: Understanding and Overcoming the Attraction of Your Broken Cisterns." *Journal of Biblical Counseling* 20, no. 3 (2002): 46–52.

Guinness, Os. "America's Last Men and Their Magnificent Talking Cure." *Journal of Biblical Counseling* 15, no. 2 (1997): 22–33.

Hadley, Richard K. "Electroshock: A Christian Option?" *Journal of Pastoral Practice* 4, no. 4 (1980): 18–25.

Hamill, Pete. "Crack the Box." *Journal of Biblical Counseling* 14, no. 3 (1996): 43–45.

Hindson, Ed. "Biblical View of Man (The Basis for Nouthetic Confrontation)." *Journal of Pastoral Practice* 3, no. 2 (1979): 33–58.

———. "Nouthetic Counseling." *Journal of Pastoral Practice* 3, no. 4 (1979): 11–31.

———. "The Use of the Scripture in Nouthetic Counseling." *Journal of Pastoral Practice* 3, no. 2 (1979): 28–39.

Hinman, Nelson E. "Healing of Memories? Inner Healing? Is There a Better Way?" *Journal of Pastoral Practice* 8, no. 4 (1987): 24–31.

Johnson, Eric L. "A Place for the Bible within Psychological Science." *Journal of Psychology and Theology* 20 (1992): 346–55.

Jones, Robert D. "Anger against God." *Journal of Biblical Counseling* 14, no. 3 (1996): 21–23.

———. "'I Just Can't Forgive Myself.'" *Journal of Pastoral Practice* 10, no. 4 (1992): 3–9.

———. "Getting to the Heart of Your Worry." *Journal of Biblical Counseling* 17, no. 3 (1999): 21–24.

———. "Resolving Conflict Christ's Way." *Journal of Biblical Counseling* 19, no. 1 (2000): 13–17.

———. "*When People Are Big and God Is Small* by Edward T. Welch." *Journal of Biblical Counseling* 16, no. 1 (1997): 56–57.

Lane, Timothy. "Normal Sunday Mornings and 24/7." *Journal of Biblical Counseling* 21, no. 2 (2003): 7–17.

Lutz, Susan. "Love One Another as I Have Loved You." *Journal of Biblical Counseling* 21, no. 3 (2003): 8–23.

MacArthur, John. "Biblical Counseling and Our Sufficiency in Christ." *Journal of Biblical Counseling* 11, no. 2 (1993): 10–15.

Mack, Wayne A. "Biblical Help for Solving Interpersonal Conflicts." *Journal of Pastoral Practice* 2, no. 1 (1978): 42–53.

———. "Biblical Help for Overcoming Despondency, Depression." *Journal of Pastoral Practice* 2, no. 2 (1978): 31–48.

———. "Some Suggestions for Preventing Homosexuality." *Journal of Pastoral Practice* 3, no. 3 (1979): 42–55.

Masri, Addam, Andy Smith, James Schaller, and Bob Smith. "Christian Doctors on Depression." *Journal of Biblical Counseling* 18, no. 3 (2000): 35–43.

Medinger, Alan P. "How Can Accountability Relationships Be Used to Encourage a Person in Biblical Change?" *Journal of Biblical Counseling* 13, no. 3 (1995): 54–55.

Megilligan, Keith. "The Ministry of Rebuking." *Journal of Pastoral Practice* 5, no. 2 (1981): 22–28.

Menand, Louis. "The Gods Are Anxious." *Journal of Biblical Counseling* 16, no. 2 (1998): 42–44.

Newheiser, Jim. "The Tenderness Trap." *Journal of Biblical Counseling* 13, no. 3 (1995): 44–47.

Nicole, Roger R. "Polemic Theology, or How to Deal with Those Who Differ from Us." *Journal of Biblical Counseling* 19, no. 1 (2000): 5–12.

Oakland, James A. "An Analysis and Critique of Jay Adams's Theory of Counseling." *Journal of the American Scientific Affiliation* (September 28, 1976): 101–9.

Patten, Randy. "A Tribute to Pastor William Goode." *Journal of Biblical Counseling* 16, no. 1 (1997): 7–8.

Piper, John. "Counseling with Suffering People." *Journal of Biblical Counseling* 21, no. 2 (2003): 18–27.

———. "God's Glory Is the Goal of Biblical Counseling." *Journal of Biblical Counseling* 20, no. 2 (2002): 8–21.

Plumlee, Gary G. "Adlerian Theory and Pastoral Counseling." *Journal of Pastoral Practice* 3, no. 4 (1979): 32–36.

Poirier, Alfred J. "Taking Up the Challenge." *Journal of Biblical Counseling* 18, no. 1 (1999): 30–37.

Powlison, David. "*I and II Corinthians* by Jay E. Adams." *Journal of Biblical Counseling* 13, no. 2 (1995): 62–63.

———. "Affirmations and Denials: A Proposed Definition of Biblical Counseling." *Journal of Biblical Counseling* 19, no. 1 (2000): 18–25.

———. "The Ambiguously Cured Soul." *Journal of Biblical Counseling* 19, no. 3 (2001): 2–7.

————. "Anger Part 2: Lies about Anger and the Transforming Truth." *Journal of Biblical Counseling* 14, no. 2 (1996): 12–21.

————. "Answers to the Human Condition: Why I Chose Seminary for Training in Counseling." *Journal of Biblical Counseling* 20, no. 1 (2001): 46–54.

————. "Biblical Counseling in Korea: An Interview with Kyu Whang and Ed Welch." *Journal of Biblical Counseling* 17, no. 3 (1999): 30–34.

————. "Biblical Ministry in a Rescue Mission: Interview with Bob Emberger." *Journal of Biblical Counseling* 17, no. 1 (1998): 15–22.

————. "Biological Psychiatry." *Journal of Biblical Counseling* 17, no. 3 (1999): 2–8.

————. "Can Philosophical Counseling Cure Psychotherapy of Its Medical Pretensions? A Review of Books on Philosophical Counseling." *Journal of Biblical Counseling* 17, no. 3 (1999): 57–59.

————. "Contemporary Confessions." *Journal of Biblical Counseling* 17, no. 1 (1998): 2–6.

————. "Counsel Ephesians." *Journal of Biblical Counseling* 17, no. 2 (1999): 2–11.

————. "Counsel the Word." *Journal of Biblical Counseling* 11, no. 2 (1993): 2–3.

————. "Counseling Is the Church." *Journal of Biblical Counseling* 20, no. 2 (2002): 2–7.

————. "Counseling Ministry Within Wider Ministry: Interview with John Babler and David Powlison." *Journal of Biblical Counseling* 18, no. 1 (1999): 17–24.

————. "Counseling under the Influence (Of the X-Chromosome!)" *Journal of Biblical Counseling* 21, no. 3 (2003): 2–7.

————. "Critiquing Modern Integrationists." *Journal of Biblical Counseling* 11, no. 3 (1993): 24–34.

————. "Crucial Issues in Contemporary Biblical Counseling." *Journal of Pastoral Practice* 9, no. 3 (1988): 53–78.

————. "Do You Have Any Idea?" *Journal of Biblical Counseling* 14, no. 1 (1995): 2–5.

———. "Do You See?" *Journal of Biblical Counseling* 11, no. 3 (1993): 3–4.

———. "Do You Ever Refer to Psychologists or Psychiatrists?" *Journal of Biblical Counseling* 13, no. 2 (1995): 64–65.

———. "Does the Shoe Fit?" *Journal of Biblical Counseling* 20, no. 3 (2002): 2–15.

———. "Don't Worry." *Journal of Biblical Counseling* 21, no. 2 (2003): 54–65.

———. "Educating, Licensing, and Overseeing Counselors." *Journal of Biblical Counseling* 25, no. 1 (2007): 29–36.

———. "Exegete the Bible; Exegete the Person: An Interview with John Street." *Journal of Biblical Counseling* 16, no. 2 (1998): 7–13.

———. "The Fear of Christ Is the Beginning of Wisdom: Ephesians 5:21–6:9." *Journal of Biblical Counseling* 17, no. 2 (1999): 49–50.

———. "Getting to the Heart of Conflict: Anger Part 3." *Journal of Biblical Counseling* 16, no. 1 (1997): 32–42.

———. "*Hebrews, James, I and II Timothy, Jude* by Jay E. Adams." *Journal of Biblical Counseling* 15, no. 1 (1996): 62–64.

———. "Hope for a 'Hopeless Case': A Case Study." *Journal of Biblical Counseling* 18, no. 2 (2000): 32–39.

———. "How Do You Help a 'Psychologized' Counselee?" *Journal of Biblical Counseling* 15, no. 1 (1996): 2–7.

———. "How Healthy Is Your Preparation?" *Journal of Biblical Counseling* 14, no. 3 (1996): 2–5.

———. "How to Hear the Gospel." *Journal of Biblical Counseling* 11, no. 2 (1993): 29–30.

———. "Human Defensiveness: The Third Way." *Journal of Pastoral Practice* 8, no. 1 (1985): 40–55.

———. "Idols of the Heart and 'Vanity Fair.'" *Journal of Biblical Counseling* 13, no. 2 (1995): 35–50.

———. "Illustrative Counseling." *Journal of Biblical Counseling* 16, no. 2 (1998): 49–53.

———. "Incarnational Ministry: An Interview with Elizabeth Hernandez." *Journal of Biblical Counseling* 16, no. 1 (1997): 20–24.

————. "Intimacy with God." *Journal of Biblical Counseling* 16, no. 2 (1998): 2–6.

————. "Is the Adonis Complex in Your Bible?" *Journal of Biblical Counseling* 22, no. 2 (2004): 42–58.

————. "The Law Written on Your Heart." *Journal of Biblical Counseling* 12, no. 2 (1994): 32.

————. "Let Me Draw a Picture: Picturing the Heart of Conflict." *Journal of Biblical Counseling* 16, no. 1 (1997): 43–45.

————. "Let's Talk!" *Journal of Biblical Counseling* 14, no. 2 (1996): 2–5.

————. "Love Speaks Many Languages Fluently." *Journal of Biblical Counseling* 21, no. 1 (2002): 2–11.

————. "Make 'Good News for the Sick' Good News for You." *Journal of Biblical Counseling* 11, no. 3 (1993): 41–42.

————. "Ministry in Mainland China." *Journal of Biblical Counseling* 19, no. 3 (2001): 31–35.

————. "Modern Therapies and the Church's Faith." *Journal of Biblical Counseling* 15, no. 1 (1996): 32–41.

————. *"Morning and Evening* by Charles Spurgeon and *The Christian Life* by Sinclair Ferguson." *Journal of Biblical Counseling* 17, no. 1 (1998): 57.

————. "A Nigerian Pastor Talks about Counseling." *Journal of Biblical Counseling* 19, no. 1 (2000): 33–39.

————. "A Nouthetic Philosophy of Ministry." *Journal of Biblical Counseling* 20, no. 3 (2002): 26–37.

————. "On a Personal Note." *Journal of Biblical Counseling* 19, no. 2 (2001): 2–3.

————. "'Peace, Be Still': Learning Psalm 131 by Heart." *Journal of Biblical Counseling* 18, no. 3 (2000): 2–10.

————. "Predator, Prey and Protector: Helping Victims Think and Act from Psalm 10." *Journal of Biblical Counseling* 16, no. 3 (1998): 27–37.

————. "Ready to Speak, with Gentleness and Fear." *Journal of Biblical Counseling* 13, no. 2 (1995): 2–8.

————. "The River of Life Flows Through the Slough of Despond." *Journal of Biblical Counseling* 18, no. 2 (2000): 2–4.

————. "The Sufficiency of Scripture to Diagnose and Cure Souls." *Journal of Biblical Counseling* 23, no. 2 (2005): 2–14.

————. "Talk Incessantly? Listen Intently!" *Journal of Biblical Counseling* 15, no. 3 (1997): 2–4.

————. "To Take the Soul to Task." *Journal of Biblical Counseling* 12, no. 3 (1994): 2–3.

————. "Troubling the Waters—and Spreading Oil on the Waves." *Journal of Biblical Counseling* 19, no. 1 (2000): 2–4.

————. "'Unconditional Love'?" *Journal of Biblical Counseling* 12, no. 3 (1994): 45–48.

————. "Understanding Anger." *Journal of Biblical Counseling* 14, no. 1 (1995): 40–53.

————. "What Do You Feel?" *Journal of Pastoral Practice* 10, no. 4 (1992): 50–61.

————. "What If Your Father Didn't Love You?" *Journal of Biblical Counseling* 12, no. 1 (1993): 2–7.

————. "What Is the Place of the Gospel and God's Grace in Biblical Counseling?" *Journal of Biblical Counseling* 13, no. 1 (1994): 53–54.

————. "Who Is God?" *Journal of Biblical Counseling* 17, no. 2 (1999): 12–23.

————. "X-ray Questions: Drawing Out the Whys and Wherefores of Human Behavior." *Journal of Biblical Counseling* 18, no. 1 (1999): 2–9.

————. "Your Looks: What the Voices Say and the Images Portray." *Journal of Biblical Counseling* 15, no. 2 (1997): 39–43.

————. "What Is 'Ministry of the Word'?" *Journal of Biblical Counseling* 21, no. 2 (2003): 2–6.

Powlison, David, Jay E. Adams, and John F. Bettler. "25 Years of Biblical Counseling: An Interview with Jay Adams and John Bettler." *Journal of Biblical Counseling* 12, no. 1 (1993): 8–13.

Powlison, David, and Ernst Gassmann. "A European Looks at Christian Counseling in America: An Interview with Ernst Gassmann." *Journal of Biblical Counseling* 15, no. 1 (1996): 21–25.

Propri, Joseph. "Hypnosis." *Journal of Pastoral Practice* 5, no. 4 (1982): 25–34.

Roberts, Robert. "Psychology and the Life of the Spirit." *Journal of Biblical Counseling* 15, no. 1 (1996): 26–31.

Rosenberger, Glen. "Alcoholism and You." *Journal of Pastoral Practice* 4, no. 4 (1980): 28–29.

Ryan, Skip. "How Jesus Transforms the Church." *Journal of Biblical Counseling* 17, no. 2 (1999): 61–64.

———. "Bond Slave—Romans 1:1–16." *Journal of Biblical Counseling* 19, no. 3 (2001): 40–46.

Sande, C. Ken. "Reconciliation through Confessing Your Sins." *Journal of Pastoral Practice* 11, no. 1 (1992): 61–62.

Scipione, George C. "Eeny, Meeny, Miny, Moe: Is Biblical Counseling It or No?" *Journal of Pastoral Practice* 9, no. 4 (1989): 44–57.

———."The Limits of Confidentiality in Counseling." *Journal of Pastoral Practice* 7, no. 2 (1984): 29–34.

Schwab, George M. "The Book of Daniel and Godly Counsel: Part 2." *Journal of Biblical Counseling* 15, no. 1 (1996): 52–61.

———. "The Book of Daniel and the Godly Counselor." *Journal of Biblical Counseling* 14, no. 2 (1996): 32–40.

———. "The Book of Job and Counsel in the Whirlwind." *Journal of Biblical Counseling* 17, no. 1 (1998): 31–42.

———. "Critique of 'Habituation' as a Biblical Model of Change." *Journal of Biblical Counseling* 21, no. 2 (2003): 67–83.

———. "Ecclesiastes and Counsel under the Sun." *Journal of Biblical Counseling* 15, no. 2 (1997): 7–16.

———."The Proverbs and the Art of Persuasion." *Journal of Biblical Counseling* 14, no. 1 (1995): 6–17.

Shogren, Gary Steven. "Recovering God in the Age of Therapy." *Journal of Biblical Counseling* 12, no. 1 (1993): 14–19.

Scott, Stuart. "Pursue the Servant's Mindset." *Journal of Biblical Counseling* 17, no. 3 (1999): 9–15.

Smith, Bill. "Authors and Arguments in Biblical Counseling: A Review and Analysis." *Journal of Biblical Counseling* 15, no. 1 (1996): 9–20.

Smith, Robert D. "Alzheimer's Disease." *Journal of Pastoral Practice* 6, no. 1 (1982): 45–56.

———. "Fearfully and Wonderfully Made." *Journal of Pastoral Practice* 8, no. 2 (1986): 2–12.

———. "God's Word and Your Health." *Journal of Pastoral Practice* 8, no. 3 (1986): 11–27.

———."Illness and a Life View." *Journal of Pastoral Practice* 1, no. 1 (1977): 80–84.

———. "It's Not What You Eat, It's What Eats You." *Journal of Pastoral Practice* 8, no. 1 (1985): 1–10.

———. "Lithium and the Biblical Counselor." *Journal of Pastoral Practice* 10, no. 1 (1989): 8–18.

———. "A Look at Psychosomatic Relationships." *Journal of Pastoral Practice* 1, no. 2 (1977): 81–87.

———. "Obtaining Medical Information from a Physician." *Journal of Pastoral Practice* 7, no. 4 (1985): 7–15.

———. "A Physician Looks at Counseling: Depression." *Journal of Pastoral Practice* 1, no. 1 (1977): 85–87.

———. "A Physician Looks at Counseling: Symptoms." *Journal of Pastoral Practice* 1, no. 1 (1977): 88–90.

———. "A Physician Looks at Fatigue." *Journal of Pastoral Practice* 2, no. 2 (1978): 63–72.

———. "Psychosomatics in the Bible." *Journal of Pastoral Practice* 1, no. 2 (1977): 88–89.

———. "Sleep." *Journal of Pastoral Practice* 4, no. 2 (1980): 36–44.

———. "What Is This Thing Called 'Chemical Imbalance'?" *Journal of Pastoral Practice* 9, no. 4 (1989): 2–7.

Smith, William. "*Totally Sufficient* by Ed Hindson and Howard Eyrich, Eds." *Journal of Biblical Counseling* 16, no. 2 (1998): 57–58.

Smith, Winston. "*Connecting: A Radical New Vision* by Larry Crabb." *Journal of Biblical Counseling* 17, no. 3 (1999): 54–56.

————. "Dichotomy or Trichotomy? How the Doctrine of Man Shapes the Treatment of Depression." *Journal of Biblical Counseling* 18, no. 3 (2000): 21–29.

————. "Wisdom in Relationships." *Journal of Biblical Counseling* 19, no. 2 (2001): 32–41.

————. *"Wrinkled but Not Ruined* by Jay E. Adams." *Journal of Biblical Counseling* 20, no. 2 (2002): 61–62.

Street, John D. "Counseling People Who Resist Change." *Journal of Biblical Counseling* 16, no. 3 (1998): 38–39.

Szasz, Thomas. "Mental Illness Is Still a Myth." *Journal of Biblical Counseling* 14, no. 1 (1995): 34–39.

Terrell, Hilton. "What about Brain Research?." *Journal of Biblical Counseling* 17, no. 3 (1999): 60–61.

Tripp, Paul D. "A Community of Good Counselors: The Fruit of Good Preaching." *Journal of Biblical Counseling* 21, no. 2 (2003): 45–53.

————. "Data Gathering Part 2: What the Counselor Brings to the Process." *Journal of Biblical Counseling* 14, no. 3 (1996): 8–14.

————. "The Great Commission: A Paradigm for Ministry in the Local Church." *Journal of Biblical Counseling* 16, no. 3 (1998): 2–4.

————. "Grumbling: A Look at a 'Little' Sin." *Journal of Biblical Counseling* 18, no. 2 (2000): 47–52.

————. "Homework and Biblical Counseling." *Journal of Biblical Counseling* 11, no. 2 (1993): 21–25.

————. "Homework and Biblical Counseling." *Journal of Biblical Counseling* 11, no. 3 (1993): 5–18.

————. "Keeping Destiny in View: Helping Counselees View Life from the Perspective of Psalm 73." *Journal of Biblical Counseling* 13, no. 1 (1994): 13–24.

————. "The Present Glories of Redemption." *Journal of Biblical Counseling* 17, no. 2 (1999): 32–37.

————. "Opening Blind Eyes: Another Look at Data Gathering." *Journal of Biblical Counseling* 14, no. 2 (1996): 6–11.

—————. "Speaking Redemptively." *Journal of Biblical Counseling* 16, no. 3 (1998): 10–18.

—————. "Strategies for Opening Blind Eyes: Data Gathering Part 3." *Journal of Biblical Counseling* 15, no. 1 (1996): 42–51.

—————. "Take Up Your Weapons: Ephesians 6:10–20." *Journal of Biblical Counseling* 17, no. 2 (1999): 58–60.

—————. "Wisdom in Counseling." *Journal of Biblical Counseling* 19, no. 2 (2001): 4–13.

Tripp, Paul, and David Powlison. "How Should You Counsel a Case of Domestic Violence? Helping the Perpetrator." *Journal of Biblical Counseling* 15, no. 2 (1997): 53–55.

Vander Veer, Joseph R. "Antipsychotic Drugs." *Journal of Pastoral Practice* 3, no. 4 (1979): 65–70.

—————. "Pastoral Psychopharmacology." *Journal of Pastoral Practice* 3, no. 2 (1979): 65–73.

Vernick, Leslie. "Getting to the Heart of the Matter in Marriage Counseling." *Journal of Biblical Counseling* 12, no. 3 (1994): 31–35.

Viars, Steve. "The Discipleship River." *Journal of Biblical Counseling* 20, no. 3 (2002): 58–60.

Wisdom, Christopher H. "Alcoholics Autonomous—A Biblical Critique of AA's View of God, Man, Sin, and Hope." *Journal of Pastoral Practice* 8, no. 2 (1986): 39–55.

Welch, Edward T. "Addictions: New Ways of Seeing, New Ways of Walking Free." *Journal of Biblical Counseling* 19, no. 3 (2001): 19–30.

—————. *"The Bible and Homosexual Practice* by Robert Gagnon." *Journal of Biblical Counseling* 20, no. 3 (2002): 67–68.

—————. "The Bondage of Sin." *Journal of Biblical Counseling* 17, no. 2 (1999): 24–31.

—————. "Counseling Those Who Are Depressed." *Journal of Biblical Counseling* 18, no. 2 (2000): 5–39.

—————. "A Discussion among Clergy: Pastoral Counseling Talks with Secular Psychology." *Journal of Biblical Counseling* 13, no. 2 (1995): 23–34.

———. "Exalting Pain? Ignoring Pain? What Do We Do with Suffering?" *Journal of Biblical Counseling* 12, no. 3 (1994): 4–19.

———. "Four Books on Homosexuality." *Journal of Biblical Counseling* 15, no. 2 (1997): 48–50.

———. "Homosexuality: Current Thinking and Biblical Guidelines." *Journal of Pastoral Practice* 13, no. 3 (1995): 19–29.

———. "How Should a Christian Counselor Think about Hypnotism?." *Journal of Biblical Counseling* 21, no. 1 (2002): 78–79.

———. "How Should You Counsel a Case of Domestic Violence? Helping the Victim." *Journal of Biblical Counseling* 15, no. 2 (1997): 51–53.

———. "How Theology Shapes Ministry: Jay Adams's View of the Flesh and an Alternative." *Journal of Biblical Counseling* 20, no. 3 (2002): 16–25.

———. "'How Valid or Useful Are Psychiatric Labels for Depression?'" *Journal of Biblical Counseling* 18, no. 2 (2000): 54–56.

———. "Insight into Multiple Personality Disorder." *Journal of Biblical Counseling* 14, no. 1 (1995): 18–28.

———. "Is Biblical-Nouthetic Counseling Legalistic? A Reexamination of a Biblical Theme." *Journal of Pastoral Practice* 11, no. 1 (1992): 4–21.

———. "Learning the Fear of the Lord: A Case Study." *Journal of Biblical Counseling* 16, no. 1 (1997): 25–27.

———. "A Letter to an Alcoholic." *Journal of Biblical Counseling* 16, no. 3 (1998): 19–26.

———. "Live as Children of Light: Ephesians 5:3–20." *Journal of Biblical Counseling* 17, no. 2 (1999): 42–48.

———. "Medical Treatments for Depressive Symptoms." *Journal of Biblical Counseling* 18, no. 3 (2000): 44–49.

———. "Memories Lost and Found: A Review of Books on Repressed Memories." *Journal of Biblical Counseling* 17, no. 1 (1998): 53–56.

———. "*Of Two Minds: The Growing Disorder in American Psychiatry* by T. M. Luhrmann." *Journal of Biblical Counseling* 19, no. 3 (2001): 55.

————. "*Prozac Backlash: Overcoming the Dangers of Prozac, Zoloft, Paxil, and Other Antidepressants with Safe, Effective Alternatives* by Joseph Glenmullen." *Journal of Biblical Counseling* 19, no. 1 (2000): 56–58.

————. "Research into the Placebo Effect." *Journal of Biblical Counseling* 21, no. 1 (2002): 76–77.

————. "Self-Control: The Battle Against 'One More.'" *Journal of Biblical Counseling* 19, no. 2 (2001): 24–31.

————. "Sin or Sickness? Biblical Counseling and the Medical Model." *Journal of Pastoral Practice* 10, no. 2 (1990): 28–39.

————. "What You Should Know about Attention Deficit Disorder." *Journal of Biblical Counseling* 14, no. 2 (1996): 26–31.

————. "Who Are We? Needs, Longings, and the Image of God in Man." *Journal of Biblical Counseling* 13, no. 1 (1994): 25–38.

————. "Why Ask, 'Why?'—Four Types of Causes in Counseling." *Journal of Pastoral Practice* 10, no. 3 (1991): 40–47.

————. "What Is Biblical Counseling, Anyway?" *Journal of Biblical Counseling* 16, no. 1 (1997): 2–6.

————. "Words of Hope for Those Who Struggle with Depression." *Journal of Biblical Counseling* 18, no. 2 (2000): 40–46.

Wendling, Woodrow W. "Pharmacology for Pastoral Counselors—Part I." *Journal of Pastoral Practice* 10, no. 1 (1989): 19–24.

————. "Pharmacology for Pastoral Counselors—Part II." *Journal of Pastoral Practice* 10, no. 2 (1990): 19–27.

————. "Pharmacology for Pastoral Counselors—Part III." *Journal of Pastoral Practice* 10, no. 3 (1991): 22–36.

Wood, William E. "When Is It 'Too Late' to Change?" *Journal of Pastoral Practice* 9, no. 1 (1987): 39–46.

Notes

Chapter 1: The Birth of a Biblical Counseling Movement

1. See the discussion on Sigmund Freud, below.

2. Integration is, arguably, the dominant approach to counseling for Christians today and, as a movement, integrationists attempt to accomplish the counseling task in a way that is theologically faithful. The theological foundation of the integration movement, however, has not been articulated in a way that makes core doctrines of redemption integral. Because of wrong emphases on the importance and value of secular psychology, misunderstandings regarding the sufficiency of Scripture, confusion regarding what constitutes general and special revelation, and the apparent inability of integrationists to integrate, the movement cannot be regarded as theologically viable.

3. Richard Baxter, *The Christian Directory*, 4 vols. (Morgan, PA: Soli Deo Gloria, 1997).

4. John Owen, *The Mortification of Sin* (Carlisle, PA: Banner of Truth, 2004).

5. William Bridge, *A Lifting Up for the Downcast* (Carlisle, PA: Banner of Truth, 2001).

6. Jonathan Edwards, *A Treatise Concerning the Religious Affections* (Sioux Falls, SD: NuVision, 2007). Many more works could be cited here, but the point is that it was the burden of those writing in the tradition of the Puritan authors to apply the truths of Scripture to the sins and sufferings of God's hurting people.

7. Ichabod Spencer, *A Pastor's Sketches* (Vestavia Hills, AL: Solid Ground, 2001).

8. This statement is worded very carefully. The point advanced here is not that Christians were not involved at all in the task of thinking about interpersonal ministry. The point is rather that this involvement was not as careful and uniquely Christian as it had been. Before this, Christians were thinking inside their community and using their resources to think through counseling issues (though they would not have called it counseling). After

this, Christians were taking their lead from secular thinkers and bringing in biblical principles almost as an afterthought.

9. David Powlison, "A Biblical Counseling View," in *Psychology and Christianity: Four Views*, ed. Eric L. Johnson and Stanton L. Jones (Downers Grove, IL: InterVarsity, 2000), 219.

10. Iain H. Murray, *Revival and Revivalism* (Carlisle, PA: Banner of Truth, 1994), *xvii.*

11. Ibid., *xviii.*

12. Kenneth O. Brown, *Holy Ground: A Study of the American Camp Meeting* (New York: Garland, 1992), *vii.*

13. See the following: Murray, *Revival and Revivalism*, 255–74; Samuel J. Baird, *A History of the New School, and of the Questions Involved in the Disruption of the Presbyterian Church in 1838* (Philadelphia, 1868), 19.

14. George M. Marsden, *Understanding Fundamentalism and Evangelicalism* (Grand Rapids, MI: Eerdmans, 1991), 12–13.

15. Benjamin Warfield, *The Inspiration and Authority of the Bible* (Phillipsburg, NJ: Presbyterian and Reformed, 1948).

16. R. A. Torrey and A. C. Dixon, eds., *The Fundamentals* (Grand Rapids, MI: Baker, 1993).

17. A fuller discussion of the modernist's affinity for counseling is not possible here. For further discussion, see Donald Capps, *Biblical Approaches to Pastoral Counseling* (Philadelphia: Westminster, 1981); Harry Emerson Fosdick, *The Living of These Days* (New York: Harper & Row, 1956), 214–15, 280; Seward Hiltner and Lowell Colston, *The Context of Pastoral Counseling* (Nashville: Abingdon, 1961).

18. E. G. Boring, *A History of Experimental Psychology*, 2nd ed. (New York: Appleton-Century-Crofts, 1950), 317, 322, 344–45.

19. Wilhelm Wundt, *Principles of Physiological Psychology*, trans. Edward Bradford Titchener (New York: Macmillan, 1904), 2.

20. Sigmund Freud, *The Question of Lay Analysis* (New York: Norton, 1950). Also see Sigmund Freud, *Psychoanalysis and Faith* (New York: Basic, 1964), 104.

21. The reasons this kind of masculinity was desirable will be discussed below.

22. E. Brooks Holifield, *A History of Pastoral Care in America* (Nashville: Abingdon, 1983), 167–68.

23. Ibid., 268–69.

24. Ibid., 167.

25. See Newman Smyth, *Christian Ethics* (New York: Charles Scribner's Sons, 1982), 479, 495; Washington Gladden, *Ruling Ideas of the Present Age* (Boston: Houghton Mifflin, 1895), 294.

26. What was called shell shock in World War I came to be called combat fatigue in World War II. Presently this identical problem is known as "posttraumatic stress disorder."

27. Holifield, *History of Pastoral Care*, 269–70.

28. There is a brief discussion of this in Holifield, *History of Pastoral Care*, 260–63.

29. Jay Adams, *Competent to Counsel* (Grand Rapids, MI: Zondervan, 1970).

30. Jay Adams, *A Theology of Christian Counseling* (Grand Rapids, MI: Zondervan, 1979), 13.

31. Jay Adams, *The Christian Counselor's Manual* (Grand Rapids, MI: Zondervan, 1973), 9–10. Though I am in fundamental agreement with Adams as he advances his case here, it is not the purpose of this project to either commend or condemn his argumentation. The purpose here is much more neutral, and it is to understand Adams's position. All of the commentary that follows will be aimed at comprehending the position; analysis will be reserved for later.

32. Adams, *Competent*, 28.

33. Adams, *Manual*, 11. Adams goes on to say that even in such an instance as this, there will be a need to work together with a biblical counselor to help alter sinful life patterns.

34. Adams, *Theology*, ix; original emphasis.

35. Adams, *Competent*, xxi. See also Adams, *Manual*, 9–11. Jay Adams, *What about Nouthetic Counseling?* (Grand Rapids, MI: Baker, 1976), 31. Jay Adams, *Counseling and the Sovereignty of God* (Philadelphia: Westminster Theological Seminary, 1975), 12.

36. Adams was inconsistent in his use of the terms *psychology* and *psychiatry*, often using them interchangeably. In this book the term *psychology* will serve as a general, catch-all category that encompasses medicine (i.e., psychiatry), theorizing, and counseling according to secular worldview commitments.

37. A comprehensive accounting of Adams's theology is impossible to provide in these pages. For a more thorough discussion see David Powlison, *Competent to Counsel? The History of the Conservative Protestant Biblical Counseling Movement* (Glenside, PA: Christian Counseling and Educational Foundation, 1996), 170–255. The following is meant to provide only a

concise summary of those most important elements of Adams's theological recovery.

38. Adams, *Manual*, 40–41.

39. Adams, *Theology*, 143.

40. Adams, *Manual*, 29.

41. Adams, *Theology*, 177.

42. Adams, *Manual*, 39.

43. It will be necessary to return to this point later in examining how the movement developed.

44. Adams, *Theology*, 177.

45. Adams, *Manual*, 178; original emphasis.

46. Jay Adams, *Shepherding God's Flock: A Handbook on Pastoral Ministry, Counseling, and Leadership* (Grand Rapids, MI: Zondervan, 1975), 174.

47. Adams, *Manual*, 11–13.

48. Adams, *Shepherding*, 172–76.

49. Adams, *Competent*, 17–19.

50. *Competent to Counsel* (1970), *The Christian Counselor's Manual* (1973), *Shepherding God's Flock* (1974), and *A Theology of Christian Counseling* (1979).

Chapter 2: Advances in How Biblical Counselors Think about Counseling

1. These concepts form the core of all of those committed to biblical counseling and demonstrate that though there has been development from the first to the second generation of biblical counseling, there is a fundamental and broad cohesion that unites both generations.

2. Jay Adams, *Competent to Counsel* (Grand Rapids, MI: Zondervan, 1970), *xvi*.

3. Ibid., 51–52.

4. Jay Adams, *The Christian Counselor's Manual* (Grand Rapids, MI: Zondervan, 1973), 124–25.

5. Adams, *Competent*, 26–36.

6. Ibid., 40. Adams did have a place (as he mentions in the footnote of the reference cited here) for organically based problems that caused difficulties. He was also clear, however, that people experiencing such problems were responsible to God even in the midst of their difficulties. Failure to do so was sinful.

7. Jay Adams, *A Theology of Christian Counseling* (Grand Rapids, MI: Zondervan, 1979), 139–40.

8. Adams even wrote two books on the topic: *How to Handle Trouble* (Phillipsburg, NJ: P&R, 1992); and *Christ and Your Problems* (Phillipsburg, NJ: P&R, 1999).

9. The critique that came from Adams's friends will come in the pages to follow. For examples of criticism from Adams's opponents see Larry Crabb, *Understanding People* (Grand Rapids, MI: Zondervan, 1987), 7–10; Tim Clinton and George Ohlschlager, *Competent Christian Counseling: Pursuing and Practicing Compassionate Soul Care* (Colorado Springs, CO: Waterbrook), 44–45.

10. For examples of criticism against Adams in this regard, see David G. Benner, *Psychotherapy and the Spiritual Quest* (Grand Rapids, MI: Baker, 1988), 46; Bruce Narramore, *No Condemnation: Rethinking Guilt Motivation in Counseling; Preaching, and Parenting* (Grand Rapids, MI: Zondervan, 1984), 129; Gary R. Collins, *The Rebuilding of Psychology: An Integration of Psychology and Christianity* (Wheaton, IL: Tyndale, 1977), 182; Gary R. Collins, *The Biblical Basis of Christian Counseling for People Helpers* (Colorado Springs, CO: NavPress, 1993), 110–12. Larry Crabb, *Inside Out* (Colorado Springs, CO: NavPress, 1988).

11. Adams, *Competent*, 29.

12. Of course Adams would admit that an organic illness would cause suffering but unfortunately never develops this idea.

13. Adams, *Manual*, 9.

14. See references above.

15. http://www.nouthetic.org/jay-e-adams/bibliography.html (accessed April 18, 2009).

16. This fact can be seen when one focuses on the three counseling books by Adams that have been the most influential and sold the most copies. As a rough gauge, consider, for example, that in *Competent to Counsel*—the book where Adams sought to lay a foundation for nouthetic counseling—there are two citations for suffering that took up four pages of the index. By contrast there are thirty-eight citations for sin that take up approximately ninety-seven pages.

In *The Christian Counselor's Manual*, Adams's unfolding of the process of biblical counseling, there is one reference each for suffering and misery, totaling two pages. There are eight references for sin totaling thirty-five pages, in addition to countless references to specific sins and an engagement of those issues. In the entire book there is no discussion of how to minister to the sufferings of a hurting person. *A Theology of Christian Counseling* includes Adams's most thorough treatment found in any of the three books. There are a combined twelve references for misery and suffering in the index. This work contains Adams's first chapter-length treatment.

In that chapter he unpacks such important themes as the inescapability of suffering, the hope that the cross brings to suffering, the temporary nature of suffering, as well as mentioning some purposes behind suffering. Such a treatment is helpful. That said, there is still much more attention given to sin, with nineteen references for sin and transgression in the index and at least six chapters dealing largely with sin.

17. Jay Adams, *Counsel from Psalm 119* (Woodruff, SC: Timeless Texts, 1998), 59.

18. Jay Adams, *Compassionate Counseling* (Woodruff, SC: Timeless Texts, 2007), 1. This work, while an effort on the part of Adams that should be appreciated, does not cover new ground. Rather, it takes themes that Adams addressed for years (e.g., the importance of counseling in the church, the importance of confronting people with their sin, the significance of showing counselees new ways of living) and argues that those things *are* compassionate. There is little development, therefore, in Adams's work in this book.

19. Adams, *Compassionate Counseling*, 1 n1.

20. It should be pointed out that, as will be demonstrated below, authors writing in the second generation of the biblical counseling movement do give much more attention to themes of suffering and compassion, though Adams does not credit their work in his statement.

21. Adams, *Competent*, 17.

22. Adams, *Manual*, 136.

23. See Job 1–2; 23:10; Ps. 94:12; Prov. 3:11–12; 5:12; 10:17; 12:1; 13:24; Jer. 31:18; Matt. 5:11–12; Luke 22:31; John 9:1–3; 11:1ff.; 21:19; Rom. 5:3–5; 8; 12:3; 1 Cor. 11:29–32; 2 Cor. 1:3–7; 8:13–15; 12:7; Phil. 1:12; 3:10; 2 Tim. 2:12; Heb. 12:7–11; James 1:2–4; 2:17; 1 Pet. 1:6–7; 4:13–14; 5:6–7; Rev. 5:12.

24. Sigmund Freud, *New Introductory Lectures on Psychoanalysis* (London: Lund Humphries, 1933), 107–43.

25. B. F. Skinner, *About Behaviorism* (New York: Knopf, 1974), 9–20.

26. Alfred Adler, *Understanding Human Nature* (New York: Greenburg, 1946), 69–90.

27. David Powlison, "Crucial Issues in Contemporary Biblical Counseling," *Journal of Pastoral Practice* 9, no. 3 (1988): 61.

28. Ibid., 62; original emphasis.

29. Ibid., 63.

30. David Powlison, "God's Grace and Your Sufferings," in *Suffering and the Sovereignty of God*, ed. John Piper and Justin Taylor (Wheaton, IL: Crossway, 2006), 157.

31. Edward Welch, "Exalting Pain? Ignoring Pain? What Do We Do with Suffering?," *Journal of Biblical Counseling* 12, no. 3 (1994): 4.

32. Ibid., 5.

33. Timothy S. Lane and Paul David Tripp, *How People Change* (Winston-Salem, NC: Punch, 2006), 133–65.

34. Ibid., 167–92.

35. Ibid., 193–223.

36. Ibid., 99.

37. Ibid., 105–6.

38. Welch is also careful to point out here that Satan is not behind all suffering. His care in this is apparent even in his multiple listings of sources for suffering.

39. Welch, "Exalting Pain? Ignoring Pain?," 6–7.

40. Paul David Tripp, *Instruments in the Redeemer's Hands* (Phillipsburg, NJ: P&R, 2002), 158.

41. Ibid., 145.

42. Ibid.

43. Welch, "Exalting Pain? Ignoring Pain?," 5.

44. Tripp, *Instruments*, 150.

45. Ibid., 155.

46. Powlison demonstrates something of this idea in *Seeing with New Eyes* (Phillipsburg, NJ: P&R, 2003), 91–108.

47. There are exceptions, of course. Mowrer's emphasis on responsibility awakened Adams to this crucial reality. Cognitive Behavioral Therapy includes an emphasis on responsibility. Even Dr. Phil (Phillip McGraw) has popularized the notion of taking responsibility for a person's problems. The problem is that when unbelievers urge the taking of responsibility, they always do so without reference to God.

48. Adams, *Theology*, 163.

49. Ibid., 161.

50. Ibid., 160–61.

51. Adams, *Manual*, 177.

52. Ibid., 178; emphasis added.

53. For Adams, this meant that the process of change through dehabituation and rehabituation was hard work and needed to be a comprehensive task—not limited to helping a counselee work through just one problem but showing how problems in one area relate to problems in another area. See Adams, *Competent*, 153–55, 156ff.

54. Adams, *Competent*, 47.

55. Ibid., 48.

56. Ibid.

57. Powlison, "Crucial Issues," 12.

58. Ibid.

59. Edward Welch, "How Theology Shapes Ministry," *Journal of Biblical Counseling* 20, no. 3 (2002):16–25; George M. Schwab, "Critique of 'Habituation' as a Biblical Model of Change," *Journal of Biblical Counseling* 14, no. 1 (1995): 67–83.

60. Welch, "How Theology Shapes Ministry," 19–20. One significant theme of Welch's article is that Adams's view of the flesh is unique among interpreters, and his assessment seems correct. See Anthony A. Hoekema, *Created in God's Image* (Grand Rapids, MI: Eerdmans, 1986), 108–9, 151, 215–16; Thomas Schreiner, *Romans,* Baker Exegetical Commentary on the New Testament, vol. 6 (Grand Rapids, MI: Baker Academic, 1998), 303–94; Douglas J. Moo, *The Epistle to the Romans*, New International Commentary on the New Testament, vol. 6 (Grand Rapids, MI: Eerdmans, 1996), 411–96; Leon Morris, *Epistle to the Romans*, Pillar New Testament Commentary, vol. 6 (Grand Rapids, MI: Eerdmans, 1988), 243–342; John Calvin, *Epistle to the Romans*, Calvin's Commentaries, vol. 14 (Grand Rapids, MI: Baker, 2003), 217–302.

61. Schwab interacts with all of Adams's proof texts including Jer. 13:23; 22:21; Rom. 7:22–23; Eph. 4:22–32; and Heb. 5:13–14 and discounts all of them, finally concluding, "Adams cites a host of other passages to illustrate his theory of habituation. But, as we have seen above, these citations are quoted out of context to mean something that has, at best, tangential relevance to the text." Schwab, "Critique of 'Habituation,'" 79.

62. Ibid.

63. Ibid., 68.

64. Ibid., 69.

65. Ibid., 22–23.

66. Ibid.

67. Adams, *Theology*, 41–42. Jay Adams, *Shepherding God's Flock: A Handbook on Pastoral Ministry, Counseling, and Leadership* (Grand Rapids, MI: Zondervan, 1975), 163–65.

68. Jay Adams, "Letter to the Editor," *Journal of Biblical Counseling* 22, no. 3 (2003): 66.

69. Adams, *Manual*, 177.

70. Ibid., 186. There is also a reference to this in Jay Adams, "Change Them? . . . Into What?" *Journal of Biblical Counseling* 13, no. 2 (1995): 17.

71. Jay Adams, *Critical Stages of Biblical Counseling* (Stanley, NC: Timeless Texts, 2002), 136.

72. David Powlison, "Idols of the Heart and 'Vanity Fair,'" *Journal of Biblical Counseling* 13, no. 2 (1995): 35.

73. Ibid., 36. Powlison also states in this context that "desires" or "lusts of the flesh" is the summary New Testament expression for the same drift that idolatry addresses in the Old Testament.

74. Ibid., 38.

75. Tedd Tripp, *Shepherding a Child's Heart* (Wapwollopen, PA: Shepherd, 1995), 21.

76. Paul David Tripp, *Instruments*, 66; original emphasis.

77. Edward T. Welch, *When People Are Big and God Is Small* (Phillipsburg, NJ: P&R, 1997), 44–45.

78. Edward T. Welch, *Addictions: A Banquet in the Grave* (Phillipsburg, NJ: P&R, 2001), 47.

79. Edward T. Welch, *Depression: A Stubborn Darkness* (Greensboro, NC: New Growth, 2004), 125.

80. Elyse Fitzpatrick, *Idols of the Heart* (Phillipsburg, NJ: P&R, 2001), 23.

81. Powlison, *Seeing with New Eyes*, 130–31.

82. Ibid., 138–39.

Chapter 3: Advances in How Biblical Counselors Do Counseling

1. Jay Adams, *The Christian Counselor's Manual* (Grand Rapids, MI: Zondervan, 1973), vii–viii.

2. Jay Adams, *Shepherding God's Flock: A Handbook on Pastoral Ministry, Counseling, and Leadership* (Grand Rapids, MI: Zondervan, 1975), 159–60.

3. Adams, *Manual*, xi–xii.

4. Of course this is a very strong statement, but, as this section will demonstrate, there is simply no example of a biblical counselor in print who does not embrace the importance of data gathering.

5. Paul David Tripp, *Instruments in the Redeemer's Hands* (Phillipsburg, NJ: P&R, 2002), 168.

6. Wayne A. Mack, "Taking Counselee Inventory: Collecting Data," in *Introduction to Biblical Counseling*, ed. John F. MacArthur Jr. and Wayne A. Mack (Nashville: W Publishing, 1994), 210.

7. David Powlison, *Speaking Truth in Love* (Winston-Salem, NC: Punch, 2005), 55–56. The questions he suggests are "What is this person

facing in life?" and "What does the Lord say that speaks directly into what you are facing?"

8. Jay Adams, *Competent to Counsel* (Grand Rapids, MI: Zondervan, 1970), 51.

9. Ibid., 45; emphasis added.

10. Carl Rogers, *Counseling and Psychotherapy: Newer Concepts in Practice* (Boston: Houghton Mifflin, 1942); Carl Rogers, *Client-Centered Therapy: Its Current Practice, Implications, and Theory* (Boston: Houghton Mifflin, 1951).

11. Adams, *Manual*, 84–85.

12. Ibid., 86.

13. Wayne A. Mack, "Providing Instruction through Biblical Counseling," in *Introduction to Biblical Counseling*, 250. Mack cites passages such as Prov. 6:23; Matt. 22:29; Eph. 4:11–12; 1 Tim. 4:6; 2 Tim. 2:16–18; and Titus 1:10–11 for biblical support.

14. Wayne A. Mack, "Implementing Biblical Instruction," in *Introduction to Biblical Counseling*, 297.

15. Paul David Tripp, "Homework and Biblical Counseling, Part 1," *Journal of Biblical Counseling* 11, no. 2 (1993): 21–25; Paul David Tripp, "Homework and Biblical Counseling, Part 2," *Journal of Biblical Counseling* 11, no. 3 (1993): 5–18.

16. Jay Adams, *How to Help People Change: The Four-Step Biblical Process* (Grand Rapids, MI: Zondervan, 1986), 169–200.

17. Tripp, *Instruments*, 239–76.

18. See chap. 2 of this work.

19. Adams, *Shepherding*, 105.

20. Ibid., 176.

21. Ibid., n15; emphasis added.

22. One is thankful that Adams says counseling should not be "officious," but one is left wondering what that means given his other language.

23. Adams's reasons for his approach will be addressed below.

24. Jay Adams, *Lectures on Counseling* (Grand Rapids, MI: Zondervan, 1977), 251–52.

25. Adams, *Competent*, 55.

26. Adams, *Competent*, 41, 42, 45, 55–59; Adams, *Manual*, 15–17; Jay Adams, *A Theology of Christian Counseling* (Grand Rapids, MI: Zondervan, 1979), 18–23; Jay Adams, *Teaching to Observe* (Hackettstown, NJ: Timeless Texts, 1995), 58–64.

27. This authoritative element will be addressed in more detail below.

28. Adams, *Competent*, 58.

29. Ibid.

30. Even his reasons for counseling in the office grew out of practical concerns that he intended to help the counselee.

31. Adams, *Manual*, 15.

32. See argument above and chap. 1.

33. Adams, *Competent*, 58.

34. Rom. 12:10, 16; 14:19; 15:7, 14; 1 Cor. 6:7; 12:25; Gal. 5:26; Eph. 4:25, 32; 5:21; Phil. 2:3; Col. 3:9, 13, 16; 1 Thess. 3:12; 4:18; 5:11, 13, 15; 1 Tim. 2:1; Heb. 10:24; James 4:11; 5:9, 16; 1 Pet. 4:9–10; 5:5, 14; 1 John 1:7.

35. David Powlison, "Crucial Issues in Contemporary Biblical Counseling," *Journal of Pastoral Practice* 9, no. 3 (1988): 65–66.

36. David Powlison, "Review of *Hebrews, James, I & II Peter, Jude,* by Jay E. Adams," *Journal of Biblical Counseling* 15, no. 1 (1996): 64.

37. David Powlison, "Familial Counseling: The Paradigm for Counselor-Counselee Relationships in 1 Thessalonians 5," *Journal of Biblical Counseling* 25, no. 3 (2007): 2.

38. Wayne A. Mack, "Developing a Helping Relationship with Counselees," in *Introduction to Biblical Counseling*, 178.

39. Powlison, "Review of *Hebrews, James, I & II Peter, Jude*," 63; original emphasis.

40. Tripp, *Instruments*, 117.

41. Ibid., 120.

42. See, e.g., Jay Adams, *Ready to Restore: The Layman's Guide to Christian Counseling* (Phillipsburg, NJ: Presbyterian & Reformed, 1981), 24–31.

43. Mack, "Developing a Helping Relationship," 173.

44. Ibid., 173–74.

45. Tripp, *Instruments*, 126.

46. Powlison, "Review of *Hebrews, James, I & II Peter, Jude*," 63.

47. Jay Adams does have an interesting discussion of this topic in the early pages of *Ready to Restore*, 7. He acknowledged that we are like those we counsel. The sense in which he addressed it, however, is different from the second generation. Adams's approach was to say that the next time, it might be the counselor who needs one-way admonishment.

48. Mack, "Developing a Helping Relationship," 179.

49. Tripp, *Instruments*, 146.

50. Ibid., 146–47.

51. Ibid., 147.

52. Mack, "Developing a Helping Relationship," 178.

53. Tripp, *Instruments*, 126–27.

54. Ibid., 127–28.

55. Adams, *Shepherding*, 159.

Chapter 4: Advances in How Biblical Counselors Talk
about Counseling

1. David Powlison, *Seeing with New Eyes* (Phillipsburg, NJ: P&R, 2003), 6.

2. There have been many efforts at this, but several noteworthy examples include Powlison, *Seeing with New Eyes*, 171–252; Douglas Bookman, "The Scriptures and Biblical Counseling," in *Introduction to Biblical Counseling*, ed. John F. MacArthur Jr. and Wayne A. Mack (Nashville: W Publishing, 1994), 63–97; Ed Hindson and Howard Eyrich, *Totally Sufficient* (Ross-Shire, Great Britain: Christian Focus, 2004); Alfred J. Poirier, "Taking Up the Challenge," *Journal of Biblical Counseling* 18, no. 1 (1999): 30–37; David Powlison, "Critiquing Modern Integrationists," *Journal of Biblical Counseling* 11, no. 3 (1993): 24–34.

3. The many occasions where this work has been done "in-house" (see previous note for examples) will not be considered here. Those occasions where Adams presented his model to various schools in the context of lectureships are also not considered here. See Jay Adams, *The Big Umbrella* (Grand Rapids, MI: Baker, 1972).

4. Jay Adams, *The Christian Counselor's Manual* (Grand Rapids, MI: Zondervan, 1973), *xiii*.

5. David Powlison, *Competent to Counsel? The History of a Conservative Protestant Biblical Counseling Movement* (Glenside, PA: Christian Counseling and Educational Foundation, 1996), 8.

6. Ibid., 8–9, for further comments on this.

7. No attempt has been made in this project to lay out in a systematic way the positions of other Christian approaches to counseling. Suffice it to say here that the integration movement seeks to help people with their problems by using the Bible as a screen to filter meaningful material from secular psychology into one consistent, Christian model of people-helping. For fuller articulations, see Stanton L. Jones and Richard E. Butman, *Modern Psychotherapies* (Downers Grove, IL: InterVarsity, 1991), 17–38.

8. The information about this event is taken exclusively from Powlison, *Competent to Counsel?*, 86–88.

9. Others in attendance included Maurice Wagner, William Donaldson, Fred Donehoo, Paul Walder, and Vernon Grounds.

10. Powlison, *Competent to Counsel?*, 87.

11. The information from this event is chronicled by Powlison, *Competent to Counsel?*, 123–32.

12. Powlison explains the fault lines with some detail; see *Competent to Counsel?*, 126–29.

13. Ibid., 130.

14. Ibid.

15. Jay Adams, "Response to the Congress on Christian Counseling," *Journal of Pastoral Practice* 10, no. 1 (1989): 3.

16. Ibid.

17. Ibid., 3–4.

18. Peter A. Magaro, *The Construction of Madness* (Elmsford, NY: Pergamon, 1976), *x*. Magaro had asked Kenneth Lux to contribute a "Mystical-Occult" understanding of schizophrenia and included this in the same "Spiritual" category as Adams. Magaro's words in this citation were intended to introduce both positions even though they bear no resemblance to one another.

19. Jay Adams, "The Christian Approach to Schizophrenia," in *The Construction of Madness*, 133.

20. Ibid.,136–37.

21. Ibid., 141. Adams said more about engaging schizophrenics in the pages that follow, but the point here is that Adams dealt with an extreme case like schizophrenia according to his characteristic understanding of sin and responsibility.

22. Jay Adams, "Change Them? . . . Into What?," *Journal of Biblical Counseling* 13, no. 2 (1995): 13–16.

23. Ibid., 15.

24. Ibid., 16–17.

25. Ibid., 16.

26. Ibid., 17.

27. David Powlison, "Crucial Issues in Contemporary Biblical Counseling," *Journal of Pastoral Practice* 9, no. 3 (1988): 70. Powlison pointed out that one particularly relevant new audience would be Christian academics. This point will be discussed below. His statement, however, would also be relevant for the opening up of new doors with integrationists and secular thinkers.

28. Edward Welch, "A Discussion among Clergy: Pastoral Counseling Talks with Secular Psychology," *Journal of Biblical Counseling* 13, no. 2 (1995): 23–34.

29. Ibid., 34.

30. A second edition of this book was published in 2010.

31. David Powlison, "A Biblical Counseling View," in *Psychology and Christianity: Four Views*, ed. Eric L. Johnson and Stanton L. Jones (Downers Grove, IL: InterVarsity, 2000), 197.

32. Ibid., 224. Notably, Powlison uses a plural noun when referring to psychology. In fact, this is one of the hallmarks of his essay, distinguishing between psychology (singular) and six different *psychologies* (plural), though the purpose here is not to spell out each of those.

33. Ibid., 192–93.

34. Gary R. Collins, "An Integration Response," in *Psychology and Christianity*, 232, 234; Robert C. Roberts, "A Christian Psychology Response," in *Psychology and Christianity*, 238–39, 242; David G. Myers, "A Levels-of-Explanation Response," in *Psychology and Christianity*, 226–31.

35. Myers, "A Levels-of-Explanation Response," 227. It is worth noting that Myers actually quoted Powlison out of context. Powlison's point in the quotation is that when the God-referential aspect of humans is taken away (i.e., the lifeblood of humanness) then they are left as a figment, beast, and so on. Powlison was saying that to the extent that psychology (or anything else) takes God away, it is removing the most important element of a human being. In other words, Powlison's point was more nuanced and careful than it appears in the Myers reference.

36. Collins, "An Integration Response," 232.

37. Mark R. McMinn and Timothy R. Phillips, "Introduction: Psychology, Theology and Care for the Soul," in *Care for the Soul*, ed. Mark R. McMinn and Timothy R. Phillips (Downers Grove, IL: InterVarsity, 2001), 12–13.

38. See various discussions in chap. 2.

39. David Powlison, "Questions at the Crossroads: The Care of Souls and Modern Psychotherapies," in *Care for the Soul*, 14–15.

40. This is true even though it must be balanced with a biblical understanding of the noetic effects of sin, which means that even truthful apprehensions have the taint of sin.

41. This also touches on another of Powlison's proposed crucial issues. His sixth crucial issue was that the relationship between secular psychology and biblical counseling needed to be publicly clarified. He said, "Perhaps it seems a paradox, but the final crucial issue for contemporary biblical counseling is the need to define more clearly the nuances in our relationship to secular thinking. . . . Biblical counseling has never developed in any detail what the properly constructed relationship would look like or do." David Powlison, "Crucial Issues in Contemporary Biblical Counseling," *Journal of Pastoral Practice* 9, no. 3 (1988): 74. Powlison went on to sketch out

some basic contours (p. 75), but these sketches were presented in an apologetic context for the first time in the *Care for Souls* project.

42. If it is any indicator that it has been over nine years since a similar engagement, then this is especially the case, although Stuart Scott is a contributor to a forthcoming book by InterVarsity Press that will do it again.

43. Powlison, "Crucial Issues," 70.

44. Powlison, *Competent to Counsel?*, 131.

45. This was part of Adams's burden when he wrote *Shepherding God's Flock: A Handbook on Pastoral Ministry, Counseling, and Leadership* (Grand Rapids, MI: Zondervan, 1975), 159–313.

46. http://www.faithlafayette.html (accessed May 10, 2009). Information about this was taken from the Faith Baptist Church website and from their strategic ministry plan, which is available for download on that site.

47. Powlison, "Questions at the Crossroads," 52ff.

48. One bit of proof that this is so is the available literature. Biblical counseling literature has exploded in the last twenty years, but most of it has been written to help deal with specific pastoral issues. There are, comparatively, few authors and few works that deal with the theory behind biblical counseling commitments.

Powlison's epistemological priorities reinforce this. With varying degrees of clarity, the leaders of the movement have articulated for forty years that biblical construction is primary while apologetic engagement is secondary or tertiary.

Chapter 5: Advances in How Biblical Counselors Think about the Bible?

1. Actually Johnson distinguishes a third school of thought as well, the Psychoheresy Awareness Network. He acknowledges, however, that this group has "little influence outside a small group of extremists." Because of that, he spends no time evaluating it. Eric Johnson, *Foundations for Soul Care: A Christian Psychology Proposal* (Downers Grove, IL: IVP Academic, 2007), 111.

2. Ibid., 109.

3. Ibid.

4. Ibid., 120.

5. Ibid., 121.

6. Ibid., 185.

7. Ibid., 113.

8. Ibid., 117. In his footnote on this statement, Johnson refers to this as a "strict Bible-only position."

9. Johnson mentions other authors such as Doug Bookman, Jay Adams, and Lance Quinn to advance his argument. Since Johnson does not rely on these men in constructing his case, however, it is necessary only to reference his use of Mack.

10. Johnson, *Foundations*, 113.

11. Ibid., 117.

12. Ibid.

13. Ibid., 118–19; 182–86.

14. Ibid., 119.

15. Ibid., 121.

16. Ibid., 187.

17. Ibid., 124.

18. Ibid., 110.

19. Ibid.

20. Ibid.

21. Ibid., 122; emphasis original.

22. Ibid.

23. Ibid.

24. David Powlison, "The Sufficiency of Scripture to Diagnose and Cure Souls," *Journal of Biblical Counseling* 23, no. 2 (2005): 2–14.

25. The same point is made in David Powlison, "A Biblical Counseling View," in *Psychology and Christianity: Four Views*, ed. Eric L. Johnson and Stanton L. Jones (Downers Grove, IL: InterVarsity, 2000), 221–24.

26. Powlison, "The Sufficiency of Scripture," 2.

27. Ibid., 2–3.

28. Powlison makes the argument in plenty of other places. See, e.g., "Is the Adonis Complex in Your Bible?," *Journal of Biblical Counseling* 22, no. 2 (2004): 42–58; "What Is Ministry of the Word?," *Journal of Biblical Counseling* 21, no. 2 (2003): 2–6; "Does the Shoe Fit?," *Journal of Biblical Counseling* 20, no. 3 (2002): 2–15. Examples could be multiplied, but the reality is that every work by Powlison appearing in the bibliography of this project either assumes or explicitly articulates a conviction regarding the comprehensive sufficiency of Scripture. But, as Johnson rightly recognizes, Powlison never means by this that Scripture is "exhaustive" or "encyclopedic."

29. Edward Welch, "What Is Biblical Counseling, Anyway?," *Journal of Biblical Counseling* 16, no. 1 (1997): 3.

30. Jay Adams, *Competent to Counsel* (Grand Rapids, MI: Zondervan, 1970), *xxi*.

31. Jay Adams, *What about Nouthetic Counseling?* (Grand Rapids, MI: Zondervan, 1976), 31.

32. Johnson, *Foundations*, 113.

33. For one of many examples, see Wayne Mack and Joshua Mack, *God's Solutions to Life's Problems* (Tulsa, OK: Hensley, 2002).

34. Wayne A. Mack, "What Is Biblical Counseling?," in *Totally Sufficient*, ed. Ed Hindson and Howard Eyrich (Ross-shire: Christian Focus, 2004), 25, 30, 39, 41, 43, 45, 46, 47, 49, 50, 51.

35. Ibid., 50; emphasis added.

36. Ibid., 51; original emphasis. In this passage Mack is interacting (as he does in other places discussed below) with statements made by Powlison, whom he believes to be advancing his same argument.

37. Ibid., 41.

38. Mack, "What Is Biblical Counseling?," 38.

39. Ibid., 50–51.

40. Johnson, *Foundations*, 122.

41. Ibid., 123.

42. Ibid.

43. James Beck, review of *Psychology and Christianity: Four Views*, ed. Eric L. Johnson and Stanton L. Jones, *Denver Journal of Biblical and Theological Studies* 4 (2001).

44. Eric L. Johnson and Stanton L. Jones eds., *Christianity and Psychology: Four Views* (Downers Grove, IL: InterVarsity, 2000).

45. David Powlison, "Does the Shoe Fit?," *Journal of Biblical Counseling* 20, no. 3 (2002): 10–12; emphasis added.

46. Jay Adams, *The Christian Counselor's Manual* (Grand Rapids, MI: Zondervan, 1973), 80 n15, 105 n5.

47. David Powlison, "Educating, Licensing, and Overseeing Counselors," *Journal of Biblical Counseling* 25, no. 1 (2007): 30.

48. See *Counseling the Hard Cases*, ed. Heath Lambert and Stuart Scott (Nashville, TN, forthcoming).

Chapter 6: An Area Still in Need of Advancement

1. As pointed out in chap. 2, David Powlison introduced this idea in "Idols of the Heart and 'Vanity Fair,'" *Journal of Biblical Counseling* 13, no. 2 (1995): 35–50.

2. Indeed, Isa. 44:20, quoted above, states that it is a deluded heart that leads to the activity so the text of Isaiah itself raises the question of what such heart issues might be.

3. See also Numbers 15; Ezekiel 23; Judges 3.

4. Moshe Halbertal and Avishai Margalit, *Idolatry* (Cambridge, MA: Harvard University Press, 1992), 13–14; emphasis added. This is also the issue at stake in Ezekiel 14. What is going on with this "idols of the heart" text is nothing new. Instead, the elders appear before Ezekiel outwardly seeming to desire a word from the Lord but secretly they are not trusting in God but in the idols of Babylon. This is what the metaphor means in the context. It is not (contra Tripp as quoted above) some new and deeper sin not seen before. See Iain M. Duguid, *Ezekiel*, NIV Application Commentary vol. 23 (Grand Rapids, MI: Zondervan, 1999), 183–84; Leslie C. Allen, *Ezekiel*, Word Biblical Commentary, vol. 29 (Dallas: Word, 1994), 205; Margaret S. Odell, *Ezekiel*, Smyth and Helwys Bible Commentary, vol. 23 (Macon, GA: Smyth and Helwys, 2005), 160.

5. In fact, one of the reasons this passage could be described as the theme verse of Philippians is that after this Paul goes on to give more examples of others who sacrificially serve, including Timothy, Epaphroditus, Paul himself, and he concludes by mentioning Jesus again.

6. This exact point is also made in Mark 10.

7. Though we are not interacting with the "Vanity Fair" element of Powlison's article, this would be the place where such interaction would occur.

8. Powlison, "Idols of the Heart," 38.

9. A. W. Tozer, *The Knowledge of the Holy* (San Francisco: Harper-Collins, 1961), 29–30.

10. David Powlison, "Crucial Issues in Contemporary Biblical Counseling," *Journal of Pastoral Practice* 9, no. 3 (1988): 57.

11. Powlison, "Idols of the Heart," 39.

12. Ibid., 45. Powlison also addresses similar realities in *Speaking Truth in Love* (Winston-Salem, NC: Punch, 2005), 33–40.

13. Edward Welch, *Addictions: A Banquet in the Grave* (Phillipsburg, NJ: P&R, 2001), 49; original emphasis.

14. See chap 2.

15. David Powlison, e-mail message to Heath Lambert, November 26, 2007.

16. Powlison, "Idols of the Heart," 36.

17. Dan B. Allender and Tremper Longman III, *Breaking the Idols of Your Heart: How to Navigate the Temptations of Life* (Deerfield, IN: InterVarsity, 2007).

Conclusion: Increasingly Competent to Counsel

1. Actually he was recovering something that had been in a place for centuries before, as chap. 1 discusses.

2. David Powlison, Jay E. Adams, and John F. Bettler, "25 Years of Biblical Counseling: An Interview with Jay Adams and John Bettler," *Journal of Biblical Counseling* 12, no. 1 (1993): 8.

3. David Powlison, *Competent to Counsel? The History of the Conservative Protestant Biblical Counseling Movement* (Glenside, PA: Christian Counseling and Educational Foundation, 1996), 36.

4. One thinks particularly of Adams's approach at the Congress of Christian Counselors mentioned in chapter 4. All can appreciate Adams's call to repentance but when done in such an insulting manner, it seems to have done more harm than good. Jay Adams, "Jay Adams's Response to the Congress on Christian Counseling," *Journal of Pastoral Practice* 10, no. 1 (1989): 2-4.

5. Jay Adams, *A Theology of Christian Counseling* (Grand Rapids, MI: Zondervan, 1979), 97. This exact point is made in different language in Jay Adams, *The Christian Counselor's Manual* (Grand Rapids, MI: Zondervan, 1973), 92–93.

6. Adams, *The Christian Counselor's Manual*, 92.

7. Jay Adams, *What about Nouthetic Counseling?* (Grand Rapids, MI: Baker, 1976), 6.

Index

abuse, 152
Adams, Jay, apologetics of,
   101–11; founding of the biblical
   counseling movement, 35–47,
   157–60; methodology of, 50–57,
   83–99, 121–22; response to
   criticism, 165–70; response to
   human motivation, 66–80
addictions, 11, 67, 77
affection, 91–92
aggressive drives, 57
alcoholism, 22–23
Allender, Dan, 153–54
anger, 151
anorexia nervosa, 133
anxiety, 151
apologetics, 46, 101–20
atheistic worldview, 39–40
authority, 87–91
avoidance, 151

Baxter, Richard, 25
Beck, James, 134
behavioral habit patterns, 67–70
behaviorism, 57, 72–73, 167–68
Bettler, John, 104, 158
Biblical Counseling Foundation,
   123
biblical suppositions, 36
biblicism, 135

Brandt, Henry, 104
Bridge, William, 25
Broger, John, 123
Buckley, Ed, 123

calling, 14, 117, 119
Carter, John, 104
change process, 60–61
chaplains, 34–35
Chicago Statement on Biblical
   Inerrancy, 130
child development, 133
Christian Counseling and Educa-
   tion Foundation, 124
Civil War, 33–34
Cognitive Behavioral Therapy, 202
Collins, Gary, 104–5, 112–13
compassion, 55–56, 64, 152–53
Congress on Christian Counseling,
   105–6
Crabb, Larry, 104

dehabituation, 42, 68–69, 133, 202
demonic activity, 38
depravity, 131–32
depression, 77, 133
desire, 142–46
Devil, 147
difficulties, 27–28
discipline, 69, 167

divine status, 145

Edwards, Jonathan, 25, 28
Emlet, Michael, 124
emotion, 11, 133
empathy, 168
"entry gates," 98
erotic drives, 57
experimental psychology, 31

faith, 12–13, 16, 49, 155, 168–69
Faith Baptist Church, 119
familial approach, 90–91
Fitzpatrick, Elyse, 78, 133
"flesh," 67–68, 72, 147, 151,
    165–70
Freud, Sigmund, 31–32, 56
Fuller Theological Seminary, 103
fundamentalism, 30–31

Glasser, William, 72
glory, 140, 151–53
Goode, William, 119
grace, 61, 66, 129, 155
Grand Unifying Theory, 148
Great Commandment, 144–45

habituation, 71–80, 170, 202
Hahnemann University, 111–12
Halbertal, Moshe, 142
Holifield, E. Brooks, 33–35
Holy Spirit, 41, 45, 73, 121, 168
human nature, 131–32
human responsibility, 57–58, 66
humility, 96

"idol hunts," 153–54
idolatry, 75–78, 139–55
illness. *See* organic illness
implementation, 86–87
Industrial Revolution, 32–33

inferiority complexes, 57
information gathering (from coun-
    selee), 83–84
inorganic mental illness, 37–38
integrationists, 22, 104–5, 112–13,
    118, 197, 207
intellectual engagement, 118, 120
International Association of Bibli-
    cal Counselors, 123
interpersonal ministry, 197
introspection, 154–55

Johnson, Eric, 112–13, 122–37
Jones, Stanton, 112–13
Journal of Biblical Counseling, 124

Krisheim symposium, 104–5

Lane, Timothy, 60–61
liberalism, 30–31
listening, 83–84
Longman, Tremper, 153–54
love, 55, 92, 145–46
lusts, 146, 151

MacArthur, John, 123
Mack, Wayne, 83–86, 90–91,
    94–98, 123–24, 129–32
Magaro, Peter, 107, 207
Margalit, Avishai, 142
Marsden, George, 30
Master's Seminary, 117, 123
McMinn, Mark, 114–15
methodology, 81–99
misery, 200
modernism, 30–31
moral responsibility, 66
moralism, 122
motivation, 45, 66–80, 139,
    150–55, 169–70
Mowrer, O. Hobart, 72

Murray, Ian, 28–29
mutuality, 87–89
Myers, David, G., 112–13, 208

Narramore, Bruce, 103–4
Narramore Christian Foundation, 103
National Association of Nouthetic Counselors, 123
National Liberty Foundation, 103
nouthetic counseling, 88, 104, 167–68, 170

obedience, 43, 145, 155
ordination, 119
organic illness, 38, 200
Owen, John, 25

pastoral authority, 87–88
pastoral ministry, 118–19
person-centered therapy, 85
person-oriented counseling, 94
Phillips, Timothy, 114–15
pornography, 152
Powlison, David, and advancements in the biblical counseling movement, 44–47, 57–66; apologetics of, 111–20; methodology of, 84, 89–91, 149–50; response to human motivation, 70–71, 75–79; and sufficiency of Scripture, 124–27, 130–31, 134–36
pride, 96, 150–51
professional responsibilities, 56–57
"progressive" biblical counseling, 122–37
progressive sanctification, 47, 162
psychiatry. *See* psychology
Psychoheresy Awareness network, 209

psychology, 26, 31–32, 38–39, 113–14, 128–31, 197, 199, 208
psychotherapists, 21–22, 111–12
psychotherapy, 32, 38
Puritans, 25–26

redemption, 41–42
rehabituation, 42, 68–69
repentance, 112–13, 152, 154, 169
revivalism, 28–30, 33
righteousness, 41–42, 121, 147
Roberts, Robert, 112–13
Rogers, Carl, 35, 85, 88, 94

sacrifice, 92–94
salvation, 41–42
sanctification, 68, 97, 167. *See also* progressive sanctification
Satan, 62
schizophrenia, 107–9, 126, 207
Schwab, George, 71
Scriptural positivism, 129–30
Scripture, authority of, 88–89; as basis for counseling methodology, 81–82; and suffering, 65–66; sufficiency of, 47, 113, 115, 123–37, 162, 210. *See also* biblical suppositions; Word of God
secular mental health professionals, 108–12
self-analysis, 154–55
self-control, 22
self-denial, 145
self-discipline, 167
self-supremacy, 146–55
seminary teaching/faculty, 116–18
sensitivity, 66
sex, 152
sin, doctrine of, 40–43, 57; and the "flesh," 165–70; and habits,

67–70, 121; and idolatry,
151–52; noetic effects of, 208;
and suffering, 62, 66, 97–98
Smith, Bob, 119
social environment, 147
Southeastern Baptist Theological
Seminary, 117
Southern Baptist Theological Semi-
nary, 117
Southwestern Baptist Theological
Seminary, 117
Spencer, Ichabod, 25–26
Stoddard, Solomon, 28
Street, John, 133
suffering, 45, 52–66, 96–98, 146,
197, 200–201
systematic theology, 60–61

temptation, 97, 144, 146
theology, 21–22, 35–37. *See also*
systematic theology
total structuring, 69
Tozer, A. W., 148–49
"traditional" biblical counseling,
122–37
Tripp, Paul, 44, 60–65, 76–77, 83,
92–93, 96–97, 124
Tripp, Ted, 76
Tweedie, Donald, 103

University Psychiatric Clinic,
108–9

Viars, Steve, 199

Warfield, B. B., 30
Welch, Ed, 44, 59–63, 71–73,
77–78, 111–12, 127, 149, 165
Westminster Theological Seminary,
117, 124
Word of God, personal ministry of,
24, 27–28; public ministry of
(preaching), 24, 27–28
World Wars I and II, 34–35
worldview, 21, 111–12, 199. *See
also* atheistic worldview
worship, 75, 78–80, 139–43, 147
Wundt, Wilhelm, 31–32